orange, floor 1
328.73
(2 copies - 1 in ---)

THE REPUBLICAN TAKEOVER OF CONGRESS

Also by Dean McSweeney

AMERICAN POLITICAL PARTIES (*with John Zvesper*)

Also by John E. Owens

AFTER FULL EMPLOYMENT (*with John Keane*)

CONGRESS AND THE PRESIDENCY (*with Michael Roley*)

The Republican Takeover of Congress

Edited by

Dean McSweeney
Principal Lecturer in Politics
University of the West of England
Bristol

and

John E. Owens
Senior Lecturer in American Politics
University of Westminster
London

First published in Great Britain 1998 by
MACMILLAN PRESS LTD
Houndmills, Basingstoke, Hampshire RG21 6XS and London
Companies and representatives throughout the world

A catalogue record for this book is available from the British Library.

ISBN 0–333–66965–7

First published in the United States of America 1998 by
ST. MARTIN'S PRESS, INC.,
Scholarly and Reference Division,
175 Fifth Avenue, New York, N.Y. 10010

ISBN 0–312–21294–1

Library of Congress Cataloging-in-Publication Data
The Republican takeover of Congress / edited by Dean McSweeney and
John E. Owens.
p. cm.
Includes bibliographical references and index.
ISBN 0–312–21294–1 (cloth)
1. Republican Party (U.S. : 1854–) 2. United States. Congress–
–Elections, 1994. 3. United States. Congress. 4. United States–
–Politics and government—1993– I. McSweeney, Dean, 1951– .
II. Owens, John E.
JK2356.R36 1998
324.2734'09'049—dc21   97–38848
                                                            CIP

Selection and editorial matter © Dean McSweeney and John E. Owens 1998
Chapters 1 and 3 © John E. Owens 1998
Chapters 7 and 9 © Dean McSweeney 1998
Chapters 2, 4, 5, 6 and 8 © Macmillan Press Ltd 1998

This book is printed on paper suitable for recycling and made from fully managed and
sustained forest sources.

10   9   8   7   6   5   4   3   2   1
07   06   05   04   03   02   01   00   99   98

Printed and bound in Great Britain by
Antony Rowe Ltd, Chippenham, Wiltshire

Contents

List of Figures and Tables

Preface and Acknowledgements

The events on Capitol Hill from late 1994 to late 1996 were momentous. The 1994 mid-term elections gave the Republican Party majorities in both houses of Congress for the first time in 40 years. For two generations our knowledge of Congress was conditioned by one, seemingly immovable, anchor point: Democratic Party control. Certainly, the Republicans had previously won control of the Senate in 1980, but their majorities endured for just six years and so could be regarded as an interruption to Democratic rule. In the House of Representatives, no such interruption occurred. The events surrounding the 104th Republican Congress are important, however, not only because Democratic majorities in the House and Senate were overturned, but also because the nature of the new Republican majorities, and the new leaders who replaced them, seemed very different from previous Democratic (and Republican) majorities and leaders, especially in the House. The sense of significant change was reinforced by the new Republican majorities' promises to change the direction of public policy, reverse the presidentialist maxim of the New Deal that the president proposes and Congress disposes, and overturn established (Democratic) organisational arrangements in Congress.

In many ways, the moment of these events is enough to warrant an entire book on a single Congress. But it is not enough. The scale and nature of events has to some extent been captured by a succession of excellent, closely observed accounts by journalists. But the dominant focus of these analyses was the interplay among the three main personalities: Newt Gingrich, Bob Dole and Bill Clinton. For political scientists interested in Congress and the broader development of American government, the sequence of events which unfolded as a result of the Republican takeover of 1994 and the scale of those events requires interpretation – not only description – and, if necessary, reappraisal in light of what we know of electoral behaviour, institutional arrangements within Congress, the conservative movement, congressional–presidential relations, minority party politics and historical experience. This collection of original essays is intended as a contribution to that interpretative analysis.

In the process of writing and editing this book we have accumulated a number of debts. The Centre for the Study of Democracy at the University of Westminster sponsored a symposium in October 1996 at which the chapters in the book were presented and subject to critical discussion. We would like to thank John Keane, Margaret Blunden, and Byron Shafer of Nuffield College, Oxford for their support. Owens would also like to thank Tom Mann, director of the Governmental Studies Program at the Brookings Institution in Washington who kindly provided valuable office facilities in 1995 and 1997. Roger H. Davidson, Richard F. Fenno, Paul Herrnson, Charles O. Jones, Tom Mann, Barbara Sinclair and Eric Uslaner at various times generously gave us the benefit of their knowledge. We would also like to thank the numerous members of Congress, White House and congressional staff assistants, Congressional Research Service officials, and journalists who provided vital detailed information for our contributions to this study. On many occasions, the impressive staff at the Reference Center at the American Embassy in London responded in a timely manner to a number of urgent requests for information. For this, we wish to thank them. The book would not have been completed without the assistance of our graduate students and research assistants who performed essential research and preparatory tasks well and with good humour. These include most notably Julian Kirby and Ali Tajvidi of the Centre for the Study of Democracy at the University of Westminster. We would also like to thank our respective institutions – the research committee of the Faculty of Economics and Social Science at the University of the West of England and the Centre for the Study of Democracy at the University of Westminster; and Tim Farmiloe, Sunder Katwala and Ruth Willats at Macmillan for their support, encouragement and professionalism in helping produce the book in final form. Finally, we both owe a huge debt to our families without whose love and support this project would not have been possible. As a token of our deep appreciation, we dedicate the book to them.

Dean McSweeney
John E. Owens
Bristol and Colchester

Notes on the Contributors

Nigel Ashford is Principal Lecturer in Politics at Staffordshire University. In 1989 and 1990, he was a Bradley Scholar at the Heritage Foundation in Washington, D.C. He is editor of *Public Policy and the Impact of the New Right* (1993) and *A Dictionary of Conservative and Libertarian Thought* (1991).

Anthony Badger is Paul Mellon Professor of American History at Cambridge University. He is author of *The New Deal: The Depression Years, 1933–40* (1989); *The New Deal and North Carolina* (1981); *Prosperity Road: The New Deal, Tobacco and North Carolina* (1980); and editor of *The Making of Martin Luther King and the Civil Rights Movement* (1996).

Michael Foley is Professor of International Politics at the University of Wales at Aberystwyth. He is co-author of *Congress and the Presidency: Institutional Politics in a Separated System* (1996); editor of *Ideas that Shape Politics* (1994); *The Rise of the British Presidency* (1993); *American Political Ideas* (1991); *Law, Men, and Machines* (1990); and *The Silence of Constitutions* (1989).

Dean McSweeney is Principal Lecturer in Politics at the University of the West of England. He is author of *American Political Parties* (1991) and various articles on party politics, and a contributor to *Political Studies*.

John E. Owens is Senior Lecturer in United States Politics in the Centre for the Study of Democracy at the University of Westminster. He is co-author of *Congress and the Presidency: Institutional Politics in a Separated System* (1996) and *After Full Employment* (1986), and author of several articles on the United States Congress, which have appeared in the *British Journal of Political Science* and *Political Studies*.

Byron E. Shafer is Andrew W. Mellon Professor of American Government at Oxford University and a Professorial Fellow in Politics at Nuffield College. He is co-author of *The Two Majorities: The Issue Context of Modern American Politics* (1995); author of *Quiet Revolution: The Struggle For the Democratic Party and the Shaping of Post-Reform*

Politics (1983); and *Bifurcated Politics: Evolution and Reform in the National Party Convention* (1988); editor of *Postwar Politics in the G7* (1996) and *Present Discontents. American Politics in the Very Late Twentieth Century* (1997) and author of numerous articles in the *American Political Science Review* and other leading journals.

Barbara Sinclair is Marvin Hoffenberg Professor of American Politics at the University of California, Los Angeles. From 1993 to 1995, she was chair of the Legislative Studies Section of the American Political Science Association. She is the author of *Unorthodox Lawmaking. New Legislative Processes in the US Congress* (1997); *Legislators, Leaders and Lawmaking* (1995); *The Transformation of the US Senate* (1989), which won the American Political Science Association's Richard F. Fenno Award and the D. B. Hardeman Prize; *Majority Leadership in the US House* (1983); *Congressional Realignment* (1982), and numerous articles which have appeared in the *American Political Science Review* and other leading journals.

1 The Republican Takeover in Context

John E. Owens

An electoral earthquake hit the American political landscape in 1994. For the first time since 1954, the Republican Party won control of the House of Representatives, and at the same time gained control of the Senate for the first time since 1986. Not for 40 years, then, had Republicans controlled both houses of Congress, and only for the third time since the beginning of the twentieth century had the Republicans won control of Congress with a Democrat incumbent in the White House.[1] When the Republicans won their majorities in 1994, they ended the longest uninterrupted period of single-party rule in the entire history of Congress. Just one member – 88-year-old Sidney Yates, a Democrat from Illinois – had ever served in a Republican-controlled House of Representatives. Republicans gained 52 seats from Democrats in the House, including those of 34 Democratic incumbents. Democratic losses in the House were the heaviest for either party in any mid-term election since Harry Truman's Democratic Party lost 55 seats in the 1946 elections. Between 1946 and 1994, the next highest losses were in 1982 following the worst recession since the 1930s, and then they were only half those of 1994. For the first time since 1952, the Democrats' percentage of the vote fell below 50 per cent. Among the Democratic casualties were House Speaker Tom Foley (D.WA), who became the first Speaker to lose his seat since 1862, former Ways and Means chair Dan Rostenkowski (D.IL), and Judiciary chair Jack Brooks (D.TX). Not a single one of the 169 House Republican incumbents lost – a feat not achieved by any party since 1948; and the party won over two-thirds of the open seats previously held by the Democrats – an unprecedented achievement since 1790.[2] In the Senate, Democratic incumbent losses were limited to two, but one of these was Senator Jim Sasser (D.TN), favoured to succeed George Mitchell (D.ME) as Senate majority leader, and for the first time since the introduction of direct election of senators in 1914 all the newly elected senators were Republicans.

Electoral surges against the president's party are not unusual in mid-term elections. In the twentieth century, they occurred in 1922, 1930,

1938, 1942, 1946, 1966 and 1974. Usually, however, they have occurred in the sixth or later – rather than the second – year of a party's control of the presidency. The exceptions are 1922 and 1994 – just two years after Democrats won control of the presidency for the first time since 1980.[3]

The events of 1994 occurred against a background of growing public distrust of Congress – and indeed, of virtually all major political and other institutions in the United States – and of a sense of disenchantment. The end of the stalemate, or 'gridlock', in American political life, supposedly ushered in by the election of Bill Clinton and the restoration of unified single-party government, had not produced the promised benefits. If we think back to the mid-1980s, it seemed that only a scandal could defeat an incumbent House member as incumbents' re-election rates climbed to 98 per cent (elections for the Senate continued to remain competitive even when incumbents were running). The public's confidence in government was relatively high, particularly when compared with the 1970s following the Watergate scandal.[4] Public approval of Congress' performance rose to 42 per cent in September 1987 – the highest level since before Watergate, although 51 per cent disapproved (net disapproval = 9 per cent).[5] By 1992, a major change had occurred. In the context of the stalemate between the Democratic Congress and President Bush over the budget deficit in 1990, the savings and loan bailout, the resignation of House Speaker Jim Wright and the Clarence Thomas hearings, the public's confidence in government fell.[6] As Congress' net disapproval ratings increased to 41 per cent, House and Senate incumbents' shares of the vote dipped sharply, although few incumbents lost their seats. 'Congress-bashing', wrote Nelson Polsby, 'is back in style.'[7] After a brief rise following the Gulf War, public approval of Congress' performance continued to slide in the wake of continuing stalemate in 1991 and 1992 over the deficit, the House 'bank' scandal and other manifestations of congressional misconduct, Ross Perot's anti-incumbent message and the nascent term-limits movement. According to Gallup, by March 1992 net disapproval of Congress had reached a massive 51 per cent. In the 1992 congressional elections, incumbents' share of the vote plunged to the lowest levels in the House since 1974 and for the Senate since 1980.[8] House Democrats lost 16 incumbents and Republicans eight. While the damage to Democratic incumbents was not major, with the benefit of hindsight, voter discontent in 1992 seemed to presage the political earthquake of 1994. With the election of Bill Clinton and the return to single-party government, net disapproval of Congress narrowed to about 40 per cent in the first half of 1994, but then, under the onslaught of a skilful national campaign against the 'corrupt' Democratic Congress led by the new House Republican Leader, Newt Gingrich (R.GA), the gap widened. An *ABC New/Washington Post* poll conducted in October 1994 showed net disapproval of Congress at 51 per cent. The result was the first Republican Congress since 1954 and a sharp rise in public approval of Congress' performance.[9]

Gingrich and Dick Armey (R.TX), chair of the House Republican Conference and subsequently Republican Majority Leader in the 104th House, devised the Contract With America as a set of specific election promises which would help overcome public distrust of Congress. The Contract – subtitled 'A Program for Accountability' – promised to bring ten specified bills to a vote on the House floor within the first 100 days of the new Congress, if the Republicans won a majority of House seats. Packaging together proposals which had been introduced by the Republicans over recent years and which were popular,[10] and framed to tap into popular emotions and voter's basic commitments,[11] the plan was intended to assure voters that Republicans could be trusted. Armey argued the value of standing up for a positive agenda to help restore the American dream and the integrity of government'.[12] The Contract signed by Republican candidates spoke of 'restor[ing] the bonds of trust between the people and their elected representatives'. 'If we break this contract,' the Contract declared, 'throw us out. We mean it.' Ohio Republican John Boehner, who became chair of the Republican Conference after the elections, argued that 'both the credibility of the party and ... the institution ... can benefit from [the Contract] ... [The public] will think that this is a place where innovation takes place.'[13] Immediately after their election victory, Gingrich spoke about Republicans initiating a 'revolution'. 'What I can do ...', he told the *Washington Times* in an interview which appeared on the opening day of the 104th Congress, 'is break up the Washington logjam, shift power back to the fifty states, break up all the liberal national organisations – and make them scramble to the state capitals ...'[14] In his opening speech to the House, he spoke of replacing 'the current welfare state with an opportunity society'.

Contrary to some critics of Congress and presidency-centred interpretations of American national government, Congress has frequently assumed a policy-initiating role. America's separated system of checks and balances has allowed – indeed, often has invited – this proactive role, particularly over recent years as split-party government has become the preferred pattern of control of Congress and the presidency.[15] In recent decades, Democratic central party leaders in the House, and to a lesser extent in the Senate, have taken a much more active role in setting and promoting the majority party's policy priorities as part of the broader efforts to wrest control of the policy agenda and national policy leadership from a (Republican) president.[16] The 104th Republican Congress represented one of those very rare examples in the twentieth century of proactive, energetic party leadership, and the only example in recent decades of a Republican leadership on Capitol Hill seeking to wrest the policy initiative from a Democratic president. Gingrich revelled in such a role – indeed, spoke in revolutionary terms of challenging explicitly the Madisonian system. 'We want to maximise the opportunity for substantial change,' he insisted. 'This is a city which is like a sponge. It absorbs waves of change, and it slows them down, and it softens them, and then one morning they cease to exist.'[17] To further the revolution, the internal organisation of Congress itself required change. House Republicans' transition task force would be 'an engine of transformation in the way this city does business – a complete redesign of the administrative and legislative processes of the House'. 'There will be a new order', which would overturn the Democrats' 'special interest state', promised the Republican leader.

This book presents a collection of original essays which seek to describe and explain the events of 1994, 1995 and 1996 in Congress, and place them in the context of broad developments in American government and politics. All eight essays are about the Republicans' takeover of Capitol Hill, but they do not focus exclusively or narrowly on events inside the House and Senate. The first, by Byron Shafer, seeks to explain the 1994 earthquake and its meaning for our understanding of contemporary electoral politics in the United States. What political messages did the 1994 mid-term results carry, and why did existing models of congressional election not work? The second, by Owens, goes to the heart of events on Capitol Hill. What institutional changes were wrought by Gingrich and his colleagues in the House? What was the thinking behind those changes? To what extent were they influenced by notions of a disciplined parliamentary party? What were the legislative consequences of institutional change? The chapter provides an interesting contrast between the responses of the House and the Senate to the 'revolution' which seems fundamental to our understanding of the contemporary Congress.

Barbara Sinclair focuses specifically on Newt Gingrich's leadership. What was, and what remains, distinctive about the Republican leader's style and strategy? How can we characterise Gingrich's leadership? How does his leadership compare with that of his Democratic predecessors, particularly Jim Wright with whom he is most often compared? What factors enabled Gingrich to compete effectively with President Clinton for the role as chief policy leader? To what extent does existing congressional leadership theory accommodate Gingrich?

Gingrich and his party colleagues in the House and Senate are political conservatives. Nigel Ashford examines the ideological substance of the Republican agenda, tracing its origins to the different strands of the conservative movement in the United States. Ashford asks, in which senses were congressional Republicans conservatives, and to what extent did the legislation enacted in the 104th Congress reflect conservatives' policy priorities?

America has a separated system, not a British-style parliamentary system. Events on Capitol Hill cannot be discussed in isolation from presidential activities. The 1994 election results were a body-blow to President Clinton. Michael Foley surveys Bill Clinton's responses to congressional Republican policy leadership. How, over the course of a single congress, was Clinton able to transform his stature from political irrelevance to partner and major policy player? What does this example of contemporary congressional–presidential dynamics tell us about the nature of contemporary presidential leadership?

Dean McSweeney examines the neglected topic of congressional minority politics. How did the initially shell-shocked congressional Democrats respond to the Republican onslaught in the 104th Congress? What strategies did they pursue to counteract Gingrich's programmatic majority and reinforcement of central party rule and with what success? How did minority Democrats interact with their Democratic president?

Chapter 8 introduces an explicitly historical perspective on the Republican takeover by examining the experience of Republican rule in the 80th Congress. It has become almost commonplace to compare the 1994 election results with 1946, and the experience of Bill Clinton in 1995 and 1996 with Harry Truman in 1947 and 1948. In his chapter, Tony Badger identifies the issues which preoccupied the parties in 1946, and examines the often bitter struggles between congressional Republicans and Truman in the 80th Congress. Despite some important similarities, the chapter provides a sharp reminder of how different congressional and presidential politics were in the 1940s.

In the final chapter, Dean McSweeney draws together the most important themes of the book and assesses the overall significance of the 104th Congress to our understanding of this complex institution. How distinctive was the 104th Republic Congress from its Democratic predecessors? How much of its distinctiveness will survive future congresses?

The purpose of this book, then, is not only to provide an interpretation of the politics of this historic congress, but also to help explain its meaning for contemporary congressional politics, and the ideological and institutional contexts in which Congress – and the presidency – operate.

NOTES

1. The other occasions were the 66th (1919–20) and 80th Congresses (1947–8). Republicans controlled both houses in the 83rd Congress, but a Republican, Dwight Eisenhower, occupied the White House. This was also the case during most of the period before 1932.
2. Walter Dean Burnham, 'Realignment Lives: The 1994 earthquake and its implications', in Colin Campbell and Bert A. Rockman, eds., *The Clinton Presidency. First Appraisals* (Chatham, NJ: Chatham House Publishers, 1995), p. 369.
3. Burnham, 'Realignment Lives', p. 367.
4. Samuel C. Patterson and Gregory A. Caldiera, 'Standing up for Congress: Variations in Public Esteem Since the 1960s', *Legislative Studies Quarterly*, 15/1 (February 1990), pp. 28–30; and John R. Hibbing and Elizabeth Theiss-Morse, *Congress as Public Enemy. Public Attitudes Toward American Political Institutions* (Cambridge and New York: Cambridge University Press, 1995), pp. 31–6.
5. CNN/USA Today/Gallup Poll, various dates.
6. Hibbing and Theiss-Morse, *Congress as Public Enemy*, p. 32.
7. Nelson W. Polsby, 'Congress-Bashing for Beginners', *Public Interest*, 100 (1990), pp. 15–23; and Nelson W. Polsby, 'Congress-Bashing through the Ages', *Roll Call*, 10 September 1990, pp. 27 and 32.
8. Samuel C. Patterson and Michael K. Barr, 'Congress Bashing in the 1992 Congressional Election', in Herbert F. Weisberg, ed., *Democracy's Feast. Elections in America* (Chatham, NJ: Chatham House Publishers, 1995), pp. 268–78.
9. CNN/USA Today/Gallup Poll, various dates. By February 1995, net disapproval of Congress had fallen to just 14 points, and throughout the entire Congress remained lower than in the 1992–4 period.
10. John B. Bader, *Taking the Initiative. Leadership Agendas in Congress and the 'Contract With America'* (Washington, DC: Georgetown University Press, 1996), pp. 185–8.
11. James Gimpel, *Fulfilling the Contract. The First 100 Days* (Needham Heights, MA: Allyn and Bacon, 1996), chapter 2.
12. Quoted in Bader, *Taking the Initiative*, p. 182.
13. Quoted in Bader, *Taking the Initiative*, p. 184.
14. Quoted in Elizabeth Drew, *Showdown. The Struggle Between the Gingrich Congress and the Clinton White House* (New York and London: Simon and Schuster, 1966), p. 26.
15. Charles O. Jones, *The Presidency in a Separated System* (Washington, D.C.: The Brookings Institution, 1994), p. 291; and Michael Foley and John E. Owens, *Congress and the Presidency: Institutional Politics in a Separated System* (Manchester and New York: Manchester University Press/St. Martin's Press, 1996), chapter 9.
16. See, for example, Barbara Sinclair, *Legislators, Leaders, and Lawmaking* (Baltimore: The Johns Hopkins University Press, 1995); David W. Rohde, *Parties and Leaders in the Postreform House* (Chicago: University of Chicago Press, 1991); and Bader, *Taking the Initiative*, chapter 1.
17. David S. Cloud, 'Gingrich Clears the Path for Republican Advance', *Congressional Quarterly Weekly Report*, 19 November 1994, p. 3322.

2 The Mid-Term Election of 1994: An Upheaval in Search of a Framework

Byron E. Shafer

A lot of cheap conventional wisdom about American politics was slain by the mid-term election of 1994. Indeed, the death of these conventional grand explanations stands as one of two unequivocally beneficial outcomes of that election. Such 'explanations' included hoary old chestnuts like 'All politics is local', and trendy insider lore like 'The House of Representatives is constitutionally Democratic'. And they included noxious new aspirants like 'It's the economy, stupid'. Their passing remains an unequivocal abstract benefit.

Even a single election cycle later, however, it is easy to forget what a practical earthquake the Republican capture of both houses of Congress seemed at the time. Within days, of course, newspapers and journals were full of commentators demonstrating that they, at least, had known it all along: showing the data that would have 'predicted' this outcome and citing all those quotations, from themselves, that were consistent with it. Yet in its time, there was also a wealth of data on the other side. Moreover, at the time professional analysts reached impressive uniformity – real closure – on a prediction of solid and portentous, but unexceptionable, Republican gains.

Table 2.1 can help to restore the sense of 'earthquake'. Particularly effective for this purpose is the column for partisan control of the House of Representatives, where Xs are Republican and Os are Democratic. Before the 1994 election, Republicans had controlled the House for exactly four of the previous 64 years. Before the 1994 election, a Democratic president had faced a fully Republican Congress for exactly two years since 1918. To say the same thing differently: in a body characterised by incumbent advantage and long careers, there was exactly one of 435 Representatives who had ever served under unified Republican control of Congress.

7

Byron E. Shafer

Table 2.1   Partisan control of the institutions of national government

	Presidency	Congress	The House
1994	0	X	X
1992	0	0	0
1990	X	0	0
1988	X	0	0
1986	X	0	0
1984	X	•	0
1982	X	•	0
1980	X	•	0
1978	0	0	0
1976	0	0	0
1974	X	0	0
1972	X	0	0
1970	X	0	0
1968	X	0	0
1966	0	0	0
1964	0	0	0
1962	0	0	0
1960	0	0	0
1958	X	0	0
1956	X	0	0
1954	X	0	0
1952	X	X	X
1950	0	0	0
1948	0	0	0
1946	0	X	X
1944	0	0	0
1942	0	0	0
1940	0	0	0
1938	0	0	0
1936	0	0	0
1934	0	0	0
1932	0	0	0

Key: 0 = Democratic control; X = Republican control; • = Split control.

Source: *Guide to U.S. Elections* (Washington, D.C.: Congressional Quarterly, 1975); Norman J. Ornstein, Thomas E. Mann and Michael J. Malbin, comps., *Vital Statistics on Congress, 1993–1994* (Washington, D.C.: Congressional Quarterly, 1994).

But before asking how to put the American election of 1994 into its proper perspective – before asking what really happened in 1994 – it is worth returning to two bits of conventional wisdom which remained in force and which thus underpin much of what follows:

1. The first is important in making sense of what did happen and concerns the institutional logic of American government. The separation of powers – separate institutions sharing powers – is *designed* to have different majorities in different institutions and to produce policy from their interaction. This fact seems all the more striking when different political parties control those different institutions. But it is *normally* present, as it was, for example, when Bill Clinton had solid Democratic majorities in both houses of Congress during the preceding two years.

2. The second piece of surviving wisdom is important in extrapolating from whatever happened, albeit important more as a cautionary note this time. What any particular electoral outcome implies for the future – what any particular incarnation of divided government implies in policy terms, as well as how these contribute to subsequent electoral outcomes – depends not so much on what the analyst or the reader can show the election to mean 'objectively' as on what those new Republican senators, but here especially those new Republican House members, *take it to mean.*

THE EVENT ITSELF

So, what did happen? Table 2.2 offers the bare outline. In the Senate, the Republicans gained (and the Democrats lost) eight seats, changing a 56–44 Democratic balance into a 52–48 Republican edge – before Richard Shelby of Alabama added insult to injury by switching parties, taking that edge to 53–47. In the House, the Republicans gained (and the Democrats lost) 53 seats, changing a 258–176–1 Democratic balance to a 229–205–1 Republican edge. These latter numbers use the results immediately after the 1992 election for comparison, and they continue to count the partisanship of a vacancy until it is changed by the next election, but no counting rules have much effect on the composite picture. Instead, what is worth recalling is that, while most analysts did not think this composite the most likely outcome, many did credit the possibility of Republican control of the Senate, few gave more than long odds on Republican control of the House.

Byron E. Shafer

Table 2.2 House and Senate election results: 1992 and 1994

	1992	1994
	Senate	
Republicans	44	53*
Democrats	56	47
Others	0	0
	House	
Republicans	176	229
Democrats	258	205
Others	1	1

Note: * After one switch of parties.

Source: Michael Barone and Grant Ujifusa, *The Almanac of American Politics 1996* (Washington, D.C.: National Journal 1995); Philip D. Duncan and Christine C. Lawrence, *Politics in America 1996: The 104th Congress* (Washington, D.C.: Congressional Quarterly Press, 1995).

Accordingly, it was the House outcome that sealed the sense of congressional upheaval. On the other hand, and not very long ago, how such an upset should be interpreted, if it did happen, at least for its directly electoral implications, would have been obvious. From the mid-term election of 1858 through the mid-term election of 1942, whenever a party recaptured Congress at the mid-term, it went on to recapture the presidency at the next election, and that interpretive fact dwarfed all others. The only exception was the congressional mid-term of 1874 and the (disputed) presidential election of 1876 – and it was politicians, not voters, who prevented the rule from holding then.

Immediately on entering the post-war world, however, the pattern collapsed. There was a genuine exception at the first opportunity, in 1946, when Republicans recaptured both the House and the Senate, but Harry Truman, the Democratic candidate, went on to win the presidency two years later and took back both houses of Congress. There was an even more debilitating exception at the next available opportunity, in 1954, when Democrats recaptured both houses of Congress from a Republican president, Dwight Eisenhower. But this led neither to the recapture of the White House by Democrats in 1956, nor to recapture of Congress by the Republicans. Since then, the most consequential link between aggregate outcomes has been in tatters.

Examined individually, each piece of Congress tells the same story. The House, of course, is the institution which actually generated these patterns, and it was the House which most effectively ended them in the post-war years. The Senate has a less predictive history here, because the Senate has been constitutionally elective only since 1911. Even then, the first genuine exception to a parallel rule – ever – was the first post-war opportunity, in 1946, when Republican senatorial capture still led two years later to a Democratic presidency and Democratic senatorial recapture. And again, the further exception was the next available opportunity, 1954, when Democratic senatorial capture did not produce a Democratic president, but when a re-elected Republican president did not recapture the Democratic Senate.

Social scientists, the specialists charged with recognising such patterns, did try to rescue a predictive element in all this by reversing the relationship, seizing on the fact that the party which won the presidency tended to lose seats in Congress at the next mid-term election. Survey research was the fresh methodological tool for this attempted resuscitation: 'surge and decline' was the name for the restored perspective.[1] What survey research revealed was that presidential years featured both increased voter turnout and increased partisan volatility, while mid-term years featured falling turnout and a return to established party loyalties. As a result, it was possible to restore some regularity to mid-term outcomes, even if the restoration no longer reached far enough to unseat (or confirm) a president.

This revised perspective worked *retrospectively* from 1858 through 1958. It was available – and published – in time for the 1962 mid-term: where it failed, when House results were minimally in accord but when the party holding the presidency, the Democrats, actually gained seats in the Senate. Once again, the choice was between abandoning the search for regularity or regrouping and reinstituting the hunt. Given the mission of the social sciences, the latter produced a further, sophisticated attempt at resuscitation – *The Presidential Pulse of Congressional Elections*, a book offering many additional and valuable insights.[2]

Methodological techniques had improved, so that statistical regression could be the basic tool this time. A powerful new predictive equation emerged, with three main contributory elements: (a) prior presidential vote; (b) current presidential popularity; and (c) the mid-term economic situation. The result was published in 1993. It restored predictability – that is, postdictability – from 1946 to 1992. And it met its fate exactly a year later. A predicted Democratic loss of 18–23 House seats and 3–5 Senate seats became another beautiful hypothesis slain by an ugly fact, or an ugly hypothesis slain by a beautiful fact, whatever you prefer.

Byron E. Shafer

TWO IMMEDIATE PARTISAN 'SPINS'

There were two forceful and immediate interpretations of the meaning of the 1994 election, well before political scientists could return to the search for periodicity. These came, inevitably, from the two political parties; they were, unsurprisingly, very much at variance. Yet not only were there elements of serious, empirically grounded, political science which could be mobilised to bolster their arguments this time. By now, partisan spokespersons themselves knew how to mobilise at least a popularised version of these elements, suggesting the extent to which they had successfully invaded the popular domain during the post-war years.

One theory, the preferred Democratic version but also the preferred version of professional *micro*-analysts, was that the outcome was most reasonably understood, despite its surface drama, as little more than a 'blip' on long-running lines. That is, it was the kind of outlying result which should be expected every half-century or so, when nothing fundamental had changed but when all the familiar but lesser influences happened to coincide in the most extreme way possible.[3] It was not difficult to array the data – some of the data – to be consistent with this view, and Tables 2.3 and 2.4 begin that task.

Table 2.3 Congressional district pluralities for president and House, 1992–4

Partisan outcome for president and House, 1992		House outcome, 1994	
		Democrats	Republicans
		No. of seats (%)	No. of seats (%)
Straight	RR	0 (0%)	126 (100%)
Split	DR	4 (8%)	42 (91%)
Split	RD	23 (46%)	27 (54%)
Straight	DD	178 (84%)	34 (16%)

Key: RR – District voted Republican for president and House;
DR – District voted Democratic for president and Republican for House;
RD – District voted Republican for president and Democratic for House;
DD – District voted Democratic for president and House.

Source: 'New Speaker, New Order', *Congressional Quarterly Weekly Report*, 12 November 1994; Barone and Ujifusa, *The Almanac of American Politics, 1996*; Duncan and Lawrence, *Politics in America, 1996*.

Table 2.4 House membership entrenchment and outcomes in 1994

Type of seat	Democratic winners N (%)	Republican winners N (%)
Republican senior incumbents	0 (0%)	112 (100%)
Republican freshmen/women	0 (0%)	46 (100%)
Republican open seats	4 (18%)	18 (82%)
Democratic open seats	10 (29%)	24 (71%)
Democratic freshmen/women	46 (74%)	16 (26%)
Democratic senior incumbents	145 (92%)	13 (8%)

Source: 'New Speaker, New Order', *Congressional Quarterly Weekly Report*, 12 November 1994; Barone and Ujifusa, *The Almanac of American Politics, 1996*; Duncan and Lawrence, *Politics in America, 1996*.

Table 2.5 Senatorial 'exposure', 1994–2000

	Democrats	Republican
1994	22	13
1996	14	18
1998	19	14
2000	14	21

Source: 'New Speaker, New Order', *Congressional Quarterly Weekly Report*, 12 November 1994.

Thus, for the House, all the old familiar findings did surface. For example, split-ticket districts – those with a presidential vote for one party and a congressional vote for the other in 1992 – were more vulnerable than were straight-ticket districts (Table 2.3). This was true within both parties, though the drift to the Republicans in each category was also evident. By the same token, open seats, those without an incumbent, were more vulnerable than were seats that had even a first-term incumbent, which were in turn more vulnerable than were those that had a more senior occupant (see Table 2.4), though again the drift to the Republicans within all three categories was also patent.

Tables 2.3 and 2.6 take the same interpretation to the Senate, where the crucial framing statistic is the degree of 'exposure'. As Table 2.5

Table 2.6 Senate incumbency, partisanship and election outcomes, 1992 and 1994

		1994	
		Democrats	Republicans
1992	Republicans		Roth (DELAWARE) Mack (FLORIDA) Lugar (INDIANA) MINNESOTA (Grams) Lott (MISSISSIPPI) MISSOURI (Ashcroft) Burns (MONTANA) Chafee (RHODE ISLAND) Hutchison (TEXAS) Hatch (UTAH) Jeffords (VERMONT) Gorton (WASHINGTON) WYOMING (Thomas)
	Democrats	Feinstein (CALIFORNIA) Lieberman (CONNECTICUT) Akaka (HAWAII) Sarbanes (MARYLAND) Kennedy (MASSACHUSETTS) Kerrey (NEBRASKA) Bryan (NEVADA) Lautenberg (NEW JERSEY) Bingaman (NEW MEXICO) Moynihan (NEW YORK) Conrad (NORTH DAKOTA) Robb (VIRGINIA) Byrd (WEST VIRGINIA) Kohl (WISCONSIN)	ARIZONA (Kyl) MAINE (Snowe) MICHIGAN (Abraham) OHIO (DeWine) OKLAHOMA (Inhofe) Santorum (PENNSYLVANIA) Frist (TENNESSEE) TENNESSEE (Thompson) {Shelby (ALABAMA)}

Source: 'New Speaker, New Order', *Congressional Quarterly Weekly Report*.

demonstrates, the Democrats had 22 seats at risk in 1994, the Republicans only 13. In 1996, by contrast, the Republicans could expect to have 18 seats at risk, the Democrats only 14. Table 2.6 lists a name first when there was an incumbent, and a state first when the seat was open, in order to show that open seats, those most vulnerable to partisan change, were also disproportionately Democratic in 1994: six Democrats versus three Republicans. This view is then capped with the point – the ostensibly clinching argument – that only two Democratic incumbents were beaten in the entire senatorial election of 1994, and one of these had been an appointive senator.

At that point, this perspective leaves the realm of theory and enters the realm of fantasy, for in order for Table 2.6 to be read this way, it is necessary to ignore the fact that there are *eight* Senate seats in the lower right-hand corner of Table 2.6 having moved from Democratic to Republican hands, and none in the upper left-hand corner, moving Republican to Democratic. And that is before the switch by Richard Shelby, also in some sense in the lower right-hand corner. Tables 2.7 and 2.8 recast the data from Tables 2.3–2.6 to underline this dissenting implication.

What the Republicans actually managed in the Senate, then, as Table 2.7 shows, was to: (a) hold all Republican incumbents; (b) hold all open Republican seats; (c) pick up all open Democratic seats; (d) invade the ranks of Democratic incumbency; and (e) add that final insult of a party switch. Overall, with just 35 seats at stake and with many of these reliably safe for one party or the other, the Republicans nevertheless managed to engineer a nine-seat shift – and a change of control over the entire body. Nevertheless, what can be said of the Senate is still overshadowed by what happened in the House, as Table 2.8 suggests.

Here, the Republicans held all their incumbents, including all those in districts carried by the Democrats for president in 1992 (the DRs of Table 2.8). They did not lose a single incumbent out of 169! On top of this, they picked

Table 2.7 1994 Senate outcomes revisited

Type of seat	Democrats N	Republicans N
Hold all Republican incumbents	0	10
Pick up all Democratic open seats	0	6
Hold all Republicans open seats	0	3
Add a party switch	0	1
Invade Democratic incumbents	14	2
Add seats not up for election	33	31
Party Totals	47	53

Source: 'New Speaker, New Order', *Congressional Quarterly Weekly Report*; Barone and Ujitusa, *The Almanac of American Politics, 1996*, Duncan and Lawrence, *Politics in America, 1996*.

Byron E. Shafer

Table 2.8   1994 House outcomes revisited

	Type of seat	Democrats N (%)	Republicans N (%)
No. Incumbent Losses	Hold all RRs – The base	0 (0%)	126 (100%)
	Hold all DRs with incumbent	0 (0%)	39 (100%)
	Pick up all open RDs	0 (0%)	10 (100%)
	Drop a few open DRs	4 (57%)	3 (43%)
	But do well with incumbent RDs	23 (58%)	17 (42%)
	Do reasonably well with DRDs	51 (65%)	27 (35%)
	Lose most DDDs – The base	127 (95%)	7 (5%)
	Party Totals	205	229

Key: For two-letter codes, first letter is 1992 vote for president; second is 1992 vote for representative. For three-letter codes, first letter is 1992 vote for president, second is 1988 vote for president, third letter is 1992 vote for representative.

Source: 'New Speaker, New Order', *Congressional Quarterly Weekly Report*; Barone and Ujifusa, *The Almanac of American Politics*; Duncan and Lawrence, *Politics in America, 1996*.

up every open seat previously held by the Democrats which had been carried by the Republican presidential candidate in 1992 (the Open RDs), and nearly half of such seats which had a Democratic incumbent running for re-election (the Incumbent RDs). In addition, they did very respectably among seats with a Democratic incumbent running for re-election where Bill Clinton had carried the district in 1992, but where Michael Dukakis had not in 1988 (the DRDs). Note that without these latter, they would not have controlled the House.

If this can be asserted to be a blip in its details, it is also arguably a tide in the aggregate – which is, again inevitably, the view consistent with the second main interpretive theory, the one preferred by partisan Republicans and professional *macro*-analysts. This is the view that 1994 might, just might, have heralded the theoretically missing 'electoral realignment'. That is, it just might have been the election expected by many analysts and practitioners since 1968, when the Republicans would become the 'new American majority party'.[4]

The data that can be mobilised – partially – on behalf of this perspective have already been displayed in Tables 2.3–2.8. All that remains to be said is that the same mixed consistency which greeted the first argument greets this second one. In the process, this perspective is perhaps even harder to sustain than its opposite number.

- First, the entire notion of a lasting, partisan, electoral realignment had by 1994 become increasingly archaic. The concept, after all, reached back to the era of genuine, strong, *organised* political parties; it depended for its applicability in the modern world on strong party loyalties in the general public – neither of which conditions prevailed in a diverse, wealthy and highly educated society.[5]

I disagree

- Second, the last time the Republicans did achieve a result comparable to 1994 was not 1930 or 1894, precursors to the two consensually recognised previous realignments and acknowledged by all those who believe that the first condition can still be met. Instead, the last Republican counterpart was *1946*, when the party not only went on to lose the next presidential election but saw both houses of Congress swept out of Republican hands.

not accord, to Burnham

On the other hand, here, a uniformly dismissive response seems wrongheaded in one crucial respect. In 1994, there was an apparent partisan realignment going on in one particular and major geographic area, namely, the American South. The once-solid South had been ratcheting towards two-party competition in its congressional representation – and hence ratcheting Republican – since the late 1960s: 1994 represented the greatest single increment to this process ever. Table 2.9 compares the last previous mid-term capture of the House of Representatives by the Republicans, in 1946, with the recapture of 1994, to show how important the South now was to the total phenomenon and how different its behaviour was.

Table 2.9 The South's contribution to Republican recaptures of the House: 1946 and 1994 compared

	1946			1994		
	Republican	Democrat	Other	Republican	Democrat	Other
South	2	103	0	65	61	0
Non-South	243	85	1	164	144	1
Total	245	188	1	229	205	1

Source: Guide to US Elections; Ornstein, Mann and Malbin, Vital Statistics on Congress, 1993–94.

Moreover, what was happening in the South was different from what was happening in the other three great political regions – the Northeast, the Midwest and the West – in ways that also bespeak partisan realignment. Most fundamentally, and unlike the situation in all these other regions, the House of Representatives was going Republican in the South for the first time in American history (if one discounts the years immediately after the Civil War when southern whites were disfranchised). But beyond that, the internal pattern to this outcome was different as well:

- In the Northeast in 1994, there was no recognisable internal trend in evidence.
- In the Midwest and West, where the Republicans also made strong gains, Republican candidates were most successful in those districts that were most conservative, the ones that could be expected to be competitive under existing partisan conditions.
- But in the South, conservative districts with conservative Democratic incumbents did not do badly; it was districts that possessed *moderate* white Democrats that fell disproportionately to the Republicans. That is a realigning, not a deviating, pattern.

In the aggregate, then, for the nation as a whole, this was surely not a classic realignment. But in the South it probably was, and that possibility does have a further reverberation for the nation at large. To wit: such an outcome, if realised, would move the partisan baseline in Congress, so that when the Democrats next regained control their 'normal' margin would be less than it had been in the entire recent past.

AN ALTERNATIVE FRAMEWORK

Most partisan and journalistic attempts to restore one of these two arguments – or indeed, to get beyond them – proceeded by analogy. 1994 was like 1930, so 1996 would be like 1932; 1994 was like 1946, so 1996 would be like 1948; 1994 was really like 1966, so 1996 would be like 1968; and so on. The problems in this are obvious. Each one of these analogies just might, of course, turn out to be (superficially) right; some such analogy has to be. But 1994 was manifestly *not* 1930, 1946 or 1966, for reasons historical, social and even demographic, so that there are no obvious prior criteria for choosing among these analogies. In that sense, any one that did turn out to be right was entitled to do so by purest accident.

What is needed instead is some larger framework – ideally one that places 1994 into a pattern involving a substantial number of other relevant elections, thereby providing the necessary grounds for asking where that pattern goes next. Any such framework is in part a hostage to fortune, as the previous surge-and-decline elaborations forcefully attest. Nevertheless, producing such a framework is the inescapable mandate in this enterprise. Ideally, besides placing 1994 in the context of a variety of preceding contests, such a framework should help to accomplish two further tasks. While these latter tasks add to the analytic load, they simultaneously help to differentiate between plausible solutions.

The first additional task is to sharpen the relevance of the subsequent choices made by those elected in 1994 to the outcome of the contests in 1996 and after, thereby making any contemporary framework contribute to future analyses. The second task is to deal with three specific aspects of the election of 1994, aspects distinctive enough to cry out for further interpretation. These include: the explanation that failed; the issue that resurged; and the social group that switched.

The 'explanation that failed' is economics. Many political analysts do believe that the state of the economy is always the dominant element driving electoral outcomes, though they differ – fracture – over whether its impact is objective or subjective, retrospective or prospective, personal or sociotropic. Many political operatives in turn believe that economics as a concern has a partisan cut: it is good for Democrats. Finally, both analysts and operatives agree that a healthy economy is beneficial to incumbents. Yet in 1994 there was a huge Democratic incumbency, in a strong and growing economy. And yet…

The 'issue that resurged' was crime. Tortured Democratic manoeuvring on a major criminal justice bill helped frame the 1994 election campaign, and pre-election polls which asked the public about the major issue facing the country frequently elicited 'crime'.[6] Yet in its way the presence of electoral damage from crime was every bit as puzzling as the absence of an electoral boost from economics. The official crime rate was down in the United States, and this seemed to be an accurate reflection of what was happening, at least, in the high-crime sector. Yet concern with crime was evidently soaring.

The 'social group that switched' was men, especially southern white men, but really all men and this was a major difference (see Table 2.10). The so-called 'gender gap' is usually small in American elections, exceeded by other social factors, and even then is sometimes an artifact of the social distribution of men and women in the voting population. In 1994, this was not the case. The gap itself – the difference between men and women in partisan voting – bulged dramatically. Moreover, all the increment was apparently contributed by men: we shall return to this below.

Table 2.10   Sex and the 1994 vote for the House

	1990		1992		1994	
	Democrats	Republicans	Democrats	Republicans	Democrats	Republicans
Men	51%	49%	52%	48%	46%	54%
Women	54%	46%	55%	45%	54%	46%

Source: 'Portrait of an Electorate: Who Voted For Whom in the House?', *New York Times*, 13 November 1994, compiled from exit polls conducted by Mitfosky International and Voters Research and Surveys.

These are some of the lesser puzzles to go with the bigger interpretive task, puzzles that make that task more demanding, of course, but that also, ideally, help in distinguishing reasonable solutions. In any case, to generate some fresh and non-partisan alternative aimed at meeting these goals, it makes sense to begin with the year 1946. That was, after all, the first post-war general election; it was the year that Republicans last seized control of both houses of Congress under a Democratic president; it was, coincidentally, the year Bill Clinton was born. What was politics about then, and how was it organised?

The substance of politics was principally focused on economic and social welfare issues, and secondarily on foreign affairs and national security. In this respect, a concern with bringing the welfare state to the United States in the 1930s and 1940s had been succeeded by a concern with bringing the full-employment state to the 1950s and 1960s; just as pursuit of the Second World War had been succeeded by the pursuit of Cold War. The basic coalitions providing a social structure to this issue conflict – the two partisan coalitions – were, then, built principally on social class. The Democrats were the party of working-class Americans, the poor, a few unpoor but sympathetic minorities, plus the entire South. The Republicans were the party of the middle class, joined by farmers outside the South.

Foreign affairs were kinder to the Republicans in such a world. Yet politics was largely centred on domestic welfare, which was much kinder to the Democrats. As a result, the Democratic Party was far more likely to win national elections, not just capturing the presidency but sweeping both houses of Congress along with it. Republicans could, however, do the same, when Democrats stumbled or when the Republicans had an especially attractive presidential candidate.

This pattern, first surfacing in the congressional election of 1930, lasted through the presidential election of 1964. It was called into question by the congressional election of 1966, and then shattered in the presidential election of 1968. Richard Nixon was the personal vehicle for its demise, but the diagnostic fact of his election was that he managed to carry neither house of Congress with him – arguably the first time in American history that an incoming president had failed to do so, though this soon became commonplace. The new pattern was to become recognised for the split partisan control of national government, which often accompanied it. The 'Late New Deal Era' thus gave way to the 'Era of Divided Government'.

Yet what was really different were the substantive issues on which this era came to centre, and the social coalitions through which it was organised. One of the great issue clusters to this era was recurrently familiar – economics and social welfare – and the economic/welfare cluster was still about the distribution of material goods in society. Yet this cluster was joined, for 1968 and through to the present day, by a set of issues incorporating foreign relations, but going far beyond it. This was a cultural/national cluster, about the intrinsic character of social life, and it picked up a huge array of matters including the public role of religion, crime and public order, sex roles and orientations, permissiveness and social control, environmentalism, the conscious taking of human life, and on and on.

The key point, however, is that the majority coalition on each of these great substantive clusters, the economic/welfare or the cultural/national clusters, was not the same as the majority coalition on the other. A liberal on economic/welfare matters, for example, could be either a liberal or a conservative on cultural/national matters, just as a conservative on cultural/national matters could be either a conservative or a liberal on economic/welfare concerns. The two dimensions were *socially* independent, thereby creating an institutionalised cross-pressure on both parties in American politics.[7]

Those parties had not actually changed their positions on these two issue clusters. The Democrats were still more liberal on both, the Republicans were still more conservative. But in an era when a second major cluster had increased in priority, the more important fact was that there were *conservative* majorities in the nation as a whole on these cultural/national concerns, and a number of practical implications followed directly from this fact. Most certainly, Republicans began to secure sustained victories in the presidency; they had a much harder time with Congress, despite those presidential victories. The new era of divided government – our era – had accordingly arrived.

There appeared to be good reasons why the normal product of this era was Republican presidencies with Democratic Congresses, and indeed, why its main secondary product was unified Democratic control of government. Foreign policy issues, for both constitutional and practical reasons, gravitated more to the presidency than to Congress. So now did cultural issues, in part by way of the powers of office, but in larger part because of the greater symbolic potential of the presidency. Yet Congress had long since cemented its ties to the social welfare bureaucracy, keeping those issues more strongly linked to the legislature than to the presidency. And Congress was always a better target when seeking the direct and divisible rewards of government – constituency service – than was the presidency.

Moreover, presidential candidates could not possibly avoid the social cross-pressures between economic/welfare and cultural/national issues in a nationwide campaign. Congressional candidates, on the other hand, often could: representing more homogeneous districts, they could adapt their positions on cultural/national issues in order to coincide with the dominant views of a single district. As a result, because there were more Democrats than Republicans in the nation as a whole, because economic/welfare issues had been central to creating these party loyalties, and because there were thus normally more Democratic incumbents in Congress: (a) Democrats normally held Congress even against a Republican tide in the presidency; and (b) in good years, they added a Democratic president to this congressional hold.

1994 IN THE FRAMEWORK

The mid-term election of 1994 is superficially a challenge to this scenario. It has the 'wrong' partisan mix, contributing a Republican Congress to a Democratic presidency; it is not therefore obvious that it does not have the 'wrong' issue associations as well. Either this challenge is sustained, then, and this framework too falls away, or 1994 can be shown to be only superficially inconsistent, so that the underlying bases of continuity actually strengthen the framework. Either way, the most direct and immediate starting point for analysis is the presidential election of 1992, and it can in fact extend the argument to 1994 without having to change the contours of the era of divided government in any way.

Most aspects of *candidate behaviour* in 1992 were fully consistent with patterns established early in the era of divided government. Thus Republicans talked about foreign policy and cultural values whenever possible, just as Democrats talked about social welfare and economic benefit, again whenever possible. Most other aspects of campaign strategy constituted simple adjustments within the same basic framework. Thus Bill Clinton pulled back consciously from previous party thematics on cultural/national issues, while pushing health insurance in particular to the fore. Less fortuitously, George Bush had to apologise for raising taxes and for a sour economy on the economic/welfare dimension, while being pulled to the right on cultural/national issues – in the very year when the Democratic candidate was trying to pull back to the centre.

Thus, a Democratic candidate positioned well, in the modern era, against a Republican candidate positioned badly. Yet there was, of course, one other thing. Ever since 1968 and the coming of the era of divided government, Democrats had been trying to push economic/welfare issues up from Congress into the presidency, just as Republicans had been trying to push cultural/national issues down from the presidency into Congress. The presidential year 1992, then, became the great Democratic success at this manoeuvre. The economy *was* the issue, just as health care was the main secondary concern. And the Democrats did, in consequence, wrest the presidency away from the Republicans.

Yet it is worth recalling, with an eye on 1994, that the Democrats actually managed to lose seats in the House, thereby reminding analysts in search of a pattern that the preconditions for a divided government did not obviously disappear with the election of Bill Clinton, or with the return of unified partisan control – all of which begins to make the congressional election of 1994 emerge from the analytic mist. For 1994 was in turn the year when Republicans finally managed *their* great triumph on the other side of the strategic manoeuvre. Which is to say: within the era of divided government, 1994 became the year when the Republicans managed to drive cultural/national issues down into Congress to such an extent that they captured both houses even without a presidential candidate at their head.

What did all this mean, in substantive terms? In many ways, the issues for the general public – and the partisan associations with these issues – continued undisturbed in 1994. In 1992, those who had been most concerned with economics or social welfare voted disproportionately Democratic, while those who had been most concerned with foreign affairs or cultural values voted disproportionately Republican. It was just that, in this particular presidential year, there had been far more of the former than the latter. By 1994, on the other hand, there was a real record of presidential responses to these preferences and perceptions, and it was uniformly pro-Republican in impact.

On those matters for which the general public had preferred the Democrats in 1992, namely economic stimulus and health care, they had gained nothing. The widely trumpeted economic stimulus plan had failed to pass, and so – incredibly – had any kind of health care reform. Yet on those matters for which the general public had never preferred the Democrats, namely foreign affairs and especially cultural values, that public had witnessed a succession of undesired initiatives: the gay military, sexual harassment, Whitewater, 'travelgate', the FBI files, even a much-publicised presidential haircut.

To this was added that framing legislative battle over an omnibus crime bill, again highlighting those aspects of the national Democratic Party – cultural liberalism, governmental fumbling – which were least appealing to the general public. To all of that was added an ongoing sequence of congressional scandals – managed, of course, by the long-dominant Democrats – in which a congressional post office scandal and an in-house banking scandal were only the most collectively noteworthy, though they were complemented by many individual cases – and excesses – as well. There were, in short, few reasons in 1994 to cast a ballot based on the economic/welfare dimension, and many reasons to cast one along the cultural/national dimension.

The regional pattern of the vote attests to the strategic success of national Republicans in exploiting this dimension. For, the four great political regions of the United States actually exemplify the cross-cutting pattern of issue preferences. In this, cultural issues are normally understood to pit the liberal coasts – that is, the Northeast and the West – against the more conservative interior – the Midwest and the South. On the other hand, the old economic coalitions, those that sustained the New Deal, also divide these regions into pairs, pitting the Northeast and South as liberals this time, against the Midwest and West as conservatives.[8]

If 1994 had been about economic/welfare issues in such a context, then the Midwest and West should have been more Republican, the Northeast and South less so. But if 1994 was about cultural/national issues instead, then the South and Midwest should have been more Republican, the Northeast and West less so – as in fact they were (Table 2.11). Indeed, ignoring the economic/welfare dimension entirely and ranking the four regions merely on cultural/national liberalism or conservatism yields a nice approximation by itself to the change in Republican support from the election of 1990, the most recent mid-term election (Table 2.12).[9]

This should not be taken to mean that economic/welfare issues went away in 1994. As Table 2.13 affirms, the relationship of a Republican or Democratic vote to family income, for example, certainly remained – and ran in the direction that it long has. On the other hand, it should also be noted that – with the exception of the bottom category, the poorest tenth of

Table 2.11   Regional preferences and the 1994 Republican Vote for the House

	Voter preference in CBS/NYT exit poll	Actual vote in contested elections
South	56%	54%
Midwest	56%	53%
Northeast	48%	50%
West	41%	48%

Source: 'Portrait of an Electorate: Who Voted For Whom in the House?', *New York Times*; 'New Speaker, New Order', *Congressional Quarterly Weekly Report*.

Table 2.12   Region, cultural values, and change in House Republicans' vote share, 1990–4

Region/cultural values	Percentage change
West/Very Liberal	–5
Northeast/Liberal	+2
Midwest/Conservative	+5
South/Very Conservative	+9

Source: 'New Speaker, New Order', *Congressional Quarterly Weekly Report*.

Table 2.13   Party vote shares for the House, by family income, 1994

Income	Percentage of All Voters	Vote Share (%)	
		Democratic	Republican
Over $50,000	39%	46%	54%
$30–50,000	30%	49%	51%
$15–30,000	20%	52%	48%
Under $15,000	11%	62%	38%

Source: 'Portrait of an Electorate: Who Voted For Whom in the House?', *New York Times*.

the electorate – the differences are not very large, and are certainly much less impressive than religious affiliation: a classic cultural locator. Here, the range on a rough continuum of Christian fundamentalism from evangelical Protestant at one end of the continuum to Jewish at the other (see Table 2.14) is imposing indeed, as is that new *sex difference* (see Table 2.9 above), which simply would not disappear in 1994.

Take, this time, educational attainment crossed with sex (Table 2.15). Again, the relationship with another key aspect of social class does not disappear. But again, except for the bottom of the distribution, where there

Table 2.14　Party vote shares for the House by religion, 1994

	Percentage of all voters	Vote share (%)	
		Democratic	Republican
Evangelic Protestants	20%	24%	76%
Liturgical Protestants	21%	44%	56%
Catholic and Orthodox	29%	52%	48%
Others and none	26%	62%	38%
Jewish	4%	76%	24%

Source: 'Portait of an Electorate: Who Voted For Whom in the House?', *New York Times*.

Table 2.15　Party vote shares for the House by education and sex, 1994

	Percentage of all voters	Vote share (%)	
		Democratic	Republican
'Some college' men	15%	44%	56%
College graduate men	23%	45%	55%
High school graduate men	9%	48%	52%
'Some college' women	17%	50%	50%
College graduate women	20%	53%	47%
High school graduate women	11%	55%	45%
High school drop-out men	2%	60%	40%
High school drop-out women	2%	70%	30%

Source: 'Portrait of an Electorate: Who Voted For Whom in the House?', *New York Times*.

are very few voters, sex trumps social class all along the line, with high-school graduate men going more Republican than college graduate women, and so on.

In any case, in an era when there are two great underlying issue dimensions to American politics, in an era when these produce two great but cross-cutting public majorities, but in an era when the two major parties hold the majority position on only one of these (two) issue dimensions, it is obviously possible to have divided government in either direction, with Republican presidencies and Democratic congresses, or Democratic presidencies and Republican congresses.

THE FRAMEWORK AND THE FINE POINTS OF 1994

Is such a conclusion also consistent with the three contemporary side-puzzles of the 1994 election – the explanation that failed (economics); the issue that resurged (crime); and the group that shifted (men)? The frame-work cannot simultaneously be a specific explanation for why these three elements moved together so forcefully in 1994. It does, however, constrain the search for such an explanation. Or at least, to be consistent, any explanatory candidate ought to focus on: (a) the differential priority between cultural/national concerns and economic/welfare matters; (b) the specific substance of those items energising the cultural/national cluster; and (c) elements which might have made the economic/welfare cluster behave, whenever it did surface in 1994, in ways parallel to the cultural/national dimension.

The first of the puzzles peculiar to the 1994 election was the 'explanation that failed', namely economics, and the larger explanation for its failure, so-called, was clear within this framework: the priority placed on economics in 1992 had been almost obliterated by 1994. Yet there is a further hypothesis, relating to the residuals. For impressive aggregate statistics on economic growth and employment, an impressive economic rebound in the aggregate, were also being greeted by the general public with a marked lack of enthusiasm. Which is to say: those who still made economics a priority in 1994 appeared to feel that while the economy might be fine in the aggregate, it was ever more unpredictable at the individual – at their personal – level.

The second of these puzzles specific to 1994 was the 'issue that resurged', namely crime. There is little need to say more about it. Crime was a classic cultural/national issue; its resurgence helped raise the priority of this entire cluster of issues; and the Democrats could hardly have played into it less effectively had they tried. But the sub-puzzle of crime in this context actually does appear to parallel the sub-puzzle of economics. To wit: crime might well be falling in the aggregate – the precise opposite of the situation on economics – but it *seemed* to be ever more randomly intrusive at the individual level at the same time.

Finally, the third puzzle peculiar to 1994 was the 'social group that switched', namely men. But here, if the gender gap has at last arrived as a major partisan feature, what the larger interpretive framework offers is a hypothesis to be applied in future elections. Put simply: the framework requires little or no elaboration in order to handle the size of this particular shift if cultural/national concerns were disproportionately important to men, and economic/welfare concerns disproportionately important to women. It must be noted that in the early post-war years, during the late New Deal era, this was not the case. Men focused on economic redistribution, women on traditional values. As a result, the former leaned to the Democrats, the latter to the Republicans. Yet there are many reasons for hypothesising a reversal in our time, from changes in family structure to changes in employment status. The point is merely that it would take at least the 1996 elections, and probably more, to evaluate this particular hypothesis.

None of this says anything directly about what the mid-term elections of 1994 implied in *policy* terms – implied for the evolution of public policy as a result of the outcome in 1994. Indeed, all such prognostications turn crucially, as we noted at the very beginning, on how the new Republican House members and senators themselves interpreted the mandate of 1994. This is not, it should be emphasised, an unusual situation. Large electoral swings are normally *away from* something; it is the job of those elected in these swings to put definition into that concern. If they get it right, they should prosper, at least until the next such large electoral swing. If they get it wrong, they are entitled to be gone as quickly as they came.

On the other hand, the fact that a framework for the era of divided government can encompass the 1994 outcome comfortably, along with the fact that the peculiarities of 1994 get at least further definition from this framework, does have implications for the fate of those new House members and senators, however they chose to interpret it. For the thrust of this framework is derived from certain institutionalised characteristics of American politics, characteristics which can be adapted but not, presumably, overridden. Within the framework, then, one major contingent implication from the election of 1994 for the election of 1996 – and beyond – is clear enough:

- If those new Republican legislators read their mandate as basically cultural, having to do with the character of ordinary American life, they were entitled to hang around. Crime and punishment, achievement and opportunity, family support and traditional values, and, yes, the character of political life too: those were among the touchstones on this dimension.
- Alternatively, if they read their mandate as basically economic, having to do with the distribution of material goods in American society, they were at risk of being gone as quickly as, say, the 1946 Republican Congress. Taxation, including its progressivity and its exemptions; social welfare, including social insurance and compensatory incentives; economic growth, including its rate and its location: those were touchstones for this alternative dimension.

Some further aspects of this choice were, in truth, already emerging by the time the results of the 1994 election were known. Thus it was clear, by the time this new Congress assembled, that the great temptation along both these dimensions was likely to come wrapped in the policies and politics of the fiscal deficit. Deficit-cutting, in and of itself, is probably best seen as falling on the cultural/national dimension. And successful reduction is likely to be seen, again in the abstract, as an unalloyed public good. Which is to say: few congressmen or women were likely to return home in two years' time and report, 'You sent me to Washington to restore traditional values, and I understood that to mean increasing the deficit.'

On the other hand, the practical situation was not so straightforward. For serious efforts to reduce the deficit, most especially for a new Republican Congress which was buttressed by conservative values on foreign affairs, really had to focus on at least the growth of entitlement programmes, and possibly on their social reach. Yet this immediately risked moving the argument onto the economic/welfare dimension, where Democrats had their natural majority and where Republicans had, for 60 years, been at their least credible. An assault on these basic social insurance programmes – or more accurately, anything which could successfully be portrayed as an assault, whether in the name of deficit reduction or of anything else – was likely to see those House members returning home in two years, permanently.

What raised the stakes in this regard – what made the situation more portentous but also more fraught – was an argument that the new Republican Congress itself had made during the election campaign, about the potential for 'leadership'. Arguing that the failures of the Clinton Administration to deliver what it had promised, along with its success at delivering some things it had not, was an evident failure of leadership, the new cohort of Republican congressional candidates promised to reassert that leadership if elected. Once elected, this promise increased the pressure. Or, said differently, if 'gridlock and inaction' had been the chief failing of the 103rd Congress, gridlock and inaction could not be allowed to characterise the 104th – despite the coupling of a Democratic president with this Republican Congress, and despite a congressional agenda at loggerheads with the president's.

What further complicated such extrapolations, however – the final cautionary note – was that they would also be the product of an interaction with the choices made by the president. A Bill Clinton who emphasised unpopular cultural/national positions might save even a Republican Congress that got its own choices wrong. Just as a Bill Clinton who repositioned himself and successfully resuscitated an economic/welfare emphasis might save at least the presidency, even if the new Republican Congress got its choices right. Or any number of intermediate mixes.

AFTERWORD ON PARTIES, INSTITUTIONS AND POLICY COMPETITION

There was, however, a prospect contributed by the mid-term election of 1994 which ran in a less conditional direction, at least in the abstract, and for which the crucial concrete preconditions had been met in the outcome of that election itself. In this, simple Republican control of Congress – the return of Republicans to majorities in both houses but especially in the House of Representatives – was already at least an essential contribution to solving one of the great problems of modern American politics. In general terms, that problem concerns the apparent demise of party competition with regard to one of the great elected institutions of American government. In specifics, it concerned the apparent inability, over two full generations, of the Republican Party to gain control of the House.

That inability was fundamentally corrupting for those Republicans who grew up within its confines. Within those confines, House Republicans gradually lost all hope of developing an alternative (Republican) programme for dealing with national problems. Having lost that hope, they had less and less reason to be accommodating, less reason to be anything other than obstructive. As a result, even successful Republican *presidents*, in the face of an increasingly intransigent partisan base in Congress, had little incentive – had little or no prospect – for addressing domestic problems generally, lacking support from either the opposition or their own party. In such a world, they had reduced incentives even to address those cultural issues which were so central to their election. The continuance of these would be essential to Republican presidential fortunes; failure at legislating on them could always be pinned on the opposition.

Yet the same situation had an equally powerful (and equally corrupting) effect on the other side of the partisan aisle. For the unfailing possibility of building majorities within their own ranks without any serious electoral interference, coupled with the increasing lack of any prospect of building coalitions across party lines, encouraged a kind of perennial 'deal-making' to knit the Democratic coalition together. Policy-making became a matter of extended side-payments within the coalition; as long as its rewards could be shared effectively, the need to address changing policy problems or changing public wishes all but disappeared. Most policy realms, from physical infrastructure to higher education to criminal justice, thus became matters to be converted into divisible goods, parcelled out to coalition members. In the process, there was no need to update a programme or even, in essence, to regenerate the larger coalition.

The 1994 election was a major contribution to sweeping away this particular problem, the absolutely essential precondition to its removal. Even then, of course, it could not do so on its own. Whether it did so over the longer run was ultimately tied up with the response of these new Republican legislators to their new governmental role. Which only increases the consequence of what they did, in and to government, when they arrived there as the 104th Congress.

NOTES

1. The fountainhead for all such work is Angus Campbell, 'Surge and Decline: A Study of Electoral Change', *Public Opinion Quarterly* 24 (Fall 1960), pp. 397–418.

2. James E. Campbell, *The Presidential Pulse of Congressional Elections* (Lexington, KY: University of Kentucky Press, 1993).

3. A huge amount of the relevant literature is mobilised, and the 1994 election placed within its context as well, in Paul R. Abramson, John H. Aldrich and David W. Rhode, *Change and Continuity in the 1992 Elections*, rev. edn (Washington, D.C.: Congressional Quarterly Press, 1995).

4. Landmarks in this perspective include Walter Dean Burnham, *Critical Elections and the Mainsprings of American Politics* (New York: W.W. Norton, 1970), and James L. Sundquist, *Dynamics of the Party System: Alignment and Realignment of Political Parties in the United States* (Washington, D.C.: The Brookings Institution, 1973)

5. The debate over its applicability can be sampled in Byron E. Shafer, ed., *The End of Realignment? Interpreting American Electoral Eras* (Madison:

University of Wisconsin Press, 1991); the attack is most richly exemplified in Joel H. Silbey, *The American Political Nation, 1838–1893* (Standford, CA: Stanford University Press, 1991).

6. For an even more portentous analysis of the crime bill and the crime issue, see Holly Idelson, 'An Era Comes to a Close: Costly victory on crime bill exposes Democratic weakness, foreshadows GOP takeover', *Congressional Quarterly Weekly Report*, 23 December 1995, pp. 3871–3.

7. Byron E. Shafer and William J. M. Claggett, *The Two Majorities: The Issue Context of Modern American Politics* (Baltimore and London: The Johns Hopkins University Press, 1995).

8. The cultural pattern – for a 'bicoastal coalition' – comes through clearly in, for example, Joel Garreau, *The Nine Nations of North America* (Boston: Houghton Mifflin, 1981); the economic coalitions stemming from the New Deal alignment are even more explicit and clearer in Everett Carll Ladd, *American Political Parties: Social Change and Political Response* (New York: W.W. Norton, 1970).

9. Regional rankings for cultural conservatism (and liberalism) are developed from the data in Shafer and Claggett, *The Two Majorities*.

3 Taking Power? Institutional Change in the House and Senate

John E. Owens

Conventionally, periods in American politics have been identified with American presidents – the Roosevelt era, the Kennedy–Johnson era, the Reagan era, and so on – rather than particular Congresses. These presidential labels are attached not only because of the prevailing presidentialism in American political science and history, but often because particular presidents are associated with detectable shifts in public policy. The events of 1995 and 1996 do not fit this pattern. As has often been the case in American government, the primary thrust for policy change came from Congress[1] not from the White House. In the past, when Congress has sought to shift public policy in a new direction members have frequently sought also to adjust their chambers' internal organisational arrangements so that they may better fulfil their policy needs and demands. When the 70 or so War Hawks elected to the 12th House in 1810 wanted to push President James Madison into waging war against Britain, they transformed the previously inert Speakership into the chamber's political leader, augmented the office's authority so as to rival the president, and elected Henry Clay as Speaker. Clay then used his new authority to appoint like-minded House members to committees and chairs in order to advance the new members' policy agenda. In 1910, Progressive Republicans in the House wished to defeat the Payne–Aldrich tariff bill and curtail the power of their autocratic leader, Speaker 'Uncle Joe' Joseph G. Cannon (R.IL, 1903–11). Progressives combined with minority Democrats to strip Cannon of his power. When Democrats organised the House in the wake of Watergate, rebellious Democrats ousted three elderly committee chairs and curbed committee chairs' powers, strengthened the powers of the Speaker, and instituted other reforms designed to enhance party accountability and flatten the authority structure within the House.

Following the resounding defeat of congressional Democrats in the 1994 mid-term elections, the new Republican House majority led by Newt

Gingrich (R.GA) followed in the footsteps of the War Hawks of 1810, the Progressives of 1910 and the Democrats of 1974 to institute changes in the organisational structures of the House and the Senate in order to enact their policy programme.

What was the nature of the organisational changes in the House? To what extent did the thrust for institutional change extend to the Senate? And what were their consequences for public policy and the legislative record of the 104th Congress? What can we learn about the nature of contemporary congressional politics from the institutional experience of 1995 and 1996?

A PARTISAN PUSH FROM THE HOUSE

There is no question that the main impetus for legislative change in the 104th Congress came from the new Republican majority in the House – rather than the Senate – at least in the first session. There were several reasons for this. First, Gingrich – the new House Republican leader – had written and fought the 1994 elections on the Contract With America – a set of legislative proposals designed to reduce the role of the federal government in American society. Second, the rules and norms of the House more than those of the Senate better facilitate more abrupt (and less incremental) policy change. House rules are designed to uphold and promote majority rule – or more accurately, majority party rule. The Senate upholds minority rule by protecting the rights and prerogatives of individual senators. For this and a host of other reasons to do with the size of the respective chambers, senators' staggered and longer terms, the effects of partisan change on the House are likely to be sharper than on the Senate. Third, House Republicans became the majority in 1994 after the longest period of single-party rule in congressional history. Finally, the partisan push from the House was fired by an ideologically homogeneous majority party. After 1988, the House Republican Conference came to be dominated by conservatives. By the 1980s, the Rockefeller liberals, so significant in the 1960s, had disappeared, while the number of moderates had declined sharply.[2] Conservative preponderance within the Conference soon led to a more united party in the 1990s (see Figure 3.1) and to the adoption of a new, more aggressive, confrontational legislative style symbolised by the election of Newt Gingrich as Republican Whip in 1989 and heir-apparent to emollient, traditional, Main Street conservative leader Bob Michel (R.IL). 'We had a choice of being attack dogs or lap dogs. We decided attack dogs are more useful,'[3] observed a House Republican. As subsequent events confirmed, Gingrich was more than a 'bomb thrower'. He was a strategically-minded politician who saw clearly the need to change House and party structures in order to advance his and his party's policy goals. An ardent admirer of Clay, Gingrich rejected explicitly the Madisonian model of congressional politics based on bargaining, negotiation and compromise, and organised institutionally round the labyrinthine, cross-cutting committee system with its imprecise, subject-of-negotiation relationship with the majority party. Republicans, he argued, should become 'party activists' rather than 'district guys' and 'committee guys'[4] and strengthen the instruments of party rule.[5]

nice

In the late 1980s and early 1990s, Gingrich's enthusiasm for party government won growing support from Republican moderates as well as conservatives. It led directly to the ten-point Contract – the party's 1994 manifesto written by Gingrich and (then Conference chair) Richard Armey (R.TX); to the imposition of the Contract's specific commitments on Republican committee members, sometimes against their wishes;[6] to a warning by Gingrich in early 1994 that ranking committee members should not take their positions for granted; and to the party's coordinated

Figure 3.1 Mean House Party Support Scores, 1954–95

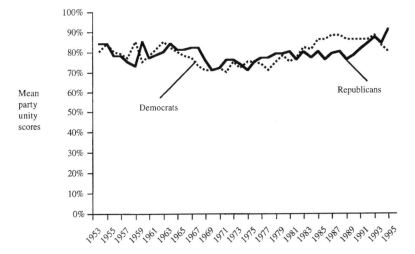

Note: Data are normalised to eliminate the effects of absences.

Source: Norman J. Ornstein, Thomas E. Mann and Michael J. Malbin, *Vital Statistics on Congress 1995–1996* (Washington, D.C.: Congressional Quarterly Press, 1996), Table 8.4. Data for 1995 recomputed from *Congressional Quarterly Weekly Report*, 27 January 1996, pp. 246–7.

national campaign led by Gingrich in which voters were invited to reject the *party* at the next available opportunity if it did not deliver on its promises.[7] After the election, Gingrich moved to implement his plans for a disciplined parliamentary party with himself as leader, or prime minister. In his daily briefings broadcast on C-SPAN and other television stations, Gingrich argued that Republicans had a mandate which should not only be accepted by the House, but also by the Senate and the president.

CONGRESS IN THE 1990s

House Republicans' enthusiastic endorsement of the principles of party government raised the important question of whether Congress in the mid-1990s was ready or amenable to this particular mode of governance. Congress often finds it difficult – even impossible – to decide on policy, at least expeditiously; witness the legislative débâcle over health reform in 1994.[8] Public and media criticism of the institution's governing capacity is widespread and often intense.[9] The reasons for Congress' difficulties need be only briefly rehearsed: the institution's fragmented structure which disperses responsibilities for collecting policy-related information and processing legislation among numerous subunits; the deliberately cumbersome, lengthy, cumulative and sequential nature of the legislative process; the existence of numerous veto points along the way; the absolute necessity for bargaining and compromise in an institution characterised by decentralisation and highly qualified party loyalty; the complexity of written and unwritten rules and procedures; and Congress' vulnerability within a separated system to influence from executive agencies (often the president), state and local government, sometimes the courts, and numerous interest groups and other 'policy watchers'.

In addition, Congress in the mid-1990s is populated by political self-starters – ambitious men and women who have come into politics on their own initiative – who as elected House members and senators expect to do business for themselves, and are not generally susceptible to the pleas of seniors or party leaders to support party policy. Perhaps individualism is not as potent in the House and Senate as it was in the 1970s and 1980s, but the individualist entrepreneurial spirit remains strong – nourished by the increasing proportion of junior members (see Figure 3.2) each determined to make his or her mark, the substantial resources made available to members' personal offices independent of party organisations and committees, and the constant demands on members to serve their individual states and districts effectively.[10]

Figure 3.2 Changing Patterns of House Service: Junior Members and Careerists, 1953–95

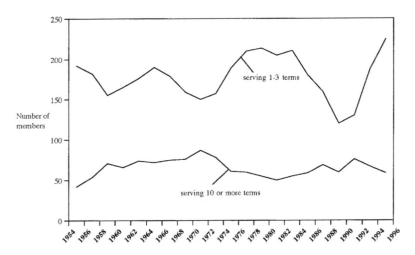

Source: Norman J. Ornstein, Thomas E. Mann, and Michael J. Malbin, *Vital Statistics on Congress, 1995–96* (Washington, D.C.: American Enterprise Institute, 1996), Table 1–6.

Yet, as these individualising, decentralising forces were strengthening, so were congressional parties. From the mid-1970s onwards, House members and senators sought to strengthen their party organisations and the powers of their central leaders. In the 1980s, more assertive House Speakers – notably Jim Wright (D.TX, 1987–9)[11] – became more than powerbrokers mediating between different wings of the Democratic Caucus. Increasingly, they shaped the House's agenda, controlled its schedule, intervened in committee work to enforce the will of the party majority[12] and spoke for the party in public – particularly on television. Even in the more stately Senate, majority leaders like George Mitchell (D.ME) and Bob Dole (R.KS) became more than managers, enablers, mediators, brokers and janitors.[13] Increasingly, they sought to exercise stronger policy leadership and to act as their party colleagues' chief spokesperson.[14] So, while House members and senators still required particularistic benefits which would help them cultivate close relations with their constituencies, equally these individualistic, entrepreneurial self-starters also came to depend increasingly on central party leaders and coordinated party efforts to tease out from an increasingly complex and conflictual Congress the collective products that the institution was expected to deliver, not least of all by their own constituents.

THE TAKEOVER IN THE HOUSE

Immediately after his party's victory, Gingrich embraced the new 'revolutionary' vanguard – the 73 newly elected freshmen and women – as the
core of his political base and the stimulus for policy change. 'I wouldn't
be Speaker if they weren't here,' he declared in an early press conference.[15] Together with 48 sophomores, Republicans elected between 1992
and 1994 represented more than half the Conference. Not only were the
newly elected members inexperienced – almost half had not previously
held elective office – most had campaigned on the kind of fierce anti-
government, anti-Washington, anti-politics-as-usual platforms advocated
by Gingrich. They were unschooled in – indeed, antithetical towards –
Congress' institutional norms, which in any case they identified with
Democratic interest group bargaining politics and/or the conventional,
compliant Main Street Republican politics symbolised by Gingrich's predecessor. 'Our class symbol should be the bumblebee,' boasted Gil
Gutknecht (R.MN). 'Aeronautical engineers say the bumblebee can't fly
… But the bumblebee flies because [sic] he never studies aeronautical
engineering.'[16] Most had signed and campaigned on the Contract and now
felt they owed Gingrich a huge debt.

With the enthusiastic support of the freshmen and women, Gingrich proceeded swiftly and methodically to implement his party government vision,
first, by consolidating his own and his party's position, and then by pushing
hard to expedite the Contract legislation through the House. Republicans, he
insisted, must change 'from a party focused on opposition to a majority
party with a responsibility for governing'. And, in order to effect that transition, 'That requires greater assets in the leader's office.'[17]

Stronger Central Leadership

Once elected as Republican leader, Gingrich quickly restructured the
Conference and consolidated his position within it. A new and powerful
Steering Committee was created modelled on the now-defunct Democratic
Steering and Policy Committee. The committee was given responsibility
for establishing the party's legislative priorities, scheduling items for
House and Conference consideration (formerly the responsibility of the
important Policy Committee), and for nominating Republican committee
members and chairs (formerly the task of the Republican's Committee on
Committees). The committee was chaired by the Speaker, who also controlled about a quarter of the votes.[18]

Having restructured the Conference and consolidated his leadership of it,
Gingrich moved decisively to strengthen party control over the standing

committees and their chairs. Under Democratics majorities, central leaders had intervened increasingly in the work of the committees, particularly when issues were very important to the party, but committees continued to be deferred to in the writing of most legislation. Before most of the newly elected Republicans had arrived in Washington, Gingrich claimed the right to name committee chairs. He had the votes in the Steering Committee to ensure that Robert Livingston (R.LA), Thomas Bliley (R.VA) and Henry Hyde (R.IL) were nominated to the chairs of Appropriations, Commerce and Judiciary rather than those committees' most senior Republicans; in Livingston's case, Gingrich passed over four more senior Republicans. All three hand-picked chairs were judged to be more assertive and dynamic (through not necessarily more conservative)[19] and less likely than those they displaced to pursue committee-defined over party-defined priorities. 'That was a strategic position', explained a staffer for Majority Leader Armey, 'and I think it ended up sending a very clear signal that you don't just rely on seniority: you've got to prove yourself as someone willing to pursue your agenda – or our agenda.'[20] Those thought incapable of exhibiting these characteristics – like Carlos Moorhead (R.CA) who was rejected as chair of both Commerce and Judiciary – were dumped. Appropriations 'cardinals' were required to pledge their loyalty to the Conference agenda on pain of removal.

Republicans' stratagem was an unequivocal attack on committee autonomy and power – and freely recognised to be so. 'We're trying to get away from the idea that all these committees are fiefdoms over which the chairmen have complete control and are jealous of each others' prerogatives,' a Gingrich ally explained.[21] And to cap central leaders' insistence that committee chairs promote the party's agenda, House rules were changed to comply with Conference rules, which imposed six-year term limits on chairs' tenure. Gingrich also used his dominant position on the Steering Committee to ensure that the 73 new members were closely involved in assigning members to committees, and that some received plum assignments – sometimes over the claims of more senior members, and sometimes against the wishes of committee chairs (notably Bill Archer, Chair of Ways and Means), who wished to limit the size of their committees.[22]

Gingrich and other central party leaders not only exercised control over committee memberships and leaders, they also restructured committee jurisdictions. Three committees with Democratic-leaning clienteles (District of Columbia, Merchant, Marine, and Fisheries, and Post Office and Civil Service) were abolished, while others lost, or were threatened with losing, some of their jurisdictions. The Commerce Committee lost about 20 per cent of its jurisdiction. A radical proposal to create an 'Empowerment Committee' was abandoned only in the face of strong opposition from senior members – but not before it gave a clear signal to committees that should they seek to assert their rights, the new Speaker had the power to deprive them of significant parts of their jurisdictions.[23] Over the objections of the new chairs of Appropriations and National Security (where staff had traditionally been organised along bipartisan lines), central leaders reduced the overall number of committee staff by one-third 'to restore accountability to the committee process'.[24] Central leaders removed various procedural protections previously accorded committees to help them win floor approval for their bills.

Following years of complaints against Democratic majorities, the new Republican-controlled Rules Committee reduced the number of closed and restricted rules. As a result, floor debate became more open.[25] Eleven of the 13 appropriations bills for 1996 were considered under open (or modified open) rules. Over the entire Congress, one in four House-approved measures were subjected to floor amendments (predominantly by minority Democrats) – up from one in six for the 99th–101st Congresses (1985–90) and about the same level as in the reform-inspired 1970s. Greater openness on the floor was designed to undermine deference to committees. Frequently, central leaders supported attempts on the floor to amend the committee's bills. One effect was to make committee leaders more dependent on central leaders for whipping and other floor assistance.[26] So, when the Judiciary Committee reported out a lobby disclosure reform bill in November 1995 the Rules Committee (presumably with central leaders' support) refused to grant a closed rule but agreed to protect from points of order two floor amendments offered by committee non-members, which were supported by the leadership. New rules abolishing rolling quorums and requiring members, including committee chairs, to obtain the majority leader's permission to offer so-called 'limitation amendments' – which seek to block motions to strike specific items in appropriations bills – had similar effects.[27] Finally, a new rule requiring the Speaker to designate a single committee 'of primary jurisdiction' when bills were referred to more than one committee was designed to encourage greater committee responsibility and better accountability to the leadership and the majority party.[28]

The new Republican majority's attempts to enhance party accountability and central leaders' power also led to greater centralisation of power within committees – thereby reversing the trend of the last 20 years towards decentralised committees operating primarily through subcommittees.[29] Thirty-one subcommittees were abolished as new rules limited most committees to five subunits; and full committee chairs regained power to appoint subcommittee members and chairs, and to set subcommittee budgets. However, far from signalling a return to the days of powerful committee chairs – to whom central leaders were required to show deference – in the 104th House

Republican committee chairs became quasi-line managers obliged to seek the permission of central leaders before making subcommittee appointments or setting agendas.[30] 'This notion that we've got to have 100 and some odd [subcommittee] fiefdoms is over,' explained Majority Whip Tom DeLay (D.TX). '[Subcommittee chairs] need to understand that they're going to be tied to the chairmen',[31] who were in turn tied to the Speaker and the Conference. In consequence, although subcommittees considered major legislation in the 104th Congress – including welfare reform, telecommunications, immigration and Superfund – their chairs were not accorded the same operational deference by full chairs as they were by their Democratic predecessors – and, indeed did not seek it.[32]

Legislating the Contract

The stated purpose of these institutional changes was to enhance party control and party accountability, and to expedite House consideration of the party's Contract which in the early months of 1995 dominated Washington's policy agenda. Immediately after his election as Republican leader, Gingrich insisted that party colleagues give priority to party-defined over committee-defined goals. Gingrich and Armey agreed a functional division of labour according to which the new Speaker would concentrate on publicising and disseminating the Contract message and develop long-term strategy and policies while the new majority leader (and other central leaders) would take responsibility for managing the daily legislative agenda. 'Newt is our visionary and primary spokesman out there,' a leading Conference staffer observed. '[He] doesn't have a clue what's on the floor today.' Once committees were organised, Armey gave chairs detailed marching orders requiring committees to give priority to reporting out Contract legislation to the floor in time for a vote within 100 days. According to *Newsweek*, so tight was central control that '[t]he chairmen could not schedule so much as a subcommittee hearing without first asking the permission of the House leadership.'[33] Judiciary chair Hyde complained, 'I'm really a sub-chairman … I am a transmission belt for the leadership.'[34] Leaders required him to ensure that his committee give expeditious consideration to congressional term limits legislation even though he disagreed fundamentally with the proposal. When one committee chair told Gingrich that he would not be able to meet Armey's deadline for consideration of a Contract bill, the Speaker warned him: 'If you can't do it, I will find someone who will.'[35] Besides setting deadlines and ensuring that they were met, Majority Leader Armey – a man not known for his subtlety or diffidence – repeatedly impressed on Republican

committee caucuses the need to minimise changes to the substance of
Contract bills.[36] In recent congresses, Democratic central leaders had intervened to ensure committee-approved legislation met the expectations and
requirements of most majority party members,[37] but not with such con-
stancy or with the same success.

Ultimately, with committees working flat out – and complaints about
impossible personal schedules and sloppy legislating abounding – central
leaders succeeding in cajoling committees to meet their deadlines to report
Contract legislation which complied with the original party manifesto
without significant amendments. Once Contract legislation was reported
out of committee, moreover, central leaders occasionally sought or supported moves to change committee legislation on the floor. When, for
example, a product liability bill reached the floor in March 1995, central
leaders supported amendments which greatly extended the legislation's
scope even beyond the original terms of the Contract. Similar attempts,
however, to amend committee-approved versions of a criminal aliens
deportation bill, the National Security Revitalisation Act and the balanced
budget legislation failed.[38]

Having written the Contract and orchestrated the party's election campaign, House leaders then adopted the role of guardians of their party's manifesto. Their guardian strategy involved performing those roles previously
assumed by Democratic leaders, but much more than in recent decades it
entailed choosing committee chairs and members; imposing strict deadlines
on committees; admonishing committees constantly to keep faith with a
manifesto; and in the event that committees failed to deliver legislation
which complied with the party programme (unless specifically sanctioned *a
priori* by the leadership) using opportunities in the Rules Committee or on
the floor to override committee decisions. Whereas in recent congresses
major involvement by central leadership in the legislative process increased
from 28 per cent in the 91st Congress (1969–70) to 60 per cent in the 100th
Congress (1989–90),[39] during the Contract period the comparable figure
approached 100 per cent – given the leadership's authorship of the Contract.
Underpinning central leaders' insistence on both deadlines and legislative
content was a new stronger, now universally recognised condition of committee leadership: that the majority party had a detailed manifesto, which
they had presented to the electorate, who had signalled their approval, and
which could not be changed significantly by committees; that committee
chairs were above all representatives of the majority party, not leaders of
semi-autonomous fiefdoms able to recommend legislation which conflicted
with the Conference's wishes; and that, should committee chairs stray any
significant distance from the party manifesto, Gingrich could invoke

Conference rules at any time, call a meeting of the Steering Committee and recommend removal of a chair. 'Committee chairmen have got to prove themselves as individuals willing to pursue their own agenda or our agenda', insisted a staffer for Armey. 'And, I really think it's one or the other.'

Experience following the first 100 days reinforced this party government interpretation. Even after all the Contract legislation was brought to a floor vote, central leaders continued to set committee agendas. Judiciary Committee chair Hyde, for example, had hoped that his committee would spend time on committee-generated issues like judicial oversight, but was required by leadership strictures to focus on central party-designated issues like Waco and immigration legislation.[40] When central leaders disagreed with a bill's content, they denied it a rule; as, for example, when Hyde's committee reported out a bill authorising more funding for the Legal Service Corporation than Gingrich and the central leadership had agreed to. More controversially, after the Commerce Committee had reported out a bipartisan telecommunication bill by 38 votes to 5, the Speaker insisted that Committee Chair Bliley sponsor a new 66-page floor manager's amendment which reversed its overall thrust. 'The leadership has forced me to change the bill in order to win consideration on the floor,' conceded Bliley.[41] The bill in its amended form passed the floor by a large margin. Later in 1995, when the reporting Subcommittee Chair and two other Agriculture Committee Republicans caused the defeat of the leadership-approved Freedom to Farm bill, Gingrich and Committee Chair Pat Roberts (R.KS) first contemplated reprisals,[42] and then persuaded the Budget Committee to include the measure in the budget reconciliation package. 'The failure of the Agriculture Committee to bring forward reconciliation instructions', warned Conference Chair John Boehner, 'puts doubts in people's minds as to the value of the committee.'

Central leaders also worked with Budget and Appropriations committee leaders to restrict, reduce, reconstitute or in some cases eliminate hundreds. of federal programmes and agencies in the process bypassing major authorising committees – partly because so much time had been consumed enacting the Contract and partly to give controversial policy issues legislation protection through the appropriations process. While the practice was far from new, the power exercised by authorisation committees and their chairs – as well as central leaders' fears that appropriations bills would be jeopardised by loading them down with controversial amendments – previously constrained its use. Committee involvement in writing Medicare legislation in 1995 was also heavily circumscribed by central leaders. The main bill was written primarily by the Speaker's 'design team' on Medicare – consisting of eight members from the leadership and Republican members of the Ways and Means and Commerce committees. 'In the process', according to *Congressional Quarterly*, 'subcommittees [with jurisdiction over the programme] became eunuchs of Medicare policy, relegated to holding hearings without a legislative proposal.'[43] The bypassing of committees continued into 1996. In the first three months of the year, the controversial Security Guarantee Act, as well as anti-terrorism and immigration legislation, did not pass through committees. By April 1996, *The Hill* reported that the Science Committee – targeted for elimination at the beginning of the Congress – had reported just one bill, compared with six in the 103rd Congress and 20 in the 102nd Congress. The Small Business Committee, also threatened with abolition, had reported no bills.[44]

Given these developments, it was not surprising that the entire status of the committee system became a matter of debate among Republican leaders. Speaker Gingrich was quoted as saying that 'eventually, it would be better if committees could be replaced by task forces.'[45] In July 1996, a Republican Task Force on Committee Review chaired by David Dreier (R.CA) recommended increased use of 'ad hoc' committees to handle major legislation, as well as other measures to strengthen party accountability further.[46] Task forces – over 25 of which were appointed by Gingrich – operate in a very different manner from standing committees: they do not have formal organisational rules, a budget or staff, and are even more directly accountable to the Speaker. Whereas previous Democratic Speakers used them to help formulate compromise legislation, manage floor strategy and encourage inclusiveness in party affairs, much to the annoyance of some committee leaders and their staff, Gingrich used them for less benign purposes, especially in 1995: to press committees to consider issues and arrive at decisions close to the leadership's positions, with the implied threat that if committees do not deliver appropriate legislation, they would be bypassed.

The strategic rationale underpinning the attack on committee power was, according to a Conference staffer, consistent with management theory and the doctrine of party responsibility: 'What's our vision? Why are we here? What's our perfect world? What's our mission for this year? And then what are our strategies to achieve our mission? What are the quantifiable goals? It's real simple.' The net result was, in the words of one critical committee staffer, a 'top-down' House decision-making style.[47]

Explaining the New Party Government

While the determination of Gingrich and other Republican leaders to run the House along party government lines goes some way to explaining this new top-down style, the unusual circumstances of 1994 and 1995 are also important. The new Republican leaders began with a clean slate. Unlike their immediate Democratic predecessors they did not have to contend with an established political directorate of powerful committee chairs or with experienced committee majorities. At the beginning of the 104th Congress, only five of the new chairs had served for more than two years as ranking minority members (the mean for all chairs was a paltry 2.7 years) while Republicans' mean committee service was just 3.7 years. The pent-up frustration and shared experiences of years in opposition, and the huge reservoir of support for, loyalty to and deference towards Gingrich were also important factors. These factors helped produce a third crucial condition. In 1995, levels of party voting and Republican Party support returned to levels not seen since the days of Cannon and party government in the 1890s and early 1900s (see Figures 3.1 and 3.3). This is explained in part by the tight ideological homogeneity of House Republicans, but partly by what Krehbiel calls 'significant party behaviour':[48] consistent with the shift to party government, the most significant increases in party support occurred among those Republicans who benefited most – and under the new conditions of

Figure 3.3 Percentage of House Votes Which Divided the Parties, 50th (1887–8) to 104th (1995) Houses

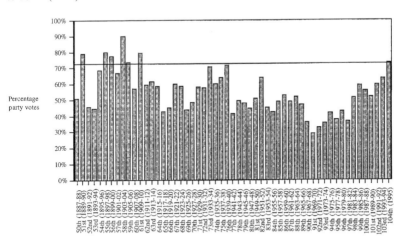

Sources: Data for the 50th through 90th Houses taken from David W. Brady, Joseph Cooper and Patricia A. Hurley, 'The Decline of Party in the US House of Representatives, 1887–1968', *Legislative Studies Quarterly*, 4 (1979), pp. 384–6. Data for the 91st through 104th Houses taken from various issues of *Congressional Quarterly Weekly Report*.

A party vote is defined as one in which more than 50 per cent of one party opposes more than 50 per cent of the other party.

their tenure stood the most to lose – from majority control: the full committee and Appropriations and Ways and Means subcommittee chairs.[49]

Even after Gingrich's huge miscalculations over the two government shutdowns in late 1995, the resultant questioning of his political judgement and style by House Republicans, lingering ethics allegations against him, the failure of much of the Contract legislation to win Senate approval, low poll ratings (just 27 per cent approval ratings in November 1995) and his self-imposed exile from the political limelight, Gingrich retained his influence and power with House Republicans although Majority Leader Armey took primary responsibility for day-to-day legislative negotiations, as during the first 100 days. Central leadership control over committees was not relaxed. Indeed, in early 1996, House Republicans codified the majority leader's unilateral power to amend committee bills before they reached the floor in their National Strategic Plan for 1996. Towards the end of 1996, leadership influence over the selection of committee chairs and members proved just as potent as at the end of 1994. In order to persuade former Congressman Bob Smith (R.OR) to contest his safe Republican district in the 1996 elections, Gingrich promised him the chair of the Agriculture Committee in the 105th Congress – even though Smith would not be the most senior Republican with the longest uninterrupted service on the committee. Earlier in 1996, Gingrich also promised former Democratic Congressman Billy Tauzin (R.LA) the chair of the important Telecommunications and Finance Subcommittee on the Commerce Committee as a reward for switching parties in 1995. In July 1996, Gingrich removed anti-abortion conservatives Robert Dornan (R.CA) and Christopher Smith (R.NJ) from a conference committee and threatened blocking any floor amendments they might want to offer, because they supported an anti-abortion candidate in the Republican primary against incumbent Sue Kelly (R.NY). And yet, in the last few months of the 104th Congress, as House leaders saw that they had to deliver some legislative products to the voters in the November elections and began to appreciate the virtues of compromise and bipartisan agreement, they allowed the committees and their chairs to write important legislation on health insurance, welfare, the environment, the minimum wage increase and business tax relief.[50]

CHANGE IN THE SENATE

While institutional change was substantial in the House, the organisational structure of the Senate remained largely unaffected by the 1994 elections, and to the extent that change did occur it was much more tentative and more attributable to leaders' individual styles than modifications to institutional rules and relationships. This is not surprising, of course, because the Senate has fewer and more flexible rules – which are designed to promote and preserve the legislative prerogatives of individual senators – so that influence within the chamber is more equally distributed and committees are less important. Taken together these features mean that shifts in electoral opinions are generally not reflected immediately in changes in public policy, and a new partisan majority's capacity to shift public policy in new directions is correspondingly weaker than in the House – much to the annoyance of House members intent on swift policy changes. During the 103rd Congress, for example, House Democrats were bitterly critical of their senatorial colleagues for what they regarded as ducking difficult decisions, especially on the budget. Immediately after the 1994 elections, Gingrich and his 'revolutionaries' expressed similar fears. Republican freshman Mark Souder (R.IN) referred to the Senate as 'the biggest graveyard in America'. Many House Republicans did not trust the party's long-serving Senate leader Bob Dole to be vigorous in advancing the 'revolution'.

Dole's Leadership and the Republican Agenda

Senate Republicans' legislative agenda – 'Seven More in '94' – was more modest than the Contract: it did not promise to consider legislation by a particular deadline, was not signed by candidates, excluded several important Contract items (notably unfunded mandates, a line-item veto, congressional compliance with workplace laws, tax allowances for adoptions, cutting capital gains tax, product liability reform and congressional term limits) and included a commitment to health care reform (which was absent from the Contract). This agenda reflected the policy priorities and legislative style of Dole, who was distinctly unenthusiastic about many Contract items or, as in the case of term limits, was a late convert to them.

By any stretch of the imagination Dole was not a revolutionary leader in the Gingrich mould, or even a policy leader in the genre of his Democratic predecessor Mitchell. While Gingrich and his conservative Republican allies were marching up to the White House in 1990 to protest at President Bush's reneging on his 'no new taxes' promise, Dole stood by his party's president. His reputation was as a staunch party loyalist and a traditional Republican conservative. His leadership was light, placing great reliance on committee chairs and other senior colleagues.

His style was pragmatic, adroitly managing the wide ideological and stylistic differences within the Republican Conference and, if necessary, reaching across the aisle to strike compromises with the Democrats. In the first 100 days – and indeed for most of 1995 – Dole seemed willing to let Gingrich and the House make the running on the major issues, including the Contract and the budget, but with a view to taking primary responsibility for working out the details thereafter. After Gingrich and House Republicans were outmanoeuvred by Clinton into shutting down the government late in 1995, Dole – by now running strongly for the presidency – effectively took charge of the party's overall strategy. Ultimately, once he was reasonably certain of the Republican nomination for president, Dole was able to negotiate a compromise with the House and the Clinton administration whereby Clinton would accept the Republicans' seven-year balanced budget goal in return for some adjustment to the underlying economic assumptions.[51]

Lacking the institutional power available to Gingrich and temperamentally unsuited to exercising coercive party leadership, Dole's management strategy was to act as a middleman or broker seeking to bridge the often sharp ideological, stylistic and generational differences among Senate Republicans. He would not or could not challenge the seniority system as Gingrich did. No freshman or woman Republican senator was awarded a seat on the prestigious Finance or Appropriations committees (although four were assigned to Foreign Relations, two to Armed Services and two to Budget). Even so, Dole was willing to use his influence over the Senate schedule to promote floor amendments supported by the younger more aggressive conservatives, even though (or perhaps because) many were bound to fail by heavy margins. Dole's toleration of the more aggressive conservatives did not extend, however, to his arch-rival for the Republican presidential nomination: in early 1995, he persuaded five more senior members to sacrifice their positions on other important committees to claim seats on the Finance Committee in order to block Senator Phil Gramm (R.TX) from claiming a seat.[52] Dole was also acutely aware of Senate arithmetic and the key strategic position occupied by the 7–9 moderate Republicans – including John Chafee (R.RI), William Cohen (R.ME) and Mark Hatfield (R.OR) – who were even less enthusiastic about the Contract than he was.[53] In the floor debate on the budget reconciliation bill in October 1995, for instance, Dole conceded ground to moderates on cuts in health, education, Medicaid and Medicare; and offered no criticism of Cohen when he provided the only Republican vote against the reconciliation bill, even though Cohen had negotiated several major concessions.

contrast House

49 contrad.

p. 48 claims 7–9 mod. Rep. senators
p. 49 claims that mod. + lib. were barely 10% (1 tenth) of Rep. senators

Hard-line Republican conservatives were less tolerant. Echoing the populist party mandate arguments of House leaders, they demanded party loyalty. 'There are some senators', complained freshman senator Rod Grams (R.MN), 'who don't think there was a November, but the voters are going to hold us accountable. We should be clear about giving the voters what they asked for.'[54]

The Growing Appetite for Combative Conservatism

As in the House, important changes had occurred in the composition of the Senate Republican Conference which suggested that an increasing number of majority senators might share Grams' view and would seek to insist on strict party discipline to match the success of the new hard-line Republican majority in the House.

From 1980 onwards, the political centre of gravity of Senate Republicans moved much further to the right. Whereas in 1980 moderates and liberals had comprised almost one third of Republican senators, after 1989 they represented barely one tenth. All of the newly elected Republicans elected in 1994 were conservatives, except Senator Olympia Snowe of Maine (see Figure 3.4). As Senate Republicans shifted to the right, party voting reached levels similar to those in the House (see Figure 3.5) and Republican party support rose (see Figure 3.6). But, as the earlier discussion noted, change was not only a matter of ideology and partisanship. As Senator Nancy Kassebaum (R.KS) observed in 1995, 'There is a different style prevalent now, and more of a desire to take a fight to the finish.' Most of the younger conservative Republicans – typically from the South and West – endorsed a more aggressive, more confrontational, hard-line approach employed by their House colleagues. Indeed, many were graduates of Gingrich's House where they suffered the frustrations of being in the minority and the often heavy hand of Democratic rule. In the Senate, the hard-line conservatives organised within the increasingly influential Steering Committee – an informal group of 35–40 Republican senators who met weekly to coordinate strategy aimed at keeping conservative issues at the centre of the party's agenda. Typically, they embraced Gingrich's notion of a Republican mandate, liked the idea of the House pushing the Senate into action[56] and often found themselves at odds with senior, more pragmatic, colleagues – including their mercurial leader Dole. Freshman senator Rick Santorum (R.PA) – a self-described 'kick-ass conservative' and Gingrich's close ally in the House – even joked that he might resign and run again for the House.[57]

John E. Owens

Figure 3.4   Republican Senators' Conservatism and Party Support, 1995

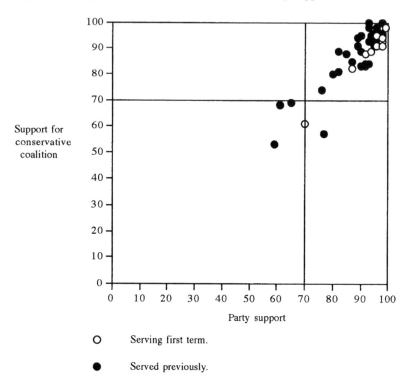

O	Serving first term.
●	Served previously.

Source: *Congressional Quarterly Weekly Report*, various dates.

   As the number of hard-line conservatives increased, their strength was
soon reflected in leadership positions. The trend began in 1993 with the
election of Trent Lott (R.MS) as Conference Secretary, the fourth-ranking
position in the leadership. From 1980 to 1989, Lott was House minority
whip and a close ally and mentor of Gingrich in the Conservative
Opportunity Society (COS). His confrontational style and aggressive conservatism placed him firmly in the Gingrich mould and frequently at odds
with traditional Republican leaders in Congress and the White House. At
the beginning of the 104th Congress, Lott capitalised further on his party's
appetite for a more aggressive approach by successfully challenging the
incumbent Republican Whip Alan Simpson (R.WY). Although Lott won
by a single vote, seven of the 11 Republican freshmen and women supported him, including moderate Olympia Snowe. Dole supported the more
conciliatory incumbent. As Dole became increasingly preoccupied with
his campaign for the presidency in 1996, much to the annoyance of the

Figure 3.5 Percentage of Senate Votes which Divided the Parties, 1954–95

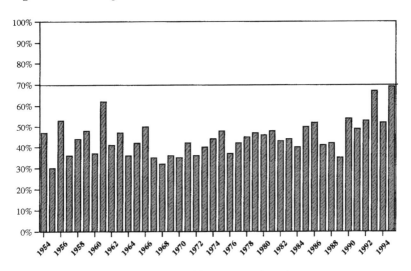

Source: *Congressional Quarterly Weekly Report*, various dates.

Figure 3.6 Mean Senate Republican and Democratic Party Support, 1954–95

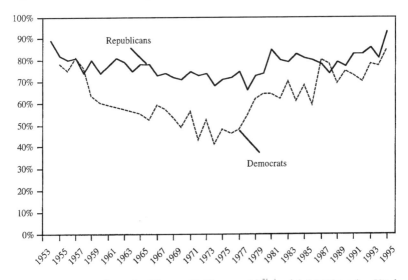

Source: Norman J. Ornstein, Thomas E. Mann and Michael J. Malbin, eds., *Vital Statistics on Congress, 1995–96* (Washington, D.C.: American Enterprise Institute, 1996), Table 8.4.

hard-line conservatives he refused to delegate the leadership exclusively to Lott, preferring instead to rely on a collective leadership comprising Policy Committee chair Nickles, Conference Chair Cochran, Conference Secretary Mack, Budget chair Pete Dominici (R.NM) and Larry Craig (R.ID), chair of the informal Steering Committee.[58] When Dole eventually retired as majority leader, Lott easily beat Thad Cochran, his more accommodating but equally conservative rival. By the end of the Congress, then, three of the Senate Republicans' four top leadership positions were held by aggressive conservatives: Lott, Majority Whip Don Nickles (R.OK) and fellow COS graduate, Conference secretary Connie Mack (R.FL). All were members of the influential Steering Committee; all were from the South. As recently as 1991, all the top four leadership positions were held by traditional conservatives.

Tighter Party Organisation

As Republican Whip, Lott made it clear in early 1995 that he would bring to his new job many of the techniques he had developed as House Whip. He promised a larger, 'very active, sort of omnipotent' whip organisation, which would include three deputy whips and five regional assistants making a whip organisation of ten senators (four more than under the Democrats). Lott's newly appointed chief deputy, Judd Gregg (R.NH) (also Lott's deputy in the House), soon made it clear that he wanted Senate Republicans to adopt a more disciplined and cohesive style. 'There has been little team spirit or sense that we need to work together,' he told the *National Journal*.[59] In future, whipping would be based on member-to-member contact, instead of relying on staff. Thus, during floor consideration of the balanced budget amendment in 1995 all ten whips – including Lott – were out in force cornering colleagues in a manner similar to House whips. Accordingly, whip counts became very accurate.[60] When Lott became majority leader and Don Nickles became Whip the new leader almost doubled funding for the historically underfunded office and provided his successor with more spacious accommodation nearer the Senate floor.[61]

In early 1995, the new Senate majority also moved to cut committee budgets: 15 per cent of committee staff and 12.5 per cent of leadership and support offices staff (but not personal offices) positions were eliminated. Dole appointed a large Republican task force on internal committee reform led by Pete Dominici and Connie Mack. Sometimes on close votes, the task force recommended reducing the number of subcommittees on 'A', or exclusive, committees to four and to two on 'B', or minor, committees in the 105th Congress; abolishing all joint committees; restricting individual senators' assignments to two 'A' committees and one 'B' committee; abolishing committees whose memberships fell below half their numbers in the 102nd Congress; further restricting the use of proxy voting (as in House Republicans' new rules) and time allotted for debate on motions to proceed (previously opposed by Dole as an encroachment on minority rights) and quorum calls (often used as a delaying tactic); and 15 per cent reductions in committee budgets. A separate Conference task force on the Senate's schedule chaired by Senator Robert Smith (R.NH) also proposed restrictions on the times of committee meetings and floor votes, and the elimination of proxy voting.

Ultimately, with Dole's support, the Dominici–Mack recommendations to reduce committee budgets and abolish subcommittees were approved by the Rules and Administration Committee – although four senior committee chairs (Strom Thurmond (R.SC) of Armed Services, Jesse Helms (R.NC) of Foreign Relations and Frank Murkowski (R.AK) of Energy and Natural Resources) lobbied successfully for smaller cuts, which were then accepted by the full Senate. (Labor and Human Resources chair Nancy Kassebaum (R.KS) voluntarily proposed a 25 per cent reduction for her committee and received a 24 per cent cut.) Despite early speculation to the contrary, the non-legislative Indian Affairs and Special Aging committees were retained. Proposed cuts in leadership budgets were subsequently rescinded following successful lobbying by party leaders, and in the FY 1997 Budget Dole (and Minority Leader Daschle) persuaded senators to increase party leadership spending by over 8 per cent and spending by whip offices and party conferences by 4 per cent.

Making the Senate More Like the House

While changes affecting Senate committees – particularly budgets and assignment procedures – received strong support from almost all Republican senators, hard-liners' demands for greater party accountability and 'streamlining' the Senate's institutional structures were inevitably much more controversial because they would bring them directly into conflict with more senior members. When he was elected majority whip, Lott appeared to recognise that the House's new 'top-down' management structure could not be applied to the Senate – promising in early 1995, for example, that committee chairs would be given 'a wide berth' in running their committees.[62] Clearly, however, pressure from hard-liners for greater party accountability was mounting.

Matters came to a head in March 1995 following the floor vote on the balanced budget constitutional amendment – a core issue for most Senate

Republicans. Senator Mark Hatfield (R.OR), chair of the Appropriations Committee and the chamber's second most senior Republican, cast the only Republican vote against the amendment,[63] thereby precipitating the party's first major legislative defeat of the 104th Congress. Hatfield was roundly castigated by Republican colleagues for disloyalty to the party's programme – and for being too close to the committee's Democratic ranking member, Robert Byrd (D.WV). Immediately after the vote, Alfonse D'Amato (R.NY), chair of the National Republican Senatorial Committee, announced that in the forthcoming 1996 elections party leaders might withhold funds for Hatfield's re-election campaign and support a primary opponent (the threat was later withdrawn and Hatfield chose to retire from the Senate). Majority Whip Lott publicly criticised Hatfield and insisted that as part of the Republican leadership committee chairs had a obligation to support the party position.[64] More seriously, Conference Secretary Mack and freshman Senator Santorum, supported by Lott and hard-line conservatives, called on the Conference to strip Hatfield of his committee chair. Echoing the rationale of Armey and other House Republicans, Santorum described the action as 'a shot across the bow' to senior colleagues who chaired committees and who might feel they could ignore the Contract.[65] Although Dole refused to take a vote in the Conference, he announced later that 'seniority ... [was] not the only factor', and suggested that in the next Congress the Conference might want to move away from a strict seniority rule.[66] Had Hatfield been stripped of his position, he would have been the first chair to suffer that fate since 1924, and the only senator ever to lose his post as a result of a single floor vote.

Moving Towards Party Government?

Although the Conference did not vote on Hatfield's removal, senators established a new task force on internal reform chaired by Mack and including Lott,[67] which recommended several organisational changes designed to strengthen party discipline and conservatives' influence. The recommendations included: giving the respective party conferences sole authority to select and remove committee members and chairs or ranking members; six-year term limits on committee chairs or ranking member-ships (as in the House); a ban on full committee chairs (except those for Appropriations, Indian Affairs, and Rules and Administration) serving simultaneously as chair of another full committee or subcommittee; a limit of two subcommittee chairs for any one Republican senator; nomination of each Republican committee chair or ranking member by the Republican leader – without necessarily following seniority (as in the House) – with ratification by the full Conference; the appointment by the Republican leader of one Republican senator to fill the vacancies on 'A' committees like Appropriations, Finance or Armed Services in the event of two or more vacancies occurring simultaneously; and a requirement – bitterly contested by moderate Republicans – that a 'Conference Legislative Agenda' be approved by a three-quarters vote in the Conference before the selection of party leaders and committee chairs, thereby allowing Senate Republicans to take into account the positions of committee chairs and leaders on Conference priorities before casting their votes on chairs.

Over the opposition of Republican moderates, all but two of the task force's recommendations were approved, albeit with modifications. Junior senators were unable to persuade the Conference to impose term limits on committee chairs to take effect from the current Congress; they took effect from January 1997. Senior Republicans – like Dole and presidential rival Gramm – as well as moderates were successful in persuading the Conference to reject the proposal to allow the leader to nominate committee chairs, arguing that too much power would be vested in the leader. Instead, Republicans gave responsibility for choosing committee chairs to committee members in secret ballots, subject to approval by the full Conference. The Conference also refused to endorse the task force's proposal to allow the leader to assign one Republican to a committee when two or more vacancies occurred.

One important effect of these changes – common to previous reform efforts – was to facilitate a politically useful redistribution of subcommittee chairs which will primarily benefit conservative junior members, particularly those elected in 1994.[68] But of greatest significance will be the fact that the Senate will make its strongest movement towards party rule and accountability than at any time in the last 70 years. The adoption of a 'Conference Legislative Agenda', in particular, will provide a mechanism whereby Republican conservatives will be able to deny committee chairs to moderate colleagues who oppose important items on the agreed party agenda.[69]

In making these changes, however, it is worth noting that Senate Republicans did not follow completely the route travelled by Gingrich and his colleagues in the House. Republican senators recoiled from violating, let alone overturning, the seniority system and from vesting their central leaders with significant powers with which to enforce party discipline. Indeed, in the remainder of the 104th Congress, the Conference clung to the seniority principle in the appointment of committee chairs. Following the resignation of Senator Bob Packwood (R.OR) from the

Senate in September 1995, Bill Roth (R.DE) became chair of the Finance
Committee, despite misgivings about his ability to lead the committee
effectively. The appointment of other committee chairs, resulting from
Packwood's resignation, also followed seniority strictly. At the beginning
of the 105th Congress (1997–8), an even more conservative Conference
ratified the promotion of Senator James Jeffords (R.VT) – the Senate's
most liberal Republican – to the chair of the Labor and Human Resources
Committee. Prudently, Jeffords moderated his liberalism in 1996 and
took the precaution of supporting Lott for the majority leadership and
Craig for chair of the Policy Committee. Yet, the conflict within the
Republican Conference between supporters of party rule and seniority
will surely continue.

Lott's More Combative Leadership

Senate Republican supporters of stronger party accountability undoubt-
edly received a boost with Lott's election as majority leader. He is an
aggressive confrontational conservative whose style differs sharply from
Dole's. As majority whip in 1995, Lott used the whip organisation to
support hard-liners' efforts to prevent liberal groups from receiving
federal grants for lobbying Congress. Later in 1995, he and others successfully undercut Dole's efforts to negotiate a compromise resolution
which would authorise US troops to go to Bosnia under certain conditions.
Lott also opposed a compromise amendment to the FY 1996 omnibus
appropriations bill to increase funding for environmental protection programmes. As majority leader in the 104th Congress, Lott showed himself
to be more confrontational and less compromising than Dole in pursuit of
a conservative agenda. Almost immediately after his election as leader, he
brought campaign finance legislation to a floor vote, but then with the
support of conservative groups such as the National Right To Life
Committee and the Christian Coalition led a fight to oppose cloture. When
the bill reached the floor, Lott made it clear to a number of committee
chairs that if they wanted leadership support for their bills they should
oppose cloture. In the final vote, only eight Republicans supported the
cloture motion; none, except Kassebaum and Simpson who would retire in
1996, were committee chairs.

Yet, like his predecessor. Lott has demonstrated a pragmatic streak
which accepts the need for both bridging the generational, ideological and
stylistic differences within the Republican Conference and cooperating
with Senate Democrats. Even in the heady days of 1995, he did not
always support the uncompromising stances of House Republicans, even

on the budget: in contrast to Dole who feared a backlash among Senate hard-liners, Lott wanted an early deal with the White House. He was also instrumental in brokering a bipartisan agreement on the landmark telecommunications bill in early 1995 – sometimes over Dole's object-ions – and, over the objections of Republican Whip Nickles and other hard-line conservatives, offered Senate Democrats a new minimum wage package coupled with new tax measures almost immediately after he was elected leader. Largely due to Lott's efforts, the legislative log-jam pre-venting enactment of other major legislation including raising the minimum wage, health care reform, welfare and immigration was unblocked[70] – much to the irritation of some party colleagues. As a party leader, Lott's management style has also been much more inclusive and accessible than Dole's. Republican moderates like Cohen and Snowe, who worked closely with Lott in the House, were willing to accept positions within the leadership organisation because they recognised his pragmatism, energy and thoroughness.

THE LEGISLATIVE CONSEQUENCES OF INSTITUTIONAL CHANGE

When legislators make changes to the way their institution operates, or when they choose new leaders or invest new powers in them, they do so because they want to advance their own or their party's political goals, including policy goals. What, then, were the consequences of the institu-tional and leadership changes in the 104th Congress for the enactment of public policy? What was the legislative record of the Republican Congress?

Energy and Confrontation

In terms of legislative pace and energy, the first months of the 104th Congress were breathtaking. During the first 100 days, the House was in session 531 hours (over nine hours a day), compared with 208 hours in the same period of the previous Congress, and a measly 74 hours (one and a half hours a day) during the 97th Congress when legislators considered proposals for the Reagan 'revolution'. In the first three months of 1995, the House passed 124 measures (compared with 53 in 1981) and recorded 302 roll call votes (just 23 in 1981). By acting on every Contract bill within the first 100 days, House Republicans fulfilled their election promises. 'Promises made, promises kept' became the Republican mantra. More than this. As they hoped, House Republicans had wrested control of

Washington's political agenda from the president and the Senate and shifted it in a new direction. By the first 100 days, the House had passed a major welfare bill which would overturn 60 years of federally controlled anti-poverty programmes, changed House rules to require a three-fifths super-majority to increase income tax rates (although not all taxes, as originally promised), given the president a form of line-item veto, prohibited US troops from operating under foreign command on UN missions, imposed a moratorium on new federal regulations, approved a new product liability law with limits on punitive damages and passed a constitutional amendment requiring a balanced budget. There seems little doubt that without a clear agenda, without the new 'top-down' institutional structure instituted by Gingrich and Armey, and without House Republicans' impressive party discipline,[71] these bills would not have moved so expeditiously through the House. And, as the Republican legislative roller-coaster surged, Congress's public approval ratings rose to 42 per cent by the end of January 1995, twice the level immediately before the elections.

Notwithstanding Republicans' impressive party discipline, the frenetic legislative pace and central leaders' success in winning floor passage of all but one of the Contract bills intact and without significant committee amendments,[72] important planks in the Republican manifesto were rejected by the House. Even before the new Congress met, it was clear that the party's line-item veto legislation would not succeed in the form proposed in the Contract; House leaders were forced to opt instead for a watered-down enhanced rescissions measure. Opposition from Agriculture chair Pat Roberts (R.KS) and Economic and Educational Opportunities chair Bill Goodling (R.PA) necessitated revisions to the Contract's proposal for converting food stamps and other nutrition programmes into block grants to the states. With the new Congress barely a few days old, the House rejected a super-majority for all tax increases. A few weeks later, the predictable clash between Republican freshmen and women and party moderates over the Contract's tax limitation provision in the balanced budget legislation ended in defeat. The leadership's attempts to cobble together an agreement on a constitutional amendment for congressional term limits failed. The Contract's plan for a 'middle-class tax cut' was made contingent on Congress approving a balanced budget plan. No amount of structural 'streamlining', brow-beating or arm-twisting of committee leaders and members, or appeals to party unity, was sufficient then to pass these important Contract provisions in tact.

While the House moved swiftly, the Senate did not. Senate committees found themselves unable to process the huge amounts of House legislation expeditiously. Predictably, senators did not accord the same high priority to Contract legislation, and on some measures reached rather different legislative solutions. They swiftly approved the Congressional Compliance Act and new floor procedures for challenging unfunded mandates. By the end of 1995, they had passed bills on welfare, budget reconciliation, the line-item veto, product liability and restrictions on US participation in UN peacekeeping in very different forms from the House; and had rejected the politically significant balanced budget amendment. The assumption of many House Republicans that the political tide was so strong that the Senate would simply accede to their demands was shown to be incredibly naive and politically damaging. Most importantly, as Republicans moved on treacherously in the post-Contract period to tackle budgetary issues and middle-class entitlements, their public standing in the polls declined (see Figure 3.7). Not only did the Senate reject many of the House Republicans' demands, but constrained by its individualistic tradition and Senator Dole's needs in the forthcoming presidential election elected for

Figure 3.7 Public Support for Republican Policies and Proposals, 1995–7

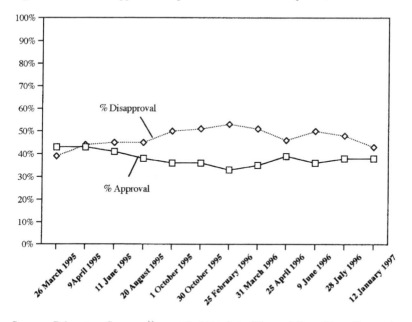

Source: Princeton Survey Research Associates/Times Mirror/Pew Research Center. The specific question was: Do you approve or disapprove of the policies and proposals of the Republican leaders in Congress?

its own legislative agenda and pace. Senators approved important immigration, telecommunications and anti-terrorism legislation which was not part of the Contract and stalled other House initiatives, including an attempt to rewrite the Clean Water Act.

Despite huge increases in the time spent and the number of roll call votes recorded by the House and Senate, by the end of the first session the legislative record of the 104th Congress looked meagre: the House had produced only 60 public bills which were signed into law (compared with 127 in the first session of the 103rd Congress); the Senate had passed 28 laws (83 two years previously). Beyond these raw data, most of congressional Republicans' major legislative objectives – including Contract bills on line-item veto/enhanced rescissions, congressional term limits, regulatory reform, legal reform, five of the six crime bills, as well as the balanced budget amendment and welfare – seemed unlikely to reach the statute book. Equally importantly, House and Senate Republican leaders fatally delayed consideration of budget and appropriations legislation in order to give priority to the Contract bills. When this 'must-pass' legislation reached the House floor, leaders allowed it to be laden with controversial extraneous amendments and other bills, then folded all the measures into one omnibus reconciliation bill, and dared Clinton to veto it. This highly risky confrontational strategy failed. The president vetoed the bill and in the ensuing *impasse*, when the federal government was shut down twice and almost defaulted on its debt, deftly outmanoeuvred congressional Republicans. As Clinton stole the issue of balancing the budget from congressional Republicans, his popularity rose sharply, that of congressional Republicans and Speaker Gingrich fell sharply.

In this new context, it was no surprise that President Clinton and congressional Democrats began referring to 'the do-nothing 104th Congress' – after Harry Truman's 1948 election slogan – and to compose their own legislative agenda in light of the forthcoming presidential election. While the House 'revolutionaries' placed the blame squarely on the Senate, much – possibly most – of the responsibility surely rested on their shoulders. Either because they lacked the experience of being the majority (no House Republican had ever served in the majority) or sheer arrogance – especially among the freshmen and women – in believing that they could change the constitutional system, they overinterpreted an election in which they had won barely 51 per cent of the popular vote, mistakenly assuming that general public support for smaller and cheaper government extended to endorsing major cuts in specific programmes and regulations. Congressional Republicans clearly overreached their electoral mandate. Internal 'streamlining' and centralising facilitated swift passage of the Contract and other legislation through the House, but it also had the important effects of exaggerating institutional and political – and subsequently policy – differences with the Senate and making it easier for voters to identify and contrast the 'extreme' forces in the House – particularly Gingrich – with a 'moderate' and politically astute president who was able to style himself successfully as the defender of Medicare and a host of other popular programmes.

The Electoral Imperative and Legislative Productivity

Concerned that their popularity would decline further, that continuing a confrontational strategy would hand new advantages to President Clinton and that they needed to demonstrate some accomplishments to the electorate in the 1996 elections, House and Senate Republicans opted consciously in 1996 for a cross-partisan incremental strategy which permitted concessions to political opponents. The Contract was replaced by Gingrich's so-called 'common sense agenda'. In early 1996, a landmark agreement to balance the budget within seven years was reached with the president; Republican proposals for spending and tax reductions in the FY 1996 budget were reduced drastically. In a late flurry of legislative activity between August and early October, the ghost of the 'do-nothing' 104th Congress was truly laid to rest. By the end of September 1996, the House and Senate had worked the longest hours of any Congress in the entire post-war period. However, the number of laws the 104th Congress produced was the lowest of any Congress since the Second World War – a total of 238 measures, over 60 per cent of them in the second session, and barely half the number enacted in the 103rd Congress, 40 per cent of the total, and only about one-third the totals for the 101st and 100th Congresses. Not surprisingly, the House was more productive than the Senate in 1995 and 1996: the House approved the largest number of measures since the 100th Congress (1987–8); the fall in productivity was entirely due to the Senate's second lowest level of productivity since the Second World War. Cursory examination shows that the decline cannot be explained either by the consolidation of smaller bills into omnibus packages or by a reduction in the number of commemorative measures. In many ways, this record reflected the House majority's short list of priorities, which as the earlier discussion showed, was rather different from those of the Senate.

Yet, the Republican Congress enacted major legislation: a landmark welfare bill which overturned the New Deal 60-year-old federal guarantee of cash assistance to all eligible low-income mothers and children; a seven-year 'Freedom to Farm' bill which replaced commodity subsidy programmes created in the 1930s; and, after years of languishing, a new federal regulatory framework for telecommunications opening up local telephone monopolies to new competitors. Perhaps most significantly, congressional Republicans also forced major cuts in non-defence spending programmes so that overall appropriations spending in 1996 was 2 per cent less than in 1995. These changes reflected an important shift in the terms of political debate in Washington and a further shift to the right in the ideological centre of gravity. Such changes would have been impossible without Republican majorities in Congress.

Besides these accomplishments, Congress enacted new weak restrictions on unfunded federal mandates; gave the president 'enhanced rescissions' (line-item veto) authority to rescind any spending item or 'limited tax benefit';[73] new anti-terrorism legislation; various relaxations of safe drinking water, pesticide and banking regulations; new restrictions on illegal immigration; and a major expansion of health insurance benefits (which imposed increased federal regulation on health insurance companies and hospitals). A number of these measures were approved with bipartisan support. Other measures – a new prohibition on late-term abortions, authorisation of a new anti-missile defence system, overhaul of Medicaid, and revisions to product liability law – were all approved by partisan majorities and vetoed by the president.

Against this record, House Republicans failed to defeat the first increase in the minimum wage since 1989 (even though the measure was coupled with modest new tax allowances for businesses); to change the Constitution to impose congressional term limits; to restrict the growth of Medicare; and to repeal the ban on assault weapons. Core items on Republicans' agenda to change the Constitution to require a balanced budget; to enact significant tax cuts, including a $500 per child tax credit for families and cuts in capital gains tax; to pass major regulatory overhaul legislation; to enact a constitutional amendment banning the physical desecration of the American flag; and to weaken the Clean Water Act – all were rejected by the Senate. Attempts to rewrite the Endangered Species and Superfund hazardous waste laws, to reform campaign finance legislation and to approve major changes to banking laws failed in both houses. Furthermore, not only did Republicans fail to win approval for their ambitious plans to balance the budget by the year 2002, fearing further adverse consequences from another federal shutdown, they were forced to agree to Clinton's request for additional domestic spending in the FY 1997 budget, restoring billions of dollars of federal spending they have hoped to cut.

CONCLUSION

Despite this long list of failures, the Republican Congress's legislative record was fairly impressive – particularly if allowance is made for degree of difficulty. Major changes were made to core areas of public policy. Undeniably, the terms of policy debate were shifted to the right. In these important respects, the 104th Congress was one of the most important in recent years. The legislative engine which drove these changes was the new House Republican majority led by Newt Gingrich, which took responsibility for formulating a clear agenda and changing the House's institutional organisation to make it better able to achieve the majority party's policy objectives. However, as events unfolded, House Republicans and their leaders came to learn that achieving policy gains required a solid policy mandate and governing skills, as well as electoral victory, a clear agenda, strict party discipline, committed leadership and institutional change. In the event, congressional Republicans overreached their mandate, badly misjudging the appetite of most American voters for cutting back favourite programmes and a hard-line confrontational approach. As a result, they suffered the political consequences in terms of public approval. Republicans also learnt that their highly partisan and overtly confrontational legislative strategy was ill-suited to a separated system which encourages power-sharing, institutional competition and compromise because such a system provides opportunities which skilful opponents in the Senate and White House can exploit to portray hard-line partisans as irresponsible and extreme.

Yet Gingrich was surely correct in arguing – as he did towards the end of the Congress – that Republicans would not have realised so many of their objectives or been so successful in shifting the political debate without the House Republicans' energy and momentum at the beginning. And, Gingrich and his colleagues changed – or were forced to change – strategy and direction and began to behave more pragmatically, less like a majority party in a parliamentary regime and more like a coordinate branch legislating together within a separated system. Equipped with this new strategy, the Republican Congress found itself with enough time to end with some important accomplishments. What this tells us about congressional politics is some familiar truths. The 104th Congress demonstrated again that in a separated system the legislative branch can influence the political agenda as much as the president, and the House as much as the Senate. But it also demonstrates that in a constitutional system characterised by power-sharing, mixed representation and institutional competition even the most determined party majority for decades could not impose its will. This stated, it seems likely that the strengthening of party rule by Republicans in the House and the Senate – begun under Democratic rule – will also be one of the lasting legacies of the 104th Congress. Although there were already indications at the end of the 104th and the beginning of the 105th Congress that central party control in the House was weakening, regardless of which party wins control in the remainder of the decade, a complex set of forces – including the need for Congress to maintain flexible and adaptable legislative processes with which to handle large complicated issues,[74] the high levels of membership turnover, the increasing ideological polarisation of the parties, and the likely continuation of split-party government – should sustain the advance.

NOTES

1.　On the role of Congress as a policy-maker, see Woodrow Wilson, *Congressional Government* (Baltimore and London: The Johns Hopkins Press, 1981; originally published 1885); Lawrence H. Chamberlain, *The President, Congress and Legislation* (New York: Columbia University Press, 1946); Ronald C. Moe and Steven C. Teel, 'Congress as Policymaker: A Necessary Reappraisal', *Political Science Quarterly*, 85 (1970), pp. 443–70; Steven A. Shull, *Domestic Policy Formation. Presidential-Congressional Partnership?* (Westport, CT: Greenwood Press, 1983); John S. Saloma, *Congress and the New Politics* (Boston: Little, Brown, 1969); James L. Sundquist, *Politics and Policy. The Eisenhower, Kennedy, and Johnson Years* (Washington, D.C.: The Brookings Institution, 1968); Gary Orfield, *Congressional Power: Congress and Social Change* (New York: Harcourt Brace, Jovanovich, 1975); and Charles O. Jones, *The Presidency in a Separated System* (Washington, D.C.: The Brookings Institution, 1994).

2.　Whereas in 1969 less than half the Republican Conference could be classified as very conservative (CQ conservative coalition scores of 84 per cent or above), since 1989 over 70 per cent have fallen into this category. See also Nicol Rae, *The Decline and Fall of the Liberal Republicans: From 1952 to the Present* (Oxford: Oxford University Press, 1989).

3.　Jacob Lamar, 'An Attack Dog, Not a Lap Dog', *Time*, 3 April 1989, p. 22.

4.　William F. Connelly and John J. Pitney, *Congress' Permanent Minority? Republicans in the US House* (Lanham, MD and London: Littlefield Adams, 1994), pp. 24–6, 62–4. For a conservative critique blaming Congress's 'irresponsible' behaviour on increasingly 'autonomous' committees and subcommittees, see, for example, Clifford M. Hardin, Kenneth A. Shepsle and Barry Weingast, *Public Policy Excesses: Government by Congressional Subcommittee* (St. Louis: Center for the Study of American Business, Washington University, 1982), p. 5. The distinction between these competing models of congressional organisation is nicely drawn in Forrest Maltzman, 'Committee–Chamber–Party Relations in the Post-Reform

House', a paper presented to the annual meeting of the Midwest Political Science Association, Chicago, 9–11 April 1992, pp. 2–3.

5. For a discussion of post-war debates on enhancing party government in Congress, see Charles O. Jones, *Party and Policymaking: The House Republican Policy Committee* (New Brunswick, NJ: Rutgers University Press, 1964), especially Chapter II. For an elaboration of party government from a conservative perspective, see Gordon S. Jones and John A. Marini, eds., *The Imperial Congress. Crisis in the Separation of Powers* (New York: Pharos Books, 1988). From an older, liberal perspective, see E. E. Schattschneider, *Party Government* (New York: Holt, Rinehart and Winston, 1941); and Austin Ranney, *The Doctrine of Responsible Party Government* (Urbana, IL: The University of Illinois Press, 1962).

6. John E. Owens, 'The Return of Party Government in the US House of Representatives: Central Leadership Committee Relations in the 104th Congress', *British Journal of Political Science*, 27/2 (April 1997), p. 361.

7. Most voters' knew little of the Contract's specific proposals. Moreover, in their 1994 election campaigns, many Republican candidates endorsed only particular parts of the Contract. See, for example, James G. Gimpel, *Fulfilling the Contract. The First 100 Days* (Needham Heights, MA: Allyn and Bacon, 1996), chapter 2; Elizabeth Drew, *Showdown. The Struggle Between the Gingrich Congress and the Clinton White House* (New York and London: Simon and Schuster, 1996), p. 30.

8. Thomas E. Mann and Norman J. Ornstein, eds., *Intensive Care. How Congress Shapes Health Policy* (Washington, D.C.: The Brookings Institution, 1995).

9. See, for example, John R. Hibbing and Elizabeth Theiss-Morse, *Congress as Public Enemy. Public Attitudes Toward American Political Institutions* (Cambridge and New York: Cambridge University Press, 1995).

10. This discussion is based on Michael Foley and John E. Owens, *Congress and the Presidency: Institutional Politics in a Separated System* (Manchester and New York: Manchester University Press/St. Martin's Press, 1996), pp. 53, 67–73, 93–5. See also Barbara Sinclair, *The Transformation of the US Senate* (Baltimore and London: The Johns Hopkins Press, 1989), especially chapter 5; Alan Ehrenhart, 'Every Man is an Island: In the Senate of the 1980s, Team Spirit Has Given Way to the Rule of Individuals', *Congressional Quarterly Weekly Report*, 4 September, 1982, pp. 2175–82; Steven S. Smith, *The American Congress* (Boston: Houghton Mifflin, 1995), pp. 17–8; Burdett A. Loomis, *The Contemporary Congress* (New York: St. Martin's Press, 1996), chapters 2–4.

11. David W. Rohde, *Parties and Leaders in the Postreform House* (Chicago: The University of Chicago Press, 1991); Lawrence C. Dodd and Bruce I. Oppenheimer, 'Consolidating Power in the House: The Rise of A New Oligarchy', in idem, *Congress Reconsidered*. Fourth edition, pp. 39–64; Barbara Sinclair, 'The Emergence of Strong Leadership in the 1980s House of Representatives', *Journal of Politics*, 54 (1992), pp. 657–84; and John Barry, *The Ambition and the Power* (New York: Penguin Books, 1989).

12. Rohde, *Parties and Leaders in the Postreform House*; Ronald M. Peters, *The American Speakership: The Office in Historical Perspective* (Baltimore: The Johns Hopkins University Press, 1990); Barbara Sinclair, *Majority*

66   John E. Owens

Leadership in the US House (Baltimore: The Johns Hopkins University Press, 1983); Sinclair, 'House Majority Leadership in the Late 1980s'; Sinclair, 'The Emergence of Strong Leadership in the 1980s House of Representatives'; Barbara Sinclair, *Legislators, Leaders, and Lawmaking. The US House of Representatives in the Postreform Era* (Baltimore and London: The Johns Hopkins University Press, 1995), pp. 189–92; Paul S. Herrnson and Kelly D. Patterson, 'Toward a More Programmatic Democratic Party? Agenda-Setting and Coalition Building in the House of Representatives', *Polity*, 27 (1995), pp. 607–28; and Barbara Sinclair, *Unorthodox Lawmaking. New Legislative Processes in the US Congress* (Washington, D.C.: Congressional Quarterly Press, 1997), especially chapter 6.

13. Roger H. Davidson, 'Senate Leaders: Janitors for an Untidy Chamber', in Dodd and Oppenheimer, eds., *Congress Reconsidered*, third edition, pp. 225–52.

14. Donald C. Baumer, 'Senate Democratic Leadership in the 101st Congress', in Allen D. Hertzke and Ronald M. Peters, eds., *The Atomistic Congress. An Interpretation of Congressional Change* (Armonk, NY and London: M.E. Sharpe, 1992), pp. 293–332, 305; Steven S. Smith, 'Forces of Change in Senate Party Leadership and Organisation', in Lawrence C. Dodd and Bruce I. Oppenheimer, *Congress Reconsidered*, fifth edition (Washington, D.C.: Congressional Quarterly Press, 1993), p. 274; and Foley and Owens, *Congress and the Presidency*, pp. 161–2.

15. Jeff Shear, 'Force Majeure?' *National Journal*, 11 March 1995, p. 602.

16. Janet Hook, 'Conservative Freshman Class Eager to Seize the Moment', *Congressional Quarterly Weekly Report*, 7 January 1995, p. 47.

17. Quoted in David S. Cloud, 'Gingrich Clears Path for Republican Advance', *Congressional Quarterly Weekly Report*, 19 November 1995, p. 3319.

18. The committee's membership comprises all House Republican leaders, the chairs of the four most important committees (chosen by Gingrich), nine regional representatives and representatives of the two most recent Republican classes. Most of the votes on the old Committee on Committees were exercised by large state delegations such as those from California and Florida.

19. Moderates such as Jim Leach (R.IA), Nancy Johnson (R.CT), and Ben Gilman (R.NY) were nominated to the chairs of the Banking, Ethics, International Relations committees evidently because they had demonstrated energy, commitment and focus in advancing the party agenda before the elections. Leach and Johnson had also supported Gingrich in the Whip election in 1969.

20. Interviews were conducted by the author in June 1995.

21. Quoted in David S. Cloud, 'Shakeup Time', *Congressional Quarterly Weekly Report*, 25 March 1995, p. 10.

22. Over half the vacancies on 'exclusive' committees were given to newcomers – including three on Ways and Means (the first since 1966), seven on Appropriations (even though the committee membership was cut by four), eight on Commerce, one on Rules (the first since 1983), and five out of nine vacancies on Budget. In the case of Appropriations, however, committee chair Livingston admitted that 'senior members weren't eager to do the

heavy lifting' on cutting spending and so did not seek the assignment. Shear, 'Force Majeure?', p. 601.

23. Owens, 'The Return of Party Government in the US House of Representatives', p. 357.

24. According to data compiled by the House Oversight committee in March 1995, the number of committee staff positions fell from 1,854 positions in the 103rd Congress to 1,233 in the 104th – a fall of 33 per cent. Committee budgets fell from $222.3 to $156.3 millions. Most reductions were borne, however, by minority Democrats while Republicans retained or slightly increased the budgets they had previously operated under.

25. Rules committee data show that during the 104th Congress just under half (46 per cent) of rules were open compared with 33 per cent in the 103rd and 34 per cent in the 102nd Congress. Data provided by Don Wolfensberger, Chief of Staff, House Rules Committee and US. Congress. House. Rules Committee. *Summary of Activities*, 104th Congress, Second Session, Report No. 104–868, 26 November 1996. Democrats' data show greater use of restrictive rules using slightly different measurement. They also argued that the percentage of open rules in the 104th House was inflated by granting open rules to non-controversial measures which might normally be considered under suspensions of the rules.

26. John E. Owens, 'How Different Was the 104th House of Representatives? Change and Continuity in Floor Amendment Activity in the Era of Party Government'. A paper presented to the annual meeting of the Southwestern Political Science Association, New Orleans, 26–9 March 1997.

27. Although used very rarely in 1995, its use generated disquiet among members of committees affected, for example, in respect of a proposal to lift the moratorium on mining patents. See Elizabeth A. Palmer, 'Empowering the Rank and File', *Congressional Quarterly Weekly Report*, 22 July 1995, p. 2165.

28. The rules change continued to allow the Speaker to refer whole bills sequentially and parts of bills to other committees. Nine of 30 Contract bills were referred sequentially to at least one other committee, and one to as many as eight different committees. However, a smaller percentage (35 per cent) of leadership bills (including all the Contract bills) were multiply referred than in three of the four previous Houses. See Owens, 'How Different Was the 104th House of Representatives?', p. 12.

29. Steven S. Smith and Christopher J. Deering, *Committees in Congress*, second edition (Washington, D.C.: Congressional Quarterly Press, 1990), p. 140.

30. Full committee chairs also lost the right to hold committee members' proxy votes, to chair a subcommittee as well and to appoint their own (so-called 5-D) staff to subcommittees in addition to those appointed by subcommittee chairs.

31. Jonathan D. Salant, 'New Chairmen Swing to the Right; Freshmen Get Choice Posts', *Congressional Quarterly Weekly Report*, 10 December 1994, pp. 3493–4.

32. See, for example, the comments of Henry Waxman (D.CA), the former activist chair of the Commerce Committee's Health and Environment Subcommittee, quoted in Jackie Koszczuk, 'Gingrich Puts More Power into

Speaker's Hands', *Congressional Quarterly Weekly Report*, 7 October 1995, p. 3052.

33. Thomas Rosenstiel, 'Why Newt is No Joke', *Newsweek*, 10 April 1995, p. 26.

34. Gabriel Kahn, 'Hyde Battles Away on Judiciary Panel', *Roll Call*, 20 February 1995, p. 15.

35. Rosenstiel, 'Why Newt is No Joke', p. 27.

36. Jennifer Babson, 'Armey Stood Guard Over the Contract', *Congressional Quarterly Weekly Report*, 8 April 1995, p. 987. Apparently in contrast, Gingrich insisted that the details of the Contract were subject to revision. See David S. Cloud, 'House GOP Shows a United Front in Crossing "Contract" Divide', *Congressional Quarterly Weekly Report*, 25 February 1995, p. 579.

37. See, for example, Sinclair, *Legislators, Leaders, and Lawmaking*, p. 163.

38. Details of this analysis are provided in Owens, 'The Return of Party Government in the US House of Representatives', pp. 360–5. A broader analysis of committee and chair success rates in winning approval of floor amendments is provided in Owens, 'How Different Was the 104th House of Representatives?', pp. 9–10. For a good journalistic account of leadership pressure on committee chairs, see David Maraniss and Michael Weisskopf, *Tell Newt to Shut Up* (New York: Touchstone, 1996).

39. Barbara Sinclair, 'House Majority Party Leadership in an Era of Divided Control', in Lawrence C. Dodd and Bruce I. Oppenheimer, eds., *Congress Reconsidered*. 5th edition (Washington, D.C.: Congressional Quarterly Press, 1993), p. 239. 'Major involvement' defined by Sinclair as leadership participating in shaping the content of legislation by talking or negotiating with or among the committees (or with the Senate or the president) fell, however, to 54 per cent in the 102nd Congress.

40. Gabriel Kahn, 'Even after Contract, House Chairs Take a Back Seat to the Leadership', *Roll Call*, 21 September 1995, pp. 3 and 22.

41. 'The New(t) Politburo', *Roll Call*, 9 October 1995, p. 4; Jon Healey, 'Leader's Last Minute Additions Offer Morsels For Everyone – Almost', *Congressional Quarterly Weekly Report*, 5 August 1995, p. 2348.

42. According to a misdirected email written by a staffer for DeLay which reached House Democrats, Gingrich spelt out specific sanctions against the three dissidents: 'Baker will be taken off [the committee] and put on Transportation. 2) Emerson (the second ranking Republican) will not become chairman if Roberts runs for the Senate. 3) Combest (the third ranking Republican) will be stripped of the Intelligence Committee chairmanship.' See Craig Winneker, 'Heard on the Hill', *Roll Call*, 28 September 1995, p. 16. Subsequently, Gingrich assured these members that he had no intention of threatening them and offered to broker a compromise with Roberts.

43. Jackie Koszczuk, 'Gingrich Puts More Power into Speaker's Hands', *Congressional Quarterly Weekly Report*, 7 October 1995, p. 3052.

44. Marcia Gelbart, 'Threatened Committees Produce Little Legislation', *The Hill*, 10 April 1996, p. 4.

45. Quoted in Gabriel Kahn, 'Gingrich Plan: End to Panels?' *Roll Call*, 9 October, 1995, p. 22. Gingrich subsequently stated that '[n]othing could

be further from the truth ... Rather than consolidating power in the leadership or funnelling it away from members, task forces actually allow for greater member participation.' See Newt Gingrich, 'Leadership Task Forces: The "Third Wave" To Consider Legislation', *Roll Call*, 16 November, 1995, p. 5.

46. These included further enhancement of central leaders' powers, stripping the Appropriations Committee of its power to set its own funding, Conference votes on subcommittee chairs 'critical to the advancement of the majority's legislative agenda in the House', reductions in the numbers of subcommittees for certain committees, and the abolition of the Joint Economic Committee.

47. Another important change reflecting this approach was the abolition of 28 legislative service organisations (including the Congressional Black Caucus, the Arms Control and Foreign Policy Caucus, the Democratic Study Group and the Older American Caucus) which according to Republican detractors were 'superfluous, wasteful and disorganised'.

48. Keith Krehbiel, 'Where's the Party?', *British Journal of Political Science*, 23 (1993), pp. 235–66.

49. See Owens, 'The Return of Party Government in the US House of Representatives', pp. 372–3.

50. Allan Freedman, 'Returning Power to Chairmen', *Congressional Quarterly Weekly Report*, 23 November 1996, p. 3300.

51. See, for example, Nancy Gibbs, 'The Inner Game', *Time*, 15 January 1996; and Maraniss and Weisskopf, *Tell Newt to Shut Up*, chapter 11.

52. Following the resignation of Finance chair Bob Packwood from the Senate in September 1995, Dole ran out of options. Gramm won an assignment to the committee.

53. Quoted in Andrew Taylor, 'House's Magnum Opus Now Subject to Senate's Tender Mercies', *Congressional Quarterly Weekly Report*, 1 April 1995, p. 913.

54. Quoted in David S. Cloud, 'GOP Moderates Refusing to Get in Line', *Congressional Quarterly Weekly Report*, 30 September 1995, p. 2963.

55. Whereas 42 per cent of Republican senators were elected from states in the South and West in 1973, by 1981 the percentage had risen to 51 per cent, and by 1995 to 55 per cent. Almost all were conservatives.

56. Quoted in Steve Langdon, '"Contract" Dwarfs Senate GOP's Pledge', *Congressional Quarterly Weekly Report*, 25 February 1995, p. 578.

57. Quoted in David S. Cloud, 'Sanitarium Pushing Senate To Be More Like House', *Congressional Quarterly Weekly Report*, 28 October 1995, p. 3255.

58. Mary Jacoby, 'With Dole Away, Lott Wants to Play Leader', *Roll Call*, 19 February 1996, pp. 1 and 40.

59. Richard E. Cohen, 'Whipping the Senate GOP into Shape', *National Journal*, 7 January 1995, p. 37.

60. David S. Cloud, 'Lott Has Pole Position in "Race" for Leader', *Congressional Quarterly Weekly Report*, 17 February 1995, p. 387.

61. Although Nickles denied any arrangement, he withdrew from the leadership race to run unopposed for Whip to replace Lott.

62. Richard E. Cohen, 'Whipping the Senate GOP into Shape', *National Journal*, 7 January 1995, p. 37.

63. Dole also voted against when he switched his vote in order to preserve his right to call for another vote on the same question.
64. Donna Cassata, 'GOP Retreats on Hatfield, but War far from Over', Congressional *Quarterly Weekly Report*, 11 March 1995, p. 729.
65. Cloud, 'Santorum Pushing Senate to be More Like House', p. 3256.
66. Mary Jacoby, 'GOP Calls off Hatfield Fight', *Roll Call*, 9 March 1995, p. 18.
67. Other task force members were Policy Committee chair, Don Nickles (R.OK), Bob Packwood (R.OR), Larry Craig (R.ID) and three freshman senators, Santorum, Fred Thompson (R.TN), John Kyl (R.AZ).
68. At the beginning of the 105th Senate, senior Republicans including Dominici (on Energy and Natural Resources), Lugar (on Foreign Relations), Helms (on Agriculture), Roth (on Governmental Affairs) and Thurmond (on Judiciary) lost subcommittee chairs. All 11 freshman/women Republicans elected in 1994 gained subcommittee chairs in 1997. Senator Fred Thompson (R.TN) even became full chair of the Governmental Affairs Committee.
69. However, in the rules eventually adopted by the Conference, it is not clear whether the votes on committee chairs occur before the establishment of the party's legislative agenda.
70. Dick Morris, *Behind the Oval Office. Winning the Presidency in the Nineties* (New York: Random House, 1997), especially chapter 16.
71. On the 33 Contract bills, 61 per cent of House Republicans, including 73 per cent of freshmen/women, voted with a majority of their party on every vote. Donna Cassata, 'Republicans Bask in Success of Rousing Performance', *Congressional Quarterly Weekly Report*, 8 April 1995, p. 986.
72. Owens, 'The Return of Party Government in the US House of Representatives', pp. 361–5.
73. Congress will be able to pass bills to 'disapprove' of the president's action, which presumably could then be vetoed by the president.
74. See, for example, Sinclair, *Unorthodox Lawmaking*.

ACKNOWLEDGEMENT

I am grateful to the Nuffield Foundation for its financial support, to the Brookings Institution for providing a congenial academic base, and to Julian Kirby for research assistance.

4 Leading the Revolution: Innovation and Continuity in Congressional Party Leadership[1]

Barbara Sinclair

At the end of the 104th Congress's first 100 days, Speaker Newt Gingrich (R.GA) was regarded by the national media and the Washington political community as a combination of Czar Reed, the president of the United States and Lenin: a powerful legislative leader, America's premier political figure and agenda-setter, and the leader of a successful revolutionary movement. His face appeared on the covers of the major newsweeklies; *Time* asked: 'Is this the most influential Republican in America?' and called him the 'Wizard of Congress'; *Newsweek* claimed that Gingrich had 'in just three months altered the basic course run by government for the past 60 years'.[2] When the House completed action on the Contract, Gingrich asked for and was granted national television time to talk to the American people, an event unprecedented for a legislative leader.

As a backbencher, Gingrich had brought down a Speaker and parlayed that feat into election as whip, the number two position in the House Republican Party hierarchy. In a short time, Gingrich had made himself the *de facto* Republican leader in the House, leaving Bob Michel (R.IL), the titular leader, little choice but to retire. He had waged a relentless campaign of Congress-bashing and, by branding the institution as insulated, arrogant and corrupt, had seemed to prepare the ground for the 1994 Republican victory. The Contract With America, the House Republican platform that most incumbents and challengers signed on to, was Gingrich's idea. When, against most expert predictions except his own, Republicans did win a House majority, he chose the committee chairs, bypassing seniority in several instances. To bring every item in the Contract to a vote within the first 100 days as promised, he set strict time limits for the committees and refused to brook significant changes in the Contract Items; when a committee did not deliver, the leadership took over and rewrote the legislation. In 1995 Speaker Gingrich dominated the agenda-setting process, not just in Congress but in the nation. No wonder the press and the political community saw him as unique.

Does Gingrich's leadership represent the abrupt discontinuity with the past that the press asserts? What factors made it possible? What, in fact, are the characteristics of Gingrich's leadership style and strategies? What accounts for its successes and its failures? Does what happened teach any larger lessons about the American political system? These are the questions this chapter seeks to answer.

HOUSE MAJORITY LEADERSHIP IN THE EARLY 1990s

Understanding Gingrich's leadership and assessing whether it is as unique as popular accounts suggest require an understanding of how the House and its majority party leadership changed in the years before the 104th Congress.

By the mid-1980s, the House majority party leadership, which was of course the Democratic leadership, showed few similarities with the weak and even peripheral party leadership of the mid-1970s. The House majority party leadership was highly active, routinely involved in all stages of the legislative process and much more engaged than its predecessors in political discourse on the national stage.[3]

Changes in the political and institutional context in the 1970s and 1980s changed the character of majority party leadership in the House by altering majority party members' expectations of their party leaders. The 1970s reforms, combined with the constraints of the 1980s political environment, greatly increased the difficulty of enacting legislation, especially legislation Democrats favour. The decline in inter-committee reciprocity and the rise in floor amending activity, split control and the huge deficits made passing major legislation more difficult.[4] The 1970s reformers, most of them liberal Democrats, had been motivated by concerns about both policy and participation. The changes they instituted would, they believed, produce better (that is, more representative and more liberal) policy *and* provide greater opportunities for the rank and file to participate in the legislative process. By the late 1970s many had concluded that unrestrained participation, particularly on the House floor, hindered rather than facilitated the production of good public policy. And in the more hostile political climate of the 1980s, the policy costs of unrestrained and un-coordinated legislative activism rose further.

Included in the 1970s reforms were provisions augmenting the party leadership's resources. The Speaker was given a greater say in the appointment of members to committee, more power over the referral of bills to committee and the right to name the majority members and the chair of the Rules Committee, subject only to Caucus ratification. In the mid-1970s, the Democratic membership had placed severe constraints on the leaders' uses of these new tools; both the party's ideological heterogeneity and members' desire fully to exploit their new participation opportunities limited the leaders' role. In the late 1970s and 1980s, in contrast, as legislating became increasingly difficult, members not only allowed but began to demand that their leaders aggressively employ the tools at their command to facilitate passing the legislation members wanted.

Members' willingness to have their party leaders exert stronger leadership was furthered by the decline, during this same period, in the effective ideological heterogeneity of the Democratic membership. The change in southern politics that the civil rights movement and the Voting Rights Act set off had, by the early 1980s, resulted in a less conservative southern Democratic House contingent. As African-Americans became able to vote and as more conservative whites increasingly voted Republican, the supportive electoral coalitions of southern Democrats began to look similar to those of their northern party colleagues.[5] Continuing members shifted their voting behaviour and, as seats became vacant, the character of the new members elected changed.

In the 1980s political environment, expensive new social programmes were ruled out by the budget deficit. This constraint upon the character of policy proposals seriously considered also contributed to the Democrats' growing ideological homogeneity which became particularly evident after 1982. As policy differences among Democrats lessened, so did fears that the exercise of stronger leadership would pose a threat to members' individual policy or re-election goals.

In response to their members' demands, the party leadership developed over time a set of strategies for coping with the new environment. Including as many members as possible in the coalition-building process became a key *modus operandi*. This 'strategy of inclusion' entailed expanding and using formal leadership structures, such as the whip system, and bringing other Democrats into the coalition-building process on an *ad hoc* basis, through bill-specific task forces, for example. In the post-reform House, the core leadership was too small to undertake the task of successful coalition-building alone; including other members provided needed assistance. At least as important, the strategy of inclusion was a way for leaders to satisfy members' expectations of significant participation in the legislative process, but to do so in a manner beneficial to the party and the leadership.

The leadership refined the quintessential legislative strategy of using its control over procedure to structure the choices members confront. By giving the Speaker control of the Rules Committee, the reforms greatly enhanced the leadership's tools for structuring floor choices. Starting in the late 1970s, the Rules Committee, in concert with the party leadership, increasingly reported rules that restricted amending activity to some extent. During the 1980s the leadership developed special rules into powerful and flexible tools for managing floor time, focusing debate and sometimes advantaging one outcome over others.

An aggressive attempt to participate in national discourse and to set the congressional agenda became another strategic thrust in the 1980s. When the opposition party controls the White House, the congressional majority will usually be dissatisfied with the president's agenda and Democrats found themselves in that position almost continuously. Furthermore, within the political climate of the 1980s and 1990s, to get their issues on the agenda House Democrats needed their leadership's aid. In the aftermath of the 1980 elections, the media anointed Speaker Tip O'Neill (D.MA) the premier Democratic spokesman and thereby increased his media access and made him more than just an inside legislative leader. President Reagan taught Democrats the importance of defining issues and party images to one's benefit. How an issue is defined often determines the electoral risk inherent in a particular vote and, consequently, the opposing sides probability of legislative success. Moreover, specific legislative battles and broader controversies may leave residues on party images. Which party ultimately benefits and which loses in the court of public opinion, which gets the credit or which bears the blame is largely determined by how the issue at controversy has been defined. Consequently, House Democrats came to expect their leadership to participate effectively in national political discourse, influencing the terms of the debate so as to further Democrats' immediate legislative goals and to protect and enhance the party's image.

THE REPUBLICAN REACTION

With an activist majority party leadership leading a relatively homogeneous membership, the minority party was increasingly relegated to the sidelines. To be sure, on many lesser issues the House still operated in a bipartisan fashion and Republicans could often influence legislation in committee. However, on most high-profile issues, the action took place

104th cong : Dem little influence even in comm.

within the majority party. Their irrelevance rankled Republicans; they increasingly charged that majority party tactics were unfair and undemocratic. A bitter partisanship became the norm on the House floor.[6]

The Republican Party had also changed, becoming more aggressively conservative in the 1980s. The House Republican membership had begun to change in the mid-and late 1970s. Not only were fewer moderates being elected, more hard-edged, ideological conservatives were entering the chamber. The elections of 1978 brought a freshman named Newt Gingrich to the House. Ensuing elections continued the trend towards Republicans who were not only conservative but more ideological and more confrontationist. Increasingly, in the 1980s the disputes within the House Republican Party were about strategy not ideology; traditional conservatives who saw their responsibility as participating in governing and therefore compromising with the majority Democrats were challenged by usually more junior party colleagues who saw compromise as a sell-out and as politically stupid besides. These 'bomb-throwers', or confrontationists, believed that becoming the majority party was possible and that it required taking the Democrats on in every way and in every forum available to them. Gingrich was the leader of the confrontationists; his winning a tight whip's race in 1989 signalled a change in the direction the party would take. The fact that a number of the small group of Republican moderates supported him in that race indicated the depth of Republican discontent with their position in the chamber.

During the 1980s and early 1990s, House Republicans had in many instances imitated House Democrats by adopting rules that decreased the autonomy of their committee leaders and strengthened their party leadership. Their committee leaders (ranking minority members when the party was in the minority, committee chairs when Republicans became the majority) were made subject to a secret ballot ratification vote in the Republican Conference, the organisation of all House Republicans; the Republican party leader was given the power to nominate Republican members of Rules and more say on the party committee that makes committee assignments. Like the Democrats, though not to the same extent, Republicans expanded their whip system. Thus, while they were still in the minority, Republicans had augmented the tools available to their party leadership.

THE 1994 ELECTIONS AND THE CONTEXT OF THE GINGRICH SPEAKERSHIP

To the astonishment of most participants and observers, the 1994 elections saw Republicans win control of the House of Representatives for the first time in 40 years. Gingrich, in the eyes of most Republicans and the media, was the miracle-maker; he was seen as responsible for the unexpected Republican victory. Gingrich had worked to build a majority for years;[7] he had recruited many of the challengers who won and had helped them with fund-raising and campaign advice; the Contract With America was Gingrich's idea and he had orchestrated its realisation.

Consequently the election results gave Gingrich enormous prestige. They also provided him with a membership that was both unusually ideologically homogeneous and determined to enact major policy change. The huge freshman class – 73-strong – consisted largely of true believers, deeply committed to cutting the size and scope of government and to balancing the budget; with the sophomores, who were very similar in outlook, they made up over half of the Republican House membership. These members and a considerable number of more senior Republicans believed themselves to be mandated to make such policy change. Even moderate Republicans strongly agreed that, for the party to maintain its majority, Republicans had to deliver on their promises.[8]

The combination of an extraordinarily ambitious agenda, a new majority united behind the agenda, and a leader with enormous prestige made the exercise of strong leadership both necessary and possible. Without strong central direction, passing the agenda would have been impossible. Without a membership united in its commitment to swift and drastic policy change, no Speaker could have exercised such strong central direction of the legislative process.

Relying on his immense prestige with House Republicans, Gingrich in the days after the elections exercised power well beyond that specified in Republican Conference rules. He designated Republicans to serve as committee chairs, bypassing seniority in several instances. He engineered a rules change to increase the party leadership's voice on the committee on committees and used that new influence to reward junior Republicans, his strongest supporters, with choice assignments. By his early actions, Gingrich augmented his own resources, but it was his prestige and the membership's belief in its mandate that made his actions possible and that constituted his greatest resources.

LEADERSHIP STYLE AND STRATEGIES

Most political scientists see congressional leaders as agents of their members; they are elected by their members and must satisfy their expectations to get re-elected. Gingrich himself and many who have written about him see him as a fundamentally different sort of leader. He has been characterised – and has characterised himself – as a 'transformational leader' whose aim is to transform how Americans think and talk about politics and thereby 'transform the political alignments, institutions, and governing policies of the nation'.[9] Gingrich himself sees the job of Speaker as combining 'grass roots organisations, mass media and legislative detail into one synergistic pattern'.[10] A leader must first be 'a visionary definer, agenda setter and value articulator for the community,' Gingrich says. Second, he should be a symbol of the community and a 'recruiter of talent and energy and gatherer of community resources'. Being an 'administrator and manager of government' comes last in importance.

Principal–agent theory conceptualises leadership in legislatures as having been instituted to ameliorate problems of collective action.[11] By assumption, members of Congress want to legislate; legislating is necessary to their advancing their individual goals. Lawmaking is, however, a complex and time-consuming enterprise and one that, if successful, produces a collective good; consequently, it presents the legislature's membership with collective action problems. Overcoming these collective action problems requires the delegation by members of powers and resources to agents. The benefits of such delegation can be great. A party leadership well endowed with powers and resources can significantly facilitate the passage of legislation that furthers its membership's policy, re-election and power goals. It can do so by providing basic coordination services, such as legislative scheduling; by facilitating, through side-payments or the coordination of tacit or explicit logrolls, for example, the passage of legislation various subgroups of its membership want; and by policy leadership, that is, using leadership powers and resources aggressively to influence the congressional agenda and the substance of legislative outputs so as to translate broadly shared legislative preferences into law.

Delegation is, however, risky for members; agents may use the powers granted them to pursue interests not those of their principal. Thus the character of the delegation and the extent to which members are willing to allow their leaders to use their delegated powers and resources aggressively depend on the costs and benefits to members of strong leadership, which in turn depend on the political and institutional environment. In particular, when members are ideologically homogeneous and committed to enacting an ambitious legislative programme they are most likely to expect their leadership to use its powers and resources expansively and more likely to augment the powers and resources delegated to the leaders.

Some scholars and most journalists object that principal agent theory with its emphasis on members' expectations as the prime determinant of leadership functioning leaves out all the richness of leaders' personality and makes them into mindless puppets. The theory does not deal with personality; in my view that is a virtue because I believe political science has little useful to say on that score. The theory does not, however, conceptualise leaders as puppets. When members perceive their leaders as both faithful and effective agents they will give them considerable leeway to be creative; that is, so long as most members are convinced the leader is furthering their goals and that the leader is skilful at doing so, those members are likely to applaud innovation on the leader's part.[12] An elected congressional leader will not, however, have the same freedom of manoeuvre as is available to a member-entrepreneur who holds no position of delegated powers.

I argue here that Gingrich like other congressional leaders can be understood as an agent of his members; he differs in that he did more than most leaders to shape the majority he leads. Because of the character of his majority, Gingrich was free to pursue his notions of transforming American politics at least during 1995; he was considerably more constrained in compromising on policy substance.

Gingrich's pursuit of a majority-building strategy from long before he entered the formal Republican House leadership differentiates him from other twentieth-century speakers and is important enough to his leadership during the 104th that it requires examination here. His leadership strategies as Speaker show more continuity with those of recent Democratic leaderships but also similarities to his pre-speakership *modus operandi* and the impact of his grandiose notion of what the speakership can be. Although Democrats had recognised the importance of participating effectively in national political discourse and had moved to increase their capabilities in the battle for public opinion, message is even more important to Gingrich's leadership. The 'buy-in' strategy is the Republican version of the strategy of inclusion, an attempt to involve a large proportion of the membership in leadership efforts and thereby give them a stake in their success. Although when they were in the minority Republicans vowed to eschew the strategy of structuring choices through the use of procedure, especially through special rules, the Republican leadership has, in fact, resorted to that strategy on a regular basis.

The Majority-Building Strategy

To say that Gingrich built his own majority is too strong; Democratic control of both Congress and the presidency and the consequent ability of voters to hold one party accountable for everything they disliked about government was almost certainly a necessary condition for the 1994 election results. Nevertheless Gingrich's majority-building activities helped to shape the character of the majority that was elected and assure that he would lead it. Gingrich carried out much of this activity, especially that part of it that was most divisive within the Republican Party, before he was elected to the party leadership and thus was no one's agent.

According to all accounts, including some contemporaneous ones, Gingrich held the goal of winning a House majority from the beginning of his House tenure and began to do something about it almost immediately. Gingrich was one of the 35-member strong Republican class of 1978, many of whom, influenced by Jack Kemp's 'supply-side' ideas and California's tax-cutting Proposition 13, had run conservative, issue-based campaigns.[13] An activist group unwilling to settle for permanent minority status, the class which elected Gingrich as its secretary met frequently; it made an attempt to expel Charles Diggs (D.MI) for ethics infractions and involved itself in the budget fight by offering its own alternative. In 1980, Kemp proposed and Gingrich ran 'Governing Team Day', an event involving Ronald Reagan and Republican congressional candidates on the Capitol steps pledging themselves to work together. Kemp and Gingrich had hoped to have candidates endorse specific policy stands but the Reagan campaign insisted on only vague campaign-style pledges.

After being involved in several precursor groups, Gingrich in 1983 formed the Conservative Opportunity Society (COS), the ultimate goal of which was to elect a Republican majority to the House; the group aggressively used floor amendments and other procedural tactics and, importantly, C-SPAN. The House is a majority-rule institution; the 'bombthrowers' might cause the majority some annoyance and even some pain, but a reasonably cohesive majority party could always defeat them. The televising of House sessions, including special orders at the end of the day in which members can talk as long as they like on the topic of their choice, gave COS a way to reach beyond the chamber and start the task Gingrich believed so important, that of framing issues and shaping the debate. Gingrich individually and through COS sought to promulgate an image of the Democratic Congress as completely divorced from the American people, arrogantly indifferent to their wants and needs while catering to special interests, wallowing in federal pork, perks and worse. By pursuing ethics charges against Speaker Jim Wright, Gingrich gained much wider publicity for his negative portrait of Congress as an institution.

In 1986 Gingrich became chairman of GOPAC, a political action committee founded by former House member and governor of Delaware Pierre duPont to recruit and assist candidates for state and local offices with the aim of strengthening the Republicans 'farm team'. Gingrich shifted GOPAC's emphasis from supplying money to supplying ideas, rationales and motivation. Gingrich sent prospective candidates audio and videotapes on tactics, strategy, ideas and issues; many Republican candidates listened to those tapes and were influenced in their view of issues and some were inspired to run for federal office.[14] Some began winning election to the House as Gingrich hoped. By the late 1980s, most Republican House freshmen had been helped and influenced by Gingrich.[15] The big 103rd Congress Republican class consisted largely of aggressive conservatives, many of whom had received help from GOPAC.

Message as Strategy

The primacy Gingrich places on the leader as 'visionary definer, agenda setter and value articulator' and the weight he puts on shaping the terms of the political debate led logically to the centrality of message to his leadership strategies. Much more than for his Democratic predecessors, message becomes strategy.

Gingrich's pre-speakership majority-building activities were based largely on message. Necessity, as well as Gingrich's larger purpose, dictated reaching out beyond the House; as a minority within a minority, Gingrich and his allies could exert little influence within the chamber. Thus the greater part of COS's effort went into disseminating its message through C-SPAN. Gingrich's attack on Wright was very much a media-based effort; he used the media's interest in the story and his own greater media access that derived therefrom to convey his Congress- and Democrat-bashing message. Through his tapes and speeches, Gingrich coached Republicans in the language to use; for example, recommending that they label Democrats as 'pathetic', 'sick' and, of course, 'corrupt'; word such as 'change', 'moral' and 'family' were to be associated with Republicans.[16]

When Gingrich became Whip, he bluntly stated that he had no intention of spending his time behind the scenes counting votes; that mundane task he delegated to his good friend Bob Walker (R.PA) and to staff, while Gingrich himself continued to concentrate on majority-building, much of it thorough message disseminating activities. When, in 1990, he opposed the budget deal negotiated by President Bush and the bipartisan congressional leadership, it was to protect the party's message he had worked to shape; only by maintaining a sharp difference between the parties and preserving the Republican's best issue – lower taxes – could the Republicans hope to win a congressional majority, Gingrich believed. A majority of the House Republican membership agreed with him and joined with liberal Democrats to defeat the deal. When the House 'bank' and post office scandals broke in 1991, Gingrich encouraged the group of junior Republicans know as the 'Gang of Seven', who took to the floor and the airwaves to demand the release of members' names; the bigger a story the scandals became the more effective they were as a vehicle for disseminating Gingrich's message about the 'corrupt Democratic Congress'.

The Contract With America was itself an elaborate effort to disseminate a bundle of messages about the Republican Party: policy messages, but also that, unlike the majority Democrats, it was dedicated to cleaning up the corrupt Congress and prepared to stake its future on fulfilling its promises. Thus the first plank dealt with congressional reform; it was called a contract to give it an aura of legal weight, and Republicans explicitly invited voters to throw them out of office if they did not fulfil their promises. The language use to name the bills in the Contract was tested through polling and focus groups; welfare reform was named the 'Personal Responsibility Act' and a cut in the capital gains tax and changes in the regulatory process aimed especially at weakening environmental regulations made up most of the 'Job Creation and Wage Enhancement Act'.

Message continued its primacy when Gingrich became Speaker. His media access was, however, much greater – a not unalloyed benefit, it turned out. Not only did Gingrich take advantage of the press's interest by granting innumerable interviews and appearing on all the interview shows, he opened the Speaker's daily press conference to television coverage. The Republican leadership insisted that all the committees hire a press secretary and coordinate message strategy with the beefed-up leadership press operation.[17] The Republican 'theme teams', members organised to use the one-minute speeches at the beginning of a day's session to promulgate the message of the day, continued to operate. Although members would later bitterly criticise the leadership for not being sufficiently effective at communication, enormous effort went into attempts to shape the perception of the Republicans' policy proposals. Thus special task forces put together media kits for use by Republican leaders and rank and file on each of the major issues. On Medicare, Republicans made an enormous effort to shift the terms of the debate – from cutting the programme to saving it by slowing the rate of increase.

The message strategy also included an effort to shut out competitors. Republicans abolished legislative service organisations such as the Congressional Black Caucus and the Democratic Study Group. They attempted to enact into law a provision aimed at liberal advocacy groups

that barred groups that receive federal funds from lobbying. Majority
Leader Dick Armey (R.TX) even tried to pressure corporations into
ceasing to make contributions to liberal organisations.[18]

The 'Buy-In' Strategy

Like the Democratic leaders before him, Gingrich knows that leading the
post-reform House requires a strategy of inclusion; the activists that make
up a substantial proportion of each party's membership expect to participate meaningfully in the legislative process; by providing that opportunity, the leadership gets help that it badly needs. Furthermore those
members involved in leadership efforts develop a stake in their success.

Gingrich sought to involve others in his majority-building efforts, to get
them to 'buy in', long before he moved into the leadership. As Whip he
continued that effort, reaching out to members with whom he had little in
common ideologically. The putting together of the Contract exemplifies
the strategy.[19] In late 1993, Gingrich began to talk about holding a Capitol
steps event during the 1994 election campaign. At the House Republicans'
retreat in Salisbury, Maryland in February 1994, members held intensive
discussions in small groups and took the first steps towards identifying the
common principles and core beliefs that would guide the drafting of the
Contract. Republican incumbents and challengers were surveyed about
what should be included. When that had been decided, working groups of
members and leadership staff put together the actual bills. Any member
who wanted to could participate, but younger activists were more likely to
do so than senior committee leaders. Still a large number of members did
have a hand in putting together the Contract and so felt some pride of
authorship. 'By the time things got to the conference, there was a great
deal of buy-in already,' Pete Hoekstra (R.MI), an activist member of the
class of 1992, reported. 'The members involved in the drafting had a great
sense of empowerment and that began to run through the Conference.'[20]

Once in the majority, Gingrich and the Republican leadership team continued the 'buy-in' strategy. Gingrich established numerous task forces to
carry out a great variety of tasks; at one point there were so many and
they had been set up so quickly that no one had a list. Some were charged
with expediting action on Contract legislation, others with coming up with
broad-based compromises on divisive issues, others with outreach beyond
Congress, and still others had an electoral purpose.[21] Inclusion – especially
of junior members – was clearly an important goal.[22] 'Newt uses task
forces to get people involved who have a common interest on something.
To get them together. Newt's very open to new ideas …,' a moderate

Republican explained. 'He wants to let everybody do their own thing, pursue their own interests.'

The Conference meets weekly, as does a large leadership group of about 20, which includes a cross-section of the party membership. Gingrich also made it a point to consult and stay in regular contact with the various party subgroups. 'He meets once a month with all the groups, the California delegation, the freshmen group, the sophomore group, the Tuesday lunch bunch, the Wednesday group, CATS, all these groups,' a member explained. 'Newt has constant meetings. Anybody can see him. After he opens the session, or is there for the opening of the session, he stays on the floor and circulates, and this is a time when people can come up and talk to him.' During the period that the Republican leadership was engaged in budget talks with the Clinton administration, Gingrich sought to keep his troops informed on a daily basis. 'After the sessions at the White House, Newt reported every day to anybody who wanted to come and hear,' according to a member. 'If the sessions went on very long, he would do it by phone. He would kind of have a phone briefing and we could call in and hear what had gone on, and he would tell us in great detail who had said what.' Summits cut most members out of the decision-making process and this breeds resentment; aware of this problem, Gingrich worked to counter it by at least keeping members informed.

Gingrich's effort to include members in the process and give them a stake in its success was especially intense with respect to the freshmen. Not only did they constitute about 30 per cent of the party's membership, they had made the party a majority and significant losses among them would make it the minority again. Thus freshmen were very heavily represented on task forces and two were included in the large leadership group that met weekly. Gingrich had made sure they received good committee assignments and, at Gingrich's behest, two even chaired subcommittees.

Structuring Choices

When Republicans were in the minority they complained bitterly about Democrats' use of procedure and especially their use of restrictive rules to structure choices. The new Republican majority in the 104th Congress had, however, promised to deliver on an ambitious agenda, much of it in the first 100 days. When Republicans brought one of the early Contract items (unfunded mandates) to the floor under an open rule, Democrats behaved just as the minority Republicans had when given the opportunity by an open rule: they offered multitudes of amendments, many designed to force vulnerable Republicans to cast difficult votes. In response and despite their

promise, Republicans began to bring most major legislation to the floor
under complex and restrictive rules. The proportion of all rules that were
restrictive did go down from 70 per cent in the 103rd Congress to 49 per
cent in 1995, though Democrats claimed Republicans manipulated the
figures by considering under open rules some non-controversial legislation
that should have been considered under the suspension procedure.

Rules were used not just to prevent obstructionism but also to structure
choices. For example, a cleverly constructed restrictive rule protected the
1995 rescission bill. The rule specified that anyone wishing to restore
spending cuts in the bill had to offset the cost by cutting something else in
the same section of the bill; thus, no money could be transferred to social
programmes from defence spending or from disaster relief for California,
in effect, protecting them from cuts. The rule for the Republicans'
omnibus tax cut bill simply disallowed an amendment on one of its most
controversial provisions – the earnings cap on eligibility for the $500 per
child tax credit. The strategic use of special rules was simply too powerful
a tool for promoting the party's legislative objectives to eschew.

PARTY ORGANISATION AND LEADERSHIP STRUCTURE

In the post-reform House, party leadership is a collective enterprise and
that remained so in the 104th Congress. Both parties have elaborate organisations and a number of leaders who share leadership responsibilities. In
recent decades, the Republican organisation had been more decentralised
than the Democratic; in addition to the Conference, the organisation of all
House Republicans, there were a number of other significant organisational entities, most of which had leaders elected independently of the
Republican Leader. The elected leadership consisted of the Republican
Leader, the Whip, the chair, vice-chair and secretary of the Conference
and the chairs of the Policy Committee, the Research Committee and the
National Republican Congressional Committee.[23] The ranking members
of the committees on Rules, Ways and Means, Appropriations and Budget
were formally recognised as part of the leadership group during the 1980s
and in 1992 a representative of the freshmen class was also included. This
structure, although more fragmented and differing in details, was quite
similar to that of the majority Democrats.

By the late 1980s, Republican confrontationists began to win leadership
posts over more traditional conservatives; after leadership elections in late
1992, confrontationists had taken over most leadership positions; only the
top position itself and the Policy Committee chairmanship were not under

their sway. The like-mindedness of most of the leaders contributed to a closer working relationship and their activism energised these entities and stimulated a number of new endeavours. In response to the Democrats' 'message board', a 'theme team' was created to disseminate the Republicans' message – usually through the daily, one-minute speeches in the House. Imitating a Clinton campaign tool, the Conference under Dick Armey formed a 'rapid response team' to respond to Clinton administration initiatives; the Conference also began producing a weekly fax newsletter sent to members on Thursday suggesting party themes to emphasise during the weekend in their districts.[24]

By and large, Republicans in the 104th Congress made only modest changes in party structure through party rules changes (the reconstitution of the Committee on Committees, renamed the Steering Committee, so as to give the leadership a considerably greater voice is the exception). Becoming the majority, of course, changed the structure by adding a top leadership position. The Speaker augmented his budget and staff. The Republican whip system expanded; in the 104th it consisted of the whip, a chief deputy whip, 13 deputy whips and 39 assistant whips – still not as big as the Democratic whip system but more similar than before. Junior representation in the leadership was expanded; one sophomore and two freshmen elected by their class were made part of the designated leadership. The greater centralisation of the 104th was not a product of structural change but of the leaders' like-mindedness and Gingrich's prestige. Other leaders and entities did not go off on their own because they agreed with the direction Gingrich was leading the party and they knew that, in case of conflict, most members would support Gingrich.

How the various leaders and organisational entities functioned was, of course, significantly affected by the Republicans' becoming the majority party. Thus, the whip system was now expected to assemble floor majorities for party priorities on an everyday basis; the communications arms – the Conference leadership and staff and the Policy Committee – now were charged with selling Republican initiatives and defending Republican actions rather than criticising those of the opposition majority. Although the responsibilities were greater, their resources were as well. By and large, how these entities went about their job did not differ in any fundamental way from their Democratic predecessors.

The Speaker's Advisory Group (SAG) has sometimes been represented as something entirely new. SAG was chaired by Gingrich's best friend Bob Walker and includes the Speaker, Majority Leader Dick Armey, Whip Tom DeLay (R,TX), Deputy Whip Dennis Hastert (R.IL), Republican Conference Chair John Boehner (R.OH), RNCC

chair Tom Paxon (R.NY) and Budget Committee Chair John Kasich
(R.OH).[25] Largely an extension of the informal leadership group that
orchestrated the development of the Contract, SAG met weekly and functioned as the core leadership directorate. Under Democratic control, a core
group that could respond quickly to unexpected events as well as talk over
problems also existed.

Gingrich's views of the appropriate division of labour between the
Speaker and the Majority Leader and his attempts to implement them do
represent a real break with the past. Gingrich, as discussed earlier, defined
himself as a visionary and his aim as transforming American politics and
society. Given the scale of the tasks he had set himself, Gingrich did not
want to get bogged down in the legislative management duties Speakers
normally perform. Consequently he delegated extensive responsibility to
Majority Leader Dick Armey. In addition to doing the scheduling of legislation for the floor, the majority leader's traditional task, Armey was
charged with working closely with the committees and task forces producing the legislation, crafting, in consultation with the Rules Committee,
the special rules for bringing legislation to the floor and negotiating post-
committee changes in legislation when necessary. All these are tasks in
which the Speaker is usually deeply involved.

During the first 100 days, the division of labour worked well. Armey
assumed much of the day-to-day responsibility and Gingrich, although a
bit more involved than he sometimes claimed, was free to concentrate on
message. During the much longer struggle over Medicare and the budget,
however, Gingrich became deeply involved in the details of the legislative
process. When that effort turned out badly, Gingrich himself and many of
his colleagues placed some of the blame on the leadership's deviation
from its successful early model. In late February 1996, Gingrich
announced a return; 'Armey will focus on the day-to-day legislation and
my focus will be on communicating to our majority – and why we need [to
retain] it,' he explained.[26]

This redefinition of the Speaker's job seems unlikely to be successful
over the long run. It worked during the Contract period because of the
consensus among House Republicans that they had to bring every item in
the Contract to a vote in the first 100 days in a form that deviated little
from the Contract language. It worked a little less well in 1996; no such
consensus agenda existed, but the majority did not attempt to pass a great
deal of legislation. It worked not at all during the budget fight when
crucial decisions about strategy, substance and priorities were closely
entangled with each other and with message; a party's top leader could not
delegate such decisions to others and remain the top leader.

DELIVERING

If House Republicans were to deliver on their ambitious promises, their party leadership would have to orchestrate the complex process of getting multiple pieces of legislation through myriad committees quickly and of mobilising votes to pass all that legislation on the floor intact.

The Party Leadership and the Committees

According to journalistic accounts, the relationship between the party leadership and congressional committees was fundamentally different in the 104th from that in previous congresses. Actually the autonomous committees with powerful and independent committee chairs that these accounts often depicted had been long gone, wiped out by the reforms, and the Democratic Party leadership in the 1980s and early 1990s had been actively involved in all stages of the legislative process. Nevertheless the relationship between party and committee leaders was different in the 104th Congress; committee leaders were clearly subordinate to party leaders on Contract bills and on much of the major legislation that went into the Republicans' attempt to balance the budget. (See John Owens' chapter in this volume for a full treatment of the relationship.)

Gingrich's enormous prestige as the majority-maker, the freshmen's ideological fervour and the Republican membership's commitment to passing the Contract allowed the leadership to play such an aggressive policy role. Before the budget débâcle, Republicans were convinced that Gingrich was a master strategist and they knew he shared their goals of making non-incremental policy change and of retaining their majority. Thus they were more than willing to let him exercise great power in order to assure that legislation was passed and in a form that would accomplish the party's objectives.

The Party Leadership and the Groups

To assist in passing the Republican agenda, the party leadership enlisted the aid of core Republican constituency groups. The National Rifle Association (NRA), small business groups, particularly the National Federation of Independent Businesses (NFIB), and especially the Christian Coalition had become increasingly important components of the Republican coalition; organised and active at the grass roots, they were key to the Republicans' victories in 1994. Many of the freshmen had strong ties to one or more of these groups.

Legislative leaders' enlisting the aid of outside groups, especially of those generally allied with the party, is by no means a new tactic. During the 1980s and early 1990s, House Democratic leaders had increasingly formalised such efforts, with specific staff aides designated to work with groups as their primary responsibility. Although not always successful, Democrats did try to put together broad-based lobbying efforts in which groups would all agree to support and work for important legislation even if it was not at the top of their own agenda.[27]

During the 104th Congress, the Thursday Group, a leadership-created entity consisting of lobbyists for both the ideological groups closely allied with the Republicans and for other business groups with a major stake in the enactment of the Republican agenda, met weekly with Republican Conference Chair John Boehner. He and Whip Tom DeLay worked to orchestrate these groups' lobbying efforts to best effect.[28] Although the character of the endeavour did not differ in a major way from that of Democrats, the Republican efforts to maintain a united front among these groups and to enlist them in lobbying for legislation not at the top of their own priority list were unusually successful, especially during the Contract period.[29] Everyone wants to be a part of a winning team. In addition, groups such as the Christian Coalition and NFIB were more successful at mobilising their grass roots to pressure members of Congress than most of the Democratic groups had been. Both were well organised at the local level and had been energised by their success in the 1994 campaigns.

Although the Republicans gained valuable help from these groups, that help and even more their electoral support came at a price. Neither the Christian Coalition nor the NRA got much of their agenda in the Contract; although they were instrumental to the Republicans' takeover of the House, both were patient in 1995; they did not push their divisive agendas and the Christian Coalition worked hard to pass the Contract. Under these circumstances, when the one Contract item the Christian Coalition cared about most became highly controversial and a liability, the Republican leadership could not compromise. Yet the refusal of Republicans to cap the family income of those eligible for the $500 per child tax credit made it easier for Democrats to paint Republican tax cuts as a giveaway to the rich. Similarly, Gingrich believed he had to deliver on his promise to the NRA to schedule a House vote on repealing the assault weapons ban even though doing so contributed to the Republicans' reputation as extremists.

MANAGING THE PARTY'S FACTIONS

During the first half of 1995, especially during the Contract period, the House Republican Party showed the world a monolithic face; the Republicans' voting cohesion was remarkable; on 33 final passage votes on the Contract items, only 4.7 members on average defected from the party position.[30] Yet the Republican Party does contain factions. An important aspect of the leadership's job is holding the party together and, given the Republicans' narrow margin, this task took on especial importance in the 104th.

Although their ideological spread is still probably less than that of Democrats, Republicans do differ ideologically; moderates, although small in number, made up enough of the membership to make the difference between a majority and a minority. Conservatives, the bulk of the party, fall along a spectrum from traditional small government conservatives to a newer brand of virulently anti-government radical. A considerable number of the 1994 freshman class fell towards the anti-government end of that spectrum. In addition to ideological divisions, Republicans can also be divided into the 'committee guys' and the party and issue activists: those who concentrate on the issues that come before their committees, often issues of importance to their districts and who were used to working with committee Democrats and, on the other hand, those whose purview was broader, who are more ideological and more focused on using issues to build and retain a majority.[31] The party and issue activists' differ among themselves in how pragmatic and how willing to compromise they are.

During 1995, the 'committee guys' were eclipsed to the point that they made few demands. To be sure, there was considerable grousing behind the scenes, from senior staff more than from members themselves. 'Many [Republican committee staffers] thought that the Contract was a joke. Basically they were happy and comfortable in the minority and they never thought that we would win a majority,' an aide to a party activist member explained. 'They don't like the legislation. They are saying, "You want us to report *this*?" And we say, "If you had been willing to work with us in developing this legislation, maybe it would be better drafted." They are unhappy because they are not in control, and that's right, they're not in control.' The headiness of being in the majority and their concern about the consequences for their careers of not seeming to be with the programme kept the 'committee guys' quiescent. In 1996, in response to increasing dissatisfaction, the leadership began to talk about giving the committees more leeway and relying on task forces less.

For managing the other factional divisions in the party, Gingrich relied heavily on the buy-in strategy. He sought through a variety of devices to include as many members as possible in the legislative process under the leadership's aegis and he worked hard at communicating with all factions and subsets of the membership (see the earlier discussion). He made himself available to members on a daily basis; 'Newt says that if you don't tell me what you're worried about, then it's your problem,' a moderate explained. 'He's essentially inviting people to talk to him.'

The party leadership also bargained with members for their support when necessary. On Contract items, the need and the willingness of the leadership to do so was very limited; on the myriad of complex legislation that made up the budget bill, the leadership did attempt to give members what they needed to support the bill. Gingrich himself conducted the negotiations on the Medicare provisions.[32]

The Contract proved to be a key resource in holding the party together and using it for that purpose was a conscious leadership strategy. By providing an agenda to which most members had pledged themselves, the Contract prevented early battles about priorities. The leaders' emphasis on the Contract was amplified by the media; even those members who had regarded the signing as just a campaign photo op (and a number of the 'committee guys' had so regarded it) realised that not delivering at least on the promise of bringing the items to a vote would be a disaster for the party. The leadership, of course, brought up the least contentious items first; but as more and more Contract items passed, the pressure to pass the rest intensified. Republicans who were less than happy with some of the bills knew that the press would have a field day if any of the items failed and that, were they responsible, their colleagues would not soon forget. (They also expected the Senate to clean up much of the sloppy language and, in some cases, block provisions altogether.)

With the strong backing of the freshmen, Gingrich extended the Contract aura to balancing the budget in seven years. Gingrich publicly committed the party to it and, given the enormous media coverage he was receiving, he made the cost of failure to the party too great to bear. Thus the leadership could use much the same arguments during the budget battle as it used during the Contract period.

Throughout 1995, an argument the leadership used, implicitly and explicitly, to keep the moderates and the 'committee guys' from straying (as well as in negotiations with the Senate and the president) was that the freshmen constrained the leadership's ability to move away from hard-line conservative positions. To be sure, in a number of cases, the leadership did persuade the freshmen to compromise; sometimes arguments based on political reality succeeded; for example, the freshmen acceded to deleting the requirement for a three-fifths vote to raise taxes from the balanced budget constitutional amendment when the leadership convinced them it would doom the amendment. In other cases, Gingrich had to rely on appeals to personal loyalty.[33] In the end, however, whether he had realised it or not, Gingrich could not control the freshmen. He could not persuade them to compromise soon enough, and the party paid a considerable price both in legislation forgone and in message. The context that had made possible persuading even cautious senior members to support a radical attempt to transform government's role also made it impossible to persuade the real revolutionaries to retreat and settle for half a loaf.

LEADING THE REVOLUTION: AN ASSESSMENT

What made Gingrich's leadership in the 104th Congress unique was not strategies, techniques or even strength, but purpose. Certainly no Speaker since Clay had attempted to use the speakership as a platform for remaking American politics. We could have predicted much about the course of the 104th Congress based on principal–agent theory and well-established generalisations about American politics; that is, much of what happened was independent of Gingrich as an individual. However, Gingrich's unique purpose also influenced the course of events and contributed to both his leadership's successes and failures.

We know that new congressional majorities tend to be more cohesive than old majorities and that majorities that believe themselves to have received an electoral mandate are more cohesive and more inclined to accept strong leadership, whether from a president of their party or internally. Freshmen members are especially likely to respond thus, since a new majority is likely to include numerous 'accidental' winners, many of whom are likely to be ideologues.

Based on these generalisations, we could have predicted on the day after the 1994 elections that the 104th Congress would see strong central leadership with the committee chairs kept on a short leash and that the new majority party would maintain high cohesion and would, in the House, quickly produce a large body of legislation responding to the new majority's purported mandate. We could also have predicted that the new House majority was very likely to overinterpret its mandate and, given the structure of the American government, that actually enacting much of the new majority's agenda would eventually require significant compromises with the Senate and the president.[34] And if we could predict these consequences, so could

Gingrich. Yet he acted as if he were unaware of the dangers of over-interpretation or of the ultimate need to compromise in order to have something to show for the effort.

Gingrich's larger purpose, in part at least, explains his approach. That purpose led him to maximise the 'revolutionary' potential of the context the 1994 elections created. He proclaimed the election represented a 'revolution' and used the multitude of forums available to him to expound on his vision. He used the 'revolutionary' zeal of the freshmen as a weapon to push other Republicans into taking actions they otherwise might well have feared went too far. Gingrich's approach had some impressive results. Probably any leader the House Republicans would conceivably have chosen could have got the Contract items through the House; passing the balanced budget legislation with its big cuts and major restructuring of numerous politically sensitive programmes very likely required the sort of revolutionary mentality Gingrich promoted through his crusade to change American politics.

The approach also, however, proved to be costly. Gingrich's rhetoric scared people; he soon became the most unpopular political figure in America. By empowering the freshmen and encouraging them in their 'revolutionary' course, Gingrich assured that, when compromise was necessary, they would be unwilling to go along. Gingrich might not have been able to control the freshmen in any case; as much as they revered Gingrich, their first allegiance was to what they perceived as their mandate. Furthermore, the freshmen were not alone in their staunch commitment to the strategy of attempting to bludgeon the president into agreeing to their policy positions by shutting the government down; even some of the Republican leadership clung to the strategy long after its disastrous impact on the Republican Party's popularity became clear.[35] Yet even this was probably influenced by Gingrich's framing the new Republican majority's mission in 'revolutionary' terms. Gingrich himself held to a hard-line strategy too long.

Why did Gingrich miscalculate? Gingrich, I believe, placed too much faith in the message strategy – in the efficacy of both the message and the messenger. His message strategy played an important role in Gingrich's rise; the resonance of his negative Congress-bashing message with the news media's definition of what constitutes a good story accounts for a large part of his media success; but not surprisingly, Gingrich attributed it to the power of his positive message and his own persuasiveness. Gingrich knew the 1994 elections did not carry an explicit mandate for the Republican's programme; he also knew that the Senate and the White House constituted potential veto points. However, Gingrich believed that he could rouse public opinion and put so much pressure on the Senate and the president that they would have to choose between going along or committing political suicide. Fulfilling the expectations of his members, especially of the junior classes, Gingrich did try to lead a revolution; it failed because he could not persuade the public that that was what it wanted.

Yet, if Gingrich's purpose was transformative policy change, he probably had to take the gamble. Breaking through the barriers to nonincremental policy change erected by the Madisonian system and the contemporary politics of cynicism, which negatively biased media feed, requires a swift frontal assault and pushing the potential of one's political resources to the maximum; a measured, cautious approach is unlikely to bear fruit. If presidents are admonished to 'hit the ground running' and to 'use it [their political capital], or lose it,' a Speaker with his much more tenuous hold on the bully pulpit is under even greater pressure to do so.[36]

Ironically, House Republicans held on to their majority at the price of reverting to incremental politics and policy-making and of Gingrich abandoning his effort to became a successful transformational leader on the national stage. The lesson the 104th Congress teaches, especially when it is considered in the light of the 103rd, is that, within the American political system, effecting major policy change is enormously and increasingly difficult.

NOTES

1. In addition to the sources cited, this essay is based on interviews conducted by the author. Unattributed quotations are from those interviews.
2. *Time*, 7 November 1994, 10 April 1995; *Newsweek*, 10 April 1995.
3. For a full presentation of the argument, see Barbara Sinclair, *Legislators, Leaders and Lawmaking* (Baltimore: Johns Hopkins University Press, 1995).
4. Barbara Sinclair, *Majority Leadership in the U.S. House* (Baltimore: The Johns Hopkins University Press, 1983) and Steven S. Smith, *Call to Order: Floor Politics in the House and Senate* (Washington, D.C.: The Brookings Institution, 1989).
5. David W. Rohde, *Parties and Leaders in the Postreform House* (Chicago: University of Chicago Press, 1991).
6. Richard B. Cheney, 'An Unruly House', *Public Opinion*, 11 (1989), pp. 41–4; and William Connelly and John Pitney, *Congress' Permanent Minority?: Republicans in the U.S. House* (Lanham, MD: Rowman & Littlefield, 1994).
7. See below, and Connelly and Pitney, *Congress' Permanent Majority?*
8. Healey, 'Jubilant GOP Strives to Keep Legislative Feet on Ground', *Congressional Quarterly Weekly Report*, 12 November 1994, pp. 3210–15.

9. Daniel Stid, 'Transformational Leadership in Congress?'. Paper prepared for delivery at the 1996 annual meeting of the American Political Science Association, San Francisco, 29 August–1 September, 1996, p. 1; and Dan Balz and Ronald Brownstein, *Storming the Gates: Protest Politics and the Republican Revival* (Boston: Little, Brown, 1996), p. 144. See also Ronald Peters, 'The Republican Speakership'. Paper prepared for delivery at the 1996 annual meeting of the American Political Science Association, San Francisco, 29 August–1 September 1996.
10. David S. Cloud, 'Speaker Wants His Platform to Rival the Presidency', *Congressional Quarterly Weekly Report*, 4 February 1995, p. 333.
11. For a fuller explication, see Sinclair, *Legislators, Leaders, and Lawmaking*, chapter 2. Also see Gary Cox and Mathew McCubbins, *Legislative Leviathan: Party Government in the House* (Berkeley: University of California Press, 1992).
12. Thus conceived, principal–agent theory does not conflict fundamentally with Randall Strahan's theory of leadership, the most sophisticated of the theories positing, to varying extents, leader autonomy. See 'Leadership in Institutional and Political Time: The case of Newt Gingrich and the 104th Congress'. Paper prepared for delivery at the annual meeting of the American Political Science Association, San Francisco, 29 August–1 September 1996. Strahan argues that there are critical moments in institutional time 'in which changes in the political environment … create demands and opportunities for actions by Congress that cannot be realised within existing institutional forms' (p. 19) and that these periods allow creative leaders to 'influence the emergence of new institutional forms' (p. 20). My emphasis and my interpretation of some important aspects of this case are, however, different.
13. John J. Pitney, 'The Conservative Opportunity Society', manuscript, December 1988.
14. Balz and Brownstein, *Storming the Gates*, pp. 144–6.
15. Douglas L. Koopman, *Hostile Takeover: The House Republican Party 1980–1995* (Lanham, MD: Rowman and Littlefield, 1996), p. 53.
16. Elizabeth Drew, *Showdown: The Struggle between the Gingrich Congress and the Clinton White House* (New York: Simon and Schuster, 1996), p. 42.
17. Douglas Koopman, 'The House of Representatives Under Republican Leadership: Changes by the New Majority'. Paper prepared for delivery at the 1995 annual meeting of the American Political Science Association, Chicago, 30 August–3 September 1995, p. 15.
18. Drew, *Showdown*, p. 261.
19. Koopman, *Hostile Takeover*, pp. 142–7; and Stid, 'Transformational Leadership', pp. 6–8.
20. Quoted in Stid, 'Transformational Leadership', p. 7.
21. Lawrence Evans and Walter J. Oleszek, *Congress under Fire: Reform Politics and the Republican Majority* (Boston: Houghton Mifflin, 1997), pp. 132–3.
22. Newt Gingrich, 'Leadership Task Forces: The "Third Wave" Way to Consider Legislation', *Roll Call*, 16 November 1995, p. 5.
23. Connelly and Pitney, *Congress' Permanent Minority*, p. 42.

24. Koopman, *Hostile Takeover*, pp. 141–2.
25. Stid, 'Transformational Leadership', p. 11.
26. Marcia Gelbart, 'Gingrich Redefines Role as Speaker,' *The Hill*, 28 February 1996, p. 1.
27. See Sinclair, *Legislators, Leaders and Lawmaking*, pp. 236–40.
28. Jonathan D. Salant, 'Alliance of Private Groups Pushes GOP "Contract"', *Congressional Quarterly Weekly Report*, 28 January 1995, pp. 261–2; and Balz and Brownstein, *Storming the Gates*, pp. 198–9.
29. Republicans do seem to have given affected interest groups a considerable greater role in drafting legislation than the Democrats ever did. See Drew, *Showdown*, pp. 116–17.
30. Calculated from data in *Congressional Quarterly Weekly Report*, 8 April 1995, p. 1006.
31. Connelly and Pitney, *Congress' Permanent Majority?*, pp. 19–40.
32. Janet Hook, 'Budget Battle Forces Gingrich into the Trenches', *Los Angeles Times*, 21 October 1995, p. A20.
33. Stid, 'Transformational Leadership', p. 12.
34. Charles O. Jones, *The Presidency in a Separated System* (Washington, D. C.: The Brookings Institution, 1994).
35. Drew, *Showdown*, pp. 305–75.
36. Paul Light, *The President's Agenda* (Baltimore: The Johns Hopkins Press, 1982).

5 The Republican Policy Agenda and the Conservative Movement
Nigel Ashford

By the 1990s both the leadership and membership of the Republican Party in the House were dominated by conservatives, as John Owens demonstrated in chapter 4. This conservatism was evinced in the policy agenda of the 104th Congress, notably in the bills arising from the Contract With America, the House Republican manifesto for the 1994 elections and the focus of the party's post-election claims to a mandate. Inspired by Republican House leader Newt Gingrich, the Contract was informed by the principles of accountability, responsibility and opportunity. Elected officials were to be more accountable, individuals were to be encouraged to take greater responsibility for their own welfare and people were offered greater economic opportunities. These principles followed from a commitment to conservative ideas which pervaded the party.[1]

The ten items of the Contract contained commitments to balance the budget, fight crime, reform welfare, support the family, cut taxes on the middle class, strengthen defence, modify social security, reduce business taxes and regulation, amend civil law and impose term limits on members of Congress. These proposals reflected only a limited list of conservative proposals, and many items that were considered were eventually excluded. The Congress also came to consider a range of issues not included in the Contract, such as telecommunications, Medicare, immigration, abortion and agriculture, which all bore a conservative imprint. However, the legislative process in Congress is notoriously difficult, with numerous obstacles to the passing of legislation. The gap between the goals and aspirations of conservatives and the legislative output of the Congress was likely to be substantial. The purpose of this chapter is to examine the extent to which conservative goals and policies were reflected in the legislative output of the 104th Congress.

96

ORIGINS OF THE CONTRACT

Four forces shaped the Contract. It had to extend the conservative agenda beyond the successes and failures of the Reagan–Bush years. It reflected debates within the conservative movement. It had to satisfy and mobilise conservative constituencies and appeal to enough voters to win control of the House for the Republican Party.

The Reagan years were hailed as a triumph by the Republicans.[2] They pointed to significant changes between 1981 to 1988: lower marginal federal income tax rates, real growth, 18.4 million new jobs, an 18 per cent increase in disposable income per capita, reductions in inflation and unemployment. They also declared that Reagan was a major contributor to the collapse of communism and the decline of the Soviet Union. However, there was also a recognition of the failings of the Reagan–Bush presidencies. The budget deficit had grown; federal expenditures had risen as a percentage of GNP; little had been achieved to reverse the widely perceived sense of cultural decline. Without a communist threat the objectives for post-Cold War foreign policy were disputed. There was a sense that the Republicans needed to go 'beyond Reagan', to bring his priorities of less government, a strong America and traditional morality into new spheres.

The Republican Party had gone through a period of crisis during the Bush Administration and after the defeat in 1992. Many Republicans, led by Gingrich, had opposed much of Bush's agenda, feeling that the former vice-president had betrayed Reagan's legacy. Conservatives disagreed on how to respond in a debate described by some commentators as 'the conservative crack-up'.[3] Bush had destroyed one of the core Republican principles by breaking his pledge of 'no new taxes'. He was also criticised for extending new regulations. The challenge for Republicans was to provide a new agenda for the late 1990s which revived the best elements of Reaganism, whilst addressing its failures and omissions, without repudiating Bush directly.

In formulating a programme Republicans drew upon dozens of think-tanks which provided ideas and specific proposals to translate conservative principles into policies. The Heritage Foundation, the American Enterprise Institute, the Cato Institute and many smaller think-tanks produced numerous reports, either derived from conservative academics or produced by their own research fellows. However, these ideas were not always complementary, consistent or prioritised.

The economic goals of the Contract were to reduce the budget deficit, balance the budget, lower taxes, curb the growth of the federal government, deregulate and control inflation. These aims were a response to a widely perceived sense of economic stagnation and declining real incomes for ordinary Americans. There were, however, conflicts between these goals with regard to priorities. For supply-siders, such as Congressman Dick Armey (R.TX) and Jack Kemp, the priority was to cut the taxes they believed to be the major obstacle to economic growth. The right type of tax cuts could lead to no loss of tax revenue in the long term. They favoured cutting capital gains taxes, which they believed discouraged saving and investment, and a flat tax, in which an income tax of 17 per cent would replace the complex maze of rules and exemptions. For deficit hawks, such as Congressman John Kasich (R.OH) and Senators Bob Dole (R.KS), Pete Dominici (R.NM) and Bob Packwood (R.OR), the priority was to reduce the budget deficit. Tax cuts would have to wait. They favoured a balanced budget amendment to the Constitution together with a commitment to the goal of a balanced budget within seven years. For budget-cutters such as Senator Phil Gramm (R.TX), reducing federal expenditure was a necessity to facilitate a balanced budget, tax cuts and a reduction in the role of the federal government.

The cultural aims of the Contract were: the restoration of traditional values through stricter anti-crime policies; the reform of welfare to discourage dependency, single parents and illegitimacy; the reduction of federal intervention; strengthening the family and mediating institutions; and decentralising responsibility to state and local government. These goals were a response to a sense of social breakdown reflected in high crime rates, illegitimacy, drug use and low educational achievement, primarily attributed by conservatives to the breakdown of the family. Conservatives saw the need to restore the 'civic virtues': hard work, self-discipline, deferred gratification, family cohesion, civic mindedness and personal responsibility.[4] However, there were differences between social conservatives such as Bill Bennett, who have no objections in principle to a positive role for government in promoting these values but are sceptical about its capacity to did so; the Christian Right such as Pat Robertson, who endorse a positive role for government in promoting Christian values; and libertarians such as Governor Bill Weld of Massachusetts, who do not believe that it is responsibility of government to promote any moral agenda. This divergence is reflected in the strategies adopted over abortion, which range from incremental reforms to discourage its use to an end to taxpayer funding, which preserves choice for those who can pay, to a complete ban via a constitutional amendment.

Another set of cultural issues disturbing conservatives ranged around multi-culturalism, immigration, affirmative action and English as a common language. Conservatives divided between those who blamed the changing cultural make-up of the United States, with the relative decline of white Europeans, and who wished to promote cultural homogeneity, and, on the other hand, those who blamed liberal ideas and interventionist policies but welcomed cultural diversity as a potential source of strength and vitality. The former were described as paleo-conservatives associated with Pat Buchanan, the television commentator and presidential candidate, his organisation the American Cause, and the journal *Chronicles* and its editor, Tom Fleming. The latter were a mixture of neo-conservatives and libertarians associated with Ben Wattenberg of the American Enterprise Institute and Julian Simon of the Cato Institute.

In the field of foreign policy and defence, the goals were a strong defence, the United States to act as a superpower, to act unilaterally, develop an anti-ballistic missile defence system and achieve greater independence from international organisations, such as the UN. In achieving these objectives conservatives divide between isolationists such as Pat Buchanan, who advocated a withdrawal from international affairs, except when US interests were directly affected; democratic globalists such as Jack Kemp, who believed that the promotion of democracy, human rights and markets throughout the world should be a primary goal of US foreign policy; and neo-realists such as Jeane Kirkpatrick, who viewed the national interest as the organising principle of US foreign policy but believed that this would involve a extensive international role, whilst expressing caution in the nation's ability to rectify the world's problems. There was consensus among conservatives that the US should have the military capacity to act independently but no agreement on what were the appropriate circumstances. However, the most notable feature of conservative foreign policy is the low priority attached to it, in contrast to the anti-communism of the post-war years. It was not prominent in the Contract.

The Contract had to mobilise a diverse range of constituencies, not only to vote Republican, but to support the agenda after the election. These constituencies included the Christian Right, the Perotistas, small business, anti-tax groups, the term limits movement, property right groups and the gun lobby. This 'community of the disaffected' was mobilised by talk show hosts such as Rush Limbaugh, whose radio show reached 659 stations with a weekly audience of 20 million; his TV show was on 250 stations, and 500,000 subscribed to the *Limbaugh Letter*.

The agenda of the Christian Right was pro-life; supportive of school prayer, education vouchers for parents to send their children to religious schools, reform of divorce laws, a constitutional amendment guaranteeing religious freedom; opposition to gay rights and euthanasia combined with an economic agenda of a balanced budget and tax cuts for families. The most prominent Christian Right group was the Christian Coalition, whose titular head was the preacher Pat Robertson, who ran unsuccessfully for the presidential nomination in 1988, but whose strategic genius and most visible public spokesman was Ralph Reed. Under his leadership, the Coalition had 1.5 million members, and active branches in all 50 states. It had built up a mass of well-trained grass-roots activists, who in the 1994 election distributed 33 million voter guides and spent $1 million in support of the Contract in 1995. Reed was an experienced Republican operative, who recognised the necessity of compromise in order to obtain a Republican Congress which would be much more sympathetic to the Coalition's agenda. The Coalition established as its priorities for the Contract: a family tax cut, school choice and a ban on taxpayer-funded abortion.[5] Other Christian Right groups, such as Focus on the Family under Jim Dobson or the Family Research Center under Gary Bauer, were critical of Reed's willingness to compromise and his emphasis on an economic rather than moral agenda.

The second biggest constituency to satisfy was the followers of Perot, who received 19 per cent of the vote in 1992 and had built up a strong cadre of activists. Republicans believed that his supporters were a natural Republican constituency who could be recruited into their coalition. The agenda of United We Stand, the Perot organisation, focused on a balanced budget amendment, term limits and campaign finance reform.

The priority for small business was lower business taxes and deregulation. Their leading voice was the National Federation of Independent Business (NFIB), with 600,000 members. The goal of the anti-tax groups, such as the National Taxpayers Union (NTU), was to block any tax increase and to support any tax cut. The group with the highest profile was Grover Norquist's Americans for Tax Reform, which coordinated over 800 state and local anti-tax groups. Best known for its 'Taxpayer Protection Pledge', the group requested candidates for office to pledge never to vote for a marginal income tax increase. By 1995, 43 per cent of House members had signed.

Another powerful force was the term limitation movement which proposed that members of the House of Representatives should be allowed to serve for no more than six years and senators for no more than 12 years. US Term Limits (USTL) was the most prominent of numerous national and state term limits groups which had persuaded over 22 states to adopt term limits for their federal representatives, usually by means of a referendum. (These state laws were declared unconstitutional by the Supreme Court in 1995.)

The property rights movement wanted protection for private property against environmental and other laws. Their intellectual origins were in 'free market environmentalism' in think-tanks such as the Political Economy Research Center and the Competitive Enterprise Institute.[6] They argued that government regulations, based on 'command and control' principles, were less effective in protecting the environment than private property rights, and were highly costly for the limited gains. The grass-roots movement was a coalition of national and state groups, such as Defenders of Property Rights and the Wise Use Movement.

The gun lobby opposed any restrictions on the ownership of guns, claiming legal restrictions unconstitutional under the Second Amendment. Americans, they argued, had a right to self-defence; gun ownership deterred crime and gun controls stopped the law-abiding owning guns but not criminals.[7] They also advocated a list of anti-crime measures such as mandatory sentences for serious offences, the death penalty, truth-in-sentencing, juvenile law reform and victims rights. The National Rifle Association (NRA) had over 3.3 million members in 1994, the ability to mobilise members into political action and spent over $3.4 million in the 1994 election.

All of these groups had their own specific agendas. What did they have in common? Grover Norquist identified them as a 'Leave Us Alone Coalition' which opposed interference by federal government into their lives, interests and values.[8] This was designed to create a sense of mutual identification so that each group would support each other's agenda. The danger was that each group would care about its own items on the agenda only and not campaign for the passage of the other items, so it was necessary to try to create a commitment to the agenda as a whole. The other problem was that the goals of these constituencies were not necessarily shared by the majority of the electorate, so they had to be brought on board without alienating other elements of the coalition or the electorate. Mobilisation of this coalition was the third condition of the Contract.

Gingrich believed that the majority of the electorate shared conservative values and principles. However they were not committed to the Republican Party. Surveys showed that they were deeply suspicious of all parties, which made them susceptible to independent candidates like Perot in 1992. The electorate was deeply alienated from politicians, believing that they would say anything to be elected, would break their promises once elected and were the captive of special interests in Washington. They remembered how Bush had broken his promise of 1988 of 'read my lips, no new taxes' and Clinton had run as a centrist New Democrat and governed as a more traditional liberal Democrat.

The Republicans therefore had to portray themselves as populists, representing the ordinary people against the 'Washington Establishment'. They had to present themselves as a party of principles. They had to commit themselves to keeping an explicit set of promises. The Contract proclaimed: 'If we break the Contract, throw us out'. They had to present a unifying agenda. The original idea to call it the Republican Contract for America was dropped as it was discovered that voters became much more sceptical when the agenda was identified with a political party. The Contract was not decided on the basis of opinion polls, as some commentators have suggested: that would have reinforced the image of politicians without principles. But the phrasing of items that were included was tested for their positive connotations to have maximum appeal to voters.

All items in the Contract met four criteria: (1), they provided a fresh agenda beyond Reagan and Bush; (2), they united the House Republicans to facilitate quick passage in the new Congress – to this end, Gingrich set up a series of task forces among House Republicans to try to build support for specific promises in the Contract; (3) they mobilised the Republican base by incorporating their ideas; and (4) focus group testing ensured items were popular. These criteria led to the exclusion from the Contract of a large number of items favoured by different elements of the party. Armey's proposal for a flat tax was not included because it had not obtained a consensus among House Republicans and would have taken too long to introduce into the House. The agenda was overwhelmingly economic in nature, but designed to satisfy the cultural constituencies as well. Religious right issues such as abortion and school prayer were excluded as too divisive within the Republican Conference and electorate, and that decision firmed up inclusion of the child tax credit that was dear to the religious right. Cultural issues such as affirmative action were excluded as detracting from the broad appeal of the Contract items. There was no mention of Medicare reform – even though health care had been a major issue in the previous Congress – because there was no consensus within the party on how to proceed and it was thought to be electorally dangerous.

LEGISLATIVE ACTION

Balancing the Budget

The proposal for a constitutional amendment required a permanent balanced budget by the year 2000 or two years after ratification. Supermajorities (three-fifths in both houses of Congress) were required to run a deficit or increase taxes. The priority given to the amendment was a victory for the deficit hawks, reflecting their perception that the deficit was the biggest failing of the Reagan–Bush years. Republicans believed that only a constitutional amendment would compel elected officials to make the government live within its means. The Contract proclaimed: 'Congress has shown itself both unwilling and incapable of balancing the budget.'[9]

In this they were influenced by the public choice school which identifies the existence of political incentives to run deficits, as they create immediate benefits while postponing the costs into the future.[10] Previous attempts to control the deficit, such as the Gramm–Rudman–Hollings Act, had been undermined by creative accounting and eventual abandonment. The amendment satisfied all three groups of economic conservatives, in placing the priority on cutting the deficit, making it difficult to raise taxes, and creating incentives to cut the budget. It appealed to economic conservatives, taxpayers, Perotistas and the business community. It also had the merit of stating the goal without identifying the means by which it was to be achieved.

Deficit hawks opposed the super-majority required to raise taxes which for supply-siders was an absolute precondition for supporting the amendment. The latter, and especially the freshmen, feared that without that item there would be new attempts to balance the budget with tax increases, as in 1990. A wavering leadership was reluctantly prepared to drop the super-majority but a freshmen revolt – 12 said that they would vote against the amendment if the clause was excluded – forced its retention. Armey stated, 'It was in the Contract, so that's it.'[11]

In the House Republican unanimity helped obtain the two-thirds vote necessary for a constitutional amendment, but it failed in the Senate by one vote. Six Democrats who had supported an amendment in 1994 voted against it in 1995. Mark Hatfield (R.OR) was the only Republican vote against, but it was a crucial one.

There was a consensus behind the line item veto, which passed both houses by comfortable margins. It provided for a presidential veto within ten days on particular line-item expenditures or targeted taxation provisions unless two-thirds majorities in both houses of Congress overrode it. Deficit hawks favoured it because it would contribute to deficit reduction by removing pork barrel projects; supply-siders favoured it because it did not increase taxes and would help to avoid the introduction of special tax favours which made the tax system more complicated; and budget-cutters saw this as a means of reducing expenditures that would achieve general approval. The emphasis on institutional reform reflected the influence of public choice analysis which identified pork as a form of 'rent-seeking', reinforced by the growing recognition among political scientists of this phenomenon as a means of incumbents improving their electoral chances.

Committed to a balanced budget amendment, the Republicans planned to eliminate the deficit in seven years. A budget was carefully constructed by the chairs of the House and Senate Budget committees, Kasich and Dominici – both deficit hawks – which included most of the financial items of the Contract agenda, such as welfare reform, the capital gains cut and child tax credits, together with a long list of budget cuts. Supply-siders were most enthusiastic about halving the capital gains tax and indexing it to inflation, believing that it depresses saving and investment, discourages the efficient allocation of capital, and is unjust as it involved double taxation of savings income, through the personal income tax and capital gains. Capital gains tax cuts would reduce the cost of capital and thereby stimulate savings and investment, increase output and growth, and thus increase revenues. It was supported by business and investors, and opposed by those fearful of the effects on the deficit and those claiming it primarily helped the rich. Supply-siders argued that it would have a positive long-term effect on the budget because of its dynamic effects on growth. However, conventional methods of estimating the effects of tax cuts viewed them as securing a revenue loss, reflecting a static model of the economy, and so would not be recognised in the estimates of the budget by official bodies such as the Congressional Budget Office. Republicans reluctantly accepted that it would be too controversial to use the dynamic model, and thus would have to reduce expenditure more than they considered necessary to achieve a balanced budget.

The Republican leadership believed that Clinton would be forced to adopt their budget. However, he refused to sign it, opposing its severity. The resulting shutdowns of the federal government, which Clinton successively managed to blame on Congress, forced Republicans to drop many of their favourite proposals, including tax cuts. They did, however, succeed in forcing Clinton to propose a balanced budget within their seven-year timeframe, reducing discretionary expenditure for the first time since 1969, reducing the deficit by $47.5 billion more than in Clinton's first budget and eliminating 270 programmes and offices.

Deregulation

The Contract's deregulatory agenda included unfunded mandates, risk assessment, property rights compensation and legal reform. Additional deregulation covered agriculture and telecommunications. The Contract promised to introduce restrictions on unfunded mandates, defined in the legislation as federal regulations costing $50 million for states and cities, or $100 million for business. More costly regulation required funding from Congress. Limiting the possibility of unfunded mandates would either reduce regulations on the states and business (as its proponents hoped), or force Congress to pay for those federal burdens by increasing the deficit or raising federal taxes (as the deficit hawks feared). The change was endorsed by state and local government, and corporations. Some Republicans favoured the principle of 'no money, no mandate', with no dollar limit; and concern was expressed at the large number of exemptions in the bill, for example for anti-discrimination laws.

The Contract proposed regulatory risk assessment and a regulatory moratorium. Conservatives protested that regulations increased prices, reduced the quality and availability of products and services, increased taxes and reduced jobs. An additional argument was that they actually caused deaths. Aaron Wildavsky claimed that an increasing standard of living contributed to longer and healthier lives.[12] Therefore, regulations which reduced growth contributed to reducing people's lives. For example, the ban on asbestos cost $111 million per life saved, but could lose 15 lives in opportunity costs. Under the Contract, government departments and agencies were to assess the cost and benefits of new regulations.

The Contract promised compensation if federal government action reduces the value of property by 20 per cent, and an offer to buy if the value is halved. Republicans claimed that it was unfair that private owners should not be compensated for losses arising from federal actions. Deficit hawks feared the difficulty of estimating the cost of compensation; state and local governments were concerned that it would eventually apply to themselves; some conservatives wanted no threshold for compensation; and the property rights movement opposed the long list of exemptions in the bill.

Legal reforms involved a cap on punitive awards on product liability; rules to discourage frivolous lawsuits through the 'loser pays' principle; and rules to discourage investor suits. Many Americans have become increasing concerned about a litigation explosion in which large sums of money have been awarded to plaintiffs more on the grounds of the deep pockets of those prosecuted than their full liability or the severity of the incident.[13] One example was the woman who successfully sued McDonald's for $3 000 000 (later reduced to $648 000) because she was scalded by a hot cup of coffee. Economists estimated that litigation costs averaged $1.6 billion per corporation in 1994.

The Federal Agricultural Improvement and Reform Act removed federal programmes that controlled the production and prices of major crops through commodity subsidies and acreage controls. Free market advocates and taxpayer groups had long sought to abolish both subsidies and controls, but reforms had been opposed by conservative representatives from rural districts. However, farmers had become increasingly dissatisfied with the unreliable and unpredictable nature of the system, and many calculated that they would be more successful in a deregulated agricultural market.

The Telecommunications Act removed barriers to competition through deregulation of the telephone, cable and broadcasting industries. The measure also included restrictions on access to the Internet designed to protect children, the so-called V-chip.

Extensive medical insurance reform was vetoed in the budget. A successful incremental reform known as the Kassebaum–Kennedy bill had a mixed reception from conservatives, who liked the provision for portability of health plans for people moving jobs, but were concerned that prohibitions on limiting coverage would increase health care costs.

The ambitious deregulation agenda obtained a mixed reception in Congress. Successes included the passage of unfunded mandates, agriculture and telecommunications legislation. Republicans failed to pass their major risk assessment and property rights compensation plans. Product liability was passed but vetoed by Clinton. An increase in the minimum wage – anathema to free marketeers but promoted by liberal Democrats – passed with support from a substantial minority of Republicans sensitive to its public popularity or a union presence in their constituencies.

Fighting Crime

Anti-crime measures included crime victim restitution; easing the rules of evidence under the exclusionary rule; prison construction grants; easier deportation of criminal aliens; block grants for law enforcement; reform of death penalty appeals; reform of appeals procedures; and limiting the process of death penalty appeals. Conservatives believe in being 'tough on crime'. Intellectual ammunition for the conservative approach was found in the work of political scientists James Q. Wilson and John DiIulio.[14] Wilson had developed polices based on a deterrence policy of incentives, and had expressed scepticism about the ability to rehabilitate hardened criminals. DeIulio, a New Democrat, was a champion of tough law enforcement and incarceration, anti-crime measures that were the best form of assistance to blacks and minorities as the chief victims of crime, contradicting the view that 'law and order' was a code word for racism. Six House anti-crime bills were passed with comfortable majorities. Additional anti-crime measures were introduced on sentencing guidelines, combating car theft, sex crimes and church arson. All these policies were adopted either as part of the 1996 Appropriations Act or in separate bills, and all were signed by Clinton. Exclusionary rule reform was blocked in the Senate.

Reforming Welfare

The intellectual foundation of Republican welfare policy was Charles Murray's study of American social policy *Losing Ground*, in which he claimed that poverty was in decline until President Johnson's War on Poverty had the unintended consequences of increasing poverty by creating incentives to become welfare-dependent.[15] Later, he went even further in calling for the abolition of all benefits for single mothers. His study was followed by a series of books attacking the welfare system, which reflected debates between those who emphasised economic disincentives and those who talked of a dysfunctional subculture; and those who believed that government welfare policy was the chief culprit and those who identified more general cultural causes.[16] Murray himself shifted from an economic incentives approach in *Losing Ground* to a more cultural interpretation in *The Bell Curve*. Myron Magnet located the problem in the social permissiveness of the 1960s, which welfare had subsidised. Marvin Olasky lamented how government had displaced private charity, which had been far more effective in preventing dependency. Robert Rector of the Heritage Foundation brought these studies to the attention of Republicans on Capitol Hill in his reports. He invented the term 'the poverty paradox': after spending $5 trillion, the poverty rate was higher than in 1965.

A central feature of the conservative case was that illegitimacy was the most significant factor behind poverty and other social problems. Murray claimed: 'Illegitimacy is the single most important social problem of our time. More important than crime, drugs, poverty, welfare or homelessness because it drives everything else.'[17] Many welfare critics pointed to evidence that children brought up by never-married single parents (thus excluding widows and the divorced) had a considerably greater chance of failing to graduate from school, taking illegal drugs and committing crimes

Six principles informed the Republican reform agenda: benefits should require work; welfare should largely be the responsibility of the states; illegitimacy should not be subsidised; welfare should be a temporary safety net not a form of dependency; welfare should not be an entitlement; private assistance should be encouraged. Specific proposals recommended the merger of 44 programmes into five block grants (cash welfare, child welfare, child care, school meals, nutrition); a freeze on federal welfare expenditures; the end of federal cash for unwed single parents aged under 18, or those already on welfare or unemployed for more than five years; and a bar on federal aid to non-citizens. These items were inspired by Republican governors Engler of Michigan and Thompson of Wisconsin. Politically, they had the merit of uniting economic conservatives – who believed that government programmes were wasteful and ineffective – and social conservatives – who worried about their contribution to moral decline. Disagreements arose among Republicans over whether federal welfare aid should be abolished to become entirely a state responsibility; the loss of an automatic entitlement for states to receive funds based on the number of their residents who qualified; the restrictions on the use of federal funds for the unwed and the unemployed; the loss of federal cash for unwed mothers which the Catholic Church feared would lead to more abortions; and the end of federal benefits to legal immigrants who pay taxes.

The House adopted the Contract version, but the Senate diverged on eligibility criteria and wanted to give the states more freedom. Clinton vetoed congressional welfare reform on two occasions, but in July 1996, facing an election and popular support for reform, the president signed a bill close to the Contract version.

Supporting the Family

Republicans perceive a crisis of the American family, the institution they see as the most important source of values such as responsibility, morality, commitment and faith. However, pro-family rhetoric has sometimes been viewed as hostile to those who do not share the agenda of the religious right, which describes itself as the pro-family movement. The Contract, therefore, was designed to address some of the concerns of the Christian Right, without arousing strong opposition. It was also designed to contrast with Hillary Clinton's interest in children's rights, as a former chair of the liberal Children's Defense Fund. Her book *It Takes a Village* was attacked as an attempt to reduce the role of parents and increase the role of government in the rearing of children.[18]

The 'pro-family' programme consisted of increased penalties for sex crimes against minors; stronger child pornography laws; stricter child support enforcement; and parental consent for child surveys. Tax incentives were family-oriented: a tax credit for families with children of an income below $200,000; a tax credit for adoption; the repeal of the marriage penalty; and incentives for Individual Retirement Accounts (IRAs). All the non-economic items were presented as strengthening the family, which satisfied constituencies such as social conservatives, the Christian Right and the pro-life movement, but also attracted moderates by their focus on protecting children. There were thus very few problems in what was potentially one of the most divisive areas. The result was their passage in a variety of bills by overwhelming majorities in both houses.

Tax incentives proved more divisive. Deficit hawks complained that tax cuts reduced revenue and thus increased the deficit; the supply-siders complained that it would not promote growth; tax reformers believed that it complicated the tax system when the goal should be to make it cleaner and simpler; and moderate Republicans feared that too much of the benefits would go to the rich. The $200,000 limit was included after protests from moderates. Criticised by the Democrats as a tax cut for the rich, Clinton proposed a lower level of $75,000 and for up to 13-year-old children only. Some Republicans proposed a lower income level to $95,000 but this was resisted as a substantial increase in the marginal tax rate and contrary to the Contract.

The $200,000 limit was adopted in the House, but the Senate concern with the effect on the deficit resulted initially in the rejection of tax cuts. Eventually, Congress agreed to a $250 tax credit for those with incomes of $110,000 or less, but with no indexation. The benefits were made retroactive so that they would be received before the 1996 elections. The marriage penalty was removed, and tax benefits for IRAs were increased for couples from $40,000 to $100,000 per annum. It was vetoed by Clinton in December 1995. IRA benefits were passed in the minimum wage bill in 1996.

Asserting Global Power

The foreign policy agenda included a general declaration for more defence expenditure, the amount to be recommended by a blue ribbon Commission on Defence; a reduction in US funds for UN peacekeeping; a bar on US troops under UN command; funding for an anti-ballistic missile (ABM) system; and enlargement of NATO to include Eastern Europe. Republicans believed that Clinton had allowed national security to decline too far and become too dependent on international opinion reflected through the UN. This agenda was a narrow one, reflecting both the decline of foreign policy as a public concern and the lack of consensus on a post-Cold War alternative.

First, the Contract called for an increase in defence expenditure, a review of defence needs by a panel of experts and the provision that any savings on defence should be earmarked for reducing the deficit rather than transferred to social programmes. The US now spent the lowest percentage of GDP on defence since the end of the Second World War. At the same time US troops were deployed more often than ever, in countries such as Haiti, Iraq, Bosnia and Rwanda. US forces would be stretched to meet one of the principles of US military strategy, known as 'win-win': the ability to win two regional conflicts at the same time. Increasing defence expenditure conflicted with the goal of reducing the deficit, which could be accomplished only by additional reductions on social programmes with the resulting political flack. Republicans were therefore cautious about how much additional expenditure was required – thus the attraction of a Commission to decide the scale of the increase.

The second commitment was to reduce US funds for UN peacekeeping and to exclude US troops from UN command. Republicans had been vocal critics of the perceived anti-Americanism, inefficiency and mismanagement of the UN, with particular concern about the growing number and cost of peacekeeping operations. For Republicans these operations damage US combat readiness. The UN lacks the legitimacy, authority, stature or procedures to organise military missions successfully, as evidenced in Somalia, and US troops could not be entrusted to them.

The third policy was to develop and deploy an ABM system which could intercept long-range missiles from 'rogue' nations, such as Iraq, through terrorism or accidents. Missiles had been used in Afghanistan, the Iran–Iraq War and the Gulf War, and were developing greater range and accuracy as to be a threat to the US in the future. The only current existing response would be nuclear retaliation. Republican critics were concerned about the cost of the programme, while Democrats claimed that it would undermine arms control and require abandoning the ABM treaty.

The fourth policy was to encourage and enlarge NATO to include Poland, Hungary and the Czech and Slovak republics by 1999, and other suitable countries later, subject to progress towards democracy, free markets and civilian control of their militaries. This would expand the NATO zone of peace and freedom, strengthen these countries in their democratic development, and send a message to Russia that Central and Eastern Europe was not a Russian sphere of influence.

The House adopted the National Security Revitalisation bill containing these provisions, less the ABM programme (defeated after 24 Republicans defected over its cost). The Senate adopted most of the Contract provisions in several bills, but dropped the proposal for a Commission. Defence authorisations were initially vetoed by Clinton because they included the funding for ABM, and his veto was narrowly upheld. The president signed a second version, with the ABM provisions deleted, even though it contained $7 billion more than he had requested, because he needed support over Bosnia.

Modifying Social Security

There is a widespread agreement amongst experts and politicians that a fundamental reform of social security entitlements is required. There is also agreement that to articulate that clearly is political death, the so-called 'third rail' that will kill anyone who touches the issue. So the Contract proposals were modest, designed to have immediate appeal to seniors, and potential long-term benefits for the deficit. They had the advantages of repealing a Clinton tax increase, reinforcing the image as a party of tax-cutters and being directed to a specific constituency that made up 12 per cent of Americans with a high turnout record. Critics protested that it had the short-term effect of reducing revenues, and that the benefits would go primarily to more prosperous seniors.

The social security reforms would: repeal the 1993 social security tax on wealthy seniors; allow seniors higher tax-free earnings; provide tax incentives to buy long-term health care insurance; and ease the laws to enable seniors to exclude children from residential retirement developments. The House adopted the Contract proposals, but the tax repeal and increase in tax-free earnings were dropped after opposition in the Senate. Clinton signed the bill increasing the earnings limit over seven years, but vetoed the budget in 1995 which included incentives for medical care insurance.

Limiting Congressional Terms

Term limits had been a very popular policy for Republican candidates on the campaign trail. Proponents claimed that a term limits constitutional amendment would increase the number of competitive elections; improve the quality of legislators; prevent political careerism and reduce corruption; and break the power of the special interests.[19]

Term limits were a controversial issue for many members of Congress. Judiciary Committee chair Henry Hyde (R.IL) led the mainly Democratic opposition, stressing the value of experience. A division among proponents existed over whether the limits should be six or 12 years. The main lobby, US Term Limits, strongly advocated the lower limit and lambasted

Republicans who favoured the 12-year maximum. Another issue was whether the limits applied to consecutive periods only or whether it should be a lifetime ban. Yet another issue was whether it should be applied retrospectively, or should apply only from the date the legislation was passed. In the House, both the lifetime ban and retrospectivity were defeated. The vote on '12 and 12' (for each house) failed to attain the two-thirds majority required to pass a constitutional amendment with 40 Republicans voting against. In the Senate term limits failed to obtain a simple majority.

Restoring a Traditional Culture

A number of bills on cultural issues were proposed, but with limited success. An ambitious programme to restrict legal and illegal immigration was amended to a very limited programme of increased border controls and speedy deportation procedures. This was due to pro-immigration forces led by Senator Spencer Abraham (R.MI). A ban on certain late-term abortions known as 'partial birth abortions' was vetoed by Clinton. An amendment to ban flag-burning to override a Supreme Court decision failed to receive a two-thirds majority. The Defence of Marriage Act (DOMA) defined marriage as involving two people of the same sex and allowed states to ignore same-sex marriages conducted in other states, so pre-empting an Hawaii court ruling. DOMA was passed overwhelmingly and signed by Clinton.

A CONSERVATIVE REVOLUTION?

How successful was the 104th Congress in furthering the conservative agenda? The answer depends on the standard of comparison. The record was disappointing for conservatives by the measure of their high expectations at the start of 1995. However, the Congress did have a high degree of success in comparison with previous congresses and the period under recent Republican presidents.

The 104th Congress was remarkably successful in furthering the conservative agenda, despite a small majority in the House, the lack of 60 votes to override a filibuster, and a more moderate Republican Conference in the Senate and a Democrat president willing to exercise the veto. Of the 40 items in the Contract, 23 were adopted. The most significant conservative successes were welfare reform (the first federal entitlement programme ever to be ended), the commitment to a balanced budget by 2002, abolition or reduction of some federal programmes, ending costly unfunded mandates, the line–item veto, agricultural and telecommunications deregulation, and anti-crime measures. There were additional conservative advances in deregulation, privatisation, reductions in funding for some federal programmes and agencies, and increased defence expenditure. Major defeats were over the balanced budget amendment, term limits, capital gains tax cuts, child tax credits, regulatory risk assessment, property rights compensation, legal reform and the minimum wage increase. There were defeats on lower priorities on ABM funding, deregulation, abortion and flag burning (for a summary see Table 5.1).

Table 5.1   The Legislative Record of the 104th Congress

	Enacted	Vetoed	Not Enacted
Balanced budget constitutional amendment			x*
Line-item veto (enhanced rescissions)	√		
Balanced budget		x	
Unfunded mandates	√		
Regulatory reform		x	
Product liability		x	
Investor lawsuits	√‡		
Agricultural reform	√		
Telecommunications deregulation	√		
Medical insurance	√		
Minimum wage increase	√		
Exclusionary rule			x
Anti-terrorism and death penalty	√		
Violent incarceration	√		
Prison litigation	√		
Welfare reform	√		
Tax cuts		x	
Defence authorisation	√		
Anti-missile defence system			x
Congressional term limits constitutional amendment			x*
Immigration reform	√		
Ban late-term abortions		x	
Flag desecration constitutional amendment			x*
Defence of Marriage Act	√		

Notes: * Failed to receive required two-thirds majorities.
    ‡ President's veto overridden by both houses.

Compared to the Reagan–Bush years, when the party held the presidency, the Republican Congress made great progress in controlling the budget, reducing the deficit, tackling welfare and deregulation. The major failures were in tax cuts, still the greatest unifier of Republicans, and in foreign policy, where conservatives have not yet defined a clear post-Cold War policy. Compared with the Bush Administration, Congress avoided tax increases, deregulated in some policy spheres and reduced discretionary spending.

To what extent will the 105th Congress and its successors follow conservative ideas? Much depends on the interpretations placed on the Republican failure to win back the presidency and its loss of House seats; as well as the party's success in resolving the conflicts among its supporting constituencies.

Following the 1996 elections, two competing theories developed among conservatives. One was that the Republicans had been too radical. The Contract had become associated with extremism, too threatening to many voters. The rhetoric of revolution had scared many voters. Newt Gingrich, in particular, had become the most disliked politician in America with his inflated rhetoric and confrontational style. The Republicans had over-interpreted their mandate in 1994, mistaking the repudiation of the corrupt Democratic Congress for a call to dismantle the federal government. This image of radicalism and excessive partisanship had damaged the party. The proposed antidote is for Republicans to seek bipartisan consensus with President Clinton and avoid a radical agenda. This was the conclusion of some Republicans, who were behind the abortive attempt to remove Newt Gingrich as Speaker prior to the beginning of the 105th Congress. *See Killian, The Freshem who contredicts this accou*

An alternative theory blamed the issue-less and colourless campaign of Bob Dole and the conservative campaign of Bill Clinton. The Contract itself has been successful. Considering the constitutional and political obstacles to passing legislation, the Republicans had done well to pass so much legislation. The congressional error had been to focus on the balanced budget, because this had revived the image of the Republicans as 'nay-sayers' and 'grouches'. One of the early damaging charges was the Democratic claim that Republicans 'wanted to deprive children of school lunches'. The commitment to a balance budget had forced the party to adopt an unpopular budget with spending cuts which would be vetoed by Clinton. The infamous government shutdowns were the decisive events in damaging the party. The Contract had forced Clinton to move to the right, for example, signing welfare reform, and he had run his presidential campaign from the right. 1995 had been a successful year because the party had remained on-message, but had been off-message in 1996. Future strategy requires new policy initiatives to avoid Clinton dominating the agenda. Many of the defeated Contract items commanded popular support amongst the public, such as the balanced budget amendment and term limits, and the party should propose them even at the risk of further defeats. Many congressional Republicans subscribe to this view, encouraging them to continue to pursue conservative policies.

Leading to the same conclusion is the need to satisfy Republican constituencies. One problem is the disappointment of the supply-siders and anti-tax groups that there had been virtually no tax cuts. The insistence on a balanced budget reduces the prospects for cuts, especially if there is a desire to agree a budget with Clinton. Dick Armey and the 1996 contender Steve Forbes will press the flat tax as the solution. Its advocates claim that a 17 per cent flat tax would be lower and simpler, and could be achieved without increasing the deficit. Deficit hawks are sceptical, especially about predicting the revenue effects.

Another problem is to how satisfy the social conservatives. The Contract successfully managed to keep the agenda focused on economics whilst tying it to social concerns with welfare reform and child tax credits. What would be necessary in order to satisfy social conservatives who feel their issues were neglected in the 104th Congress, for example abortion and affirmative action? Republican leaders will attempt to identify more areas where economic and social conservatives can unite, such as decentralisation to state and local governments, school choice and defunding the National Endowments of the Arts and the Humanities.

A third group to be considered is the coalition of deregulators, combining free market advocates, small and big businesses and property rights supporters. Deregulation was successfully portrayed by its opponents as the surrender of reasonable protection of the environment and consumers. It is likely to remain a priority, but will be approached either on a narrower front, as with agriculture and telecommunications, or under the Tenth Amendment giving more power and flexibility to state and local governments, as in the control of pesticides and drinking water.

The 105th Congress is likely to be dominated by policy proposals that were first introduced in the 104th Congress such as a balanced budget amendment, term limits and deregulation. The agenda will be based on a consensus amongst conservatives but with a greater attention to marketing strategy to preempt critics. The 1996 elections left a House Republican Conference smaller but more homogeneously conservative, a Republican Senate under Trent Lott (R.MS) much more conservative than its predecessor, and a president eager to ensure the election of his successor in Al Gore, and therefore keen to maintain a centrist image. America will continue to move right.

NOTES

1. Nigel Ashford, 'The Right after Reagan', in Alan Grant, ed., *Contemporary American Politics* (Aldershot: Dartmouth, 1995) pp. 117–43.
2. Nigel Ashford, 'The Conservative Agenda and the Reagan Administration', in Joseph Hogan, ed., *The Reagan Years* (Manchester: Manchester University Press, 1990), pp. 189–213; Robert Bartley, *The Seven Fat Years* (New York: Free Press, 1992).
3. Ashford, 'The Right after Reagan'.
4. Gertrude Himmelfarb, *The De-Moralisation of Society* (London: Institute of Economic Affairs, 1995).
5. Ralph Reed, *Active Faith: How Christians are Changing the Soul of American Politics* (New York: Free Press, 1996).
6. Terry Anderson and Donald Leal, *Free Market Environmentalism* (Boulder, CO: Westview Press, 1991).
7. Wayne LaPierre, *Guns, Crime and Freedom* (New York: HarperCollins, 1995).
8. Grover Norquist, *Rock the House* (Fort Lauderdale, FL: Vytis Press, 1995)
9. Newt Gingrich, Dick Armey and the House Republicans, *The Contract with America* (New York: Times Books, 1994), p. 13.
10. Nigel Ashford, 'The Ideas of the New Right', in Grant Jordan and Nigel Ashford, eds., *Public Policy and the Impact of the New Right* (London: Pinter, 1993) pp. 31–3.
11. Jennifer Babson, 'Armey Stood Guard over Contract', *Congressional Quarterly Weekly Report*, 8 April 1995, p. 987.
12. Aaron Wildavsky, *Searching for Safety* (New Brunswick NJ: Transaction, 1988), ch. 3.
13. Walter Olson, *The Litigation Explosion* (New York: Plume, 1992); Peter Huber, *Liability* (New York: Basic Books, 1988).
14. James Q. Wilson, *Thinking about Crime* (New York: Basic Books, 1985); James Q. Wilson and Richard Herrnstein, *Crime and Human Nature* (New York: Simon and Schuster, 1985); John DeIulio, 'White Lies About Black Crime', *Public Interest*, Winter 1995.
15. Charles Murray, *Losing Ground: American Social Policy, 1950–1980* (New York: Basic Books, 1984); Murray, 'The Coming White Underclass', *Wall Street Journal*, 29 October 1993; Charles Murray and Richard Herrnstein, *The Bell Curve* (New York: Free Press, 1994).
16. Myron Magnet, *The Dream and the Nightmare: the Sixties Legacy to the Underclass* (New York: Quill, 1993); Marvin Olasky, *The Tragedy of American Compassion* (New York: Regnery, 1992); Robert Rector and William Lauber, *America's Failed $5.4 Trillion War on Poverty* (Washington, D.C.: The Heritage Foundation, 1995).
17. Murray, 'The Coming White Underclass'.
18. Hillary Clinton, *It Takes a Village* (New York: Simon & Schuster, 1996). For a critical review, see *Commentary*, March 1996.
19. Alan Grant, 'Legislative Careerism and the Term Limitation Movement', in Grant, *Contemporary American Politics*, pp. 80–2.

6 Split-Party Control: Clinton On the Defensive

Michael Foley

The transition from the 103rd Congress to the 104th Congress represented not only an uncomfortable adjustment for President Clinton, but a highly unusual turn in legislative–executive relations. The election of Bill Clinton in 1992 had provided a much heralded return to 'unified government', when the first Democrat to enter the White House since 1977 would be in a position to cooperate with Democratic majorities in the House and Senate and, thereby, ostensibly to optimise the system's capacity for coherent policy-making and effective governance. Clinton's victory had been marginal in nature and led the president to adopt a leadership strategy designed to compensate for the limitations of his mandate.[1] In spite of his efforts to neutralise the deficiencies of the 1992 result, it was safe to assume on the basis of previous patterns of incoming administrations that President Clinton would face a progressive series of problems in his second Congress. In the event, he was confronted by a wholesale transformation in his position. The president, who had only two years earlier marked the end of 12 years of Republican hegemony in the White House, had not only lost the Democratic majorities in Congress but had inherited a resurgent Republican Party in Washington committed to a more radical programme of government reduction than President Reagan's agenda in 1980–1. Other presidents had experienced mid-term reversals before, but not in these circumstances and not on this scale in the cycle of party alternation. President Truman suffered a loss of party control in Congress in his first mid-term election as president in 1946 (losing 55 seats in the House and 12 in the Senate), but such a reversal could be explained partly by the unusual political conditions immediately following the end of the Second World War and partly by the general trend towards a recovery of Republican seats following the high water mark of Democratic Party representation during the New Deal in 1936. Moreover, Truman had the disadvantage of having inherited the office after a prolonged period of Democratic control and after the demise of a highly authoritative president whom he could not hope to emulate especially given the limited

117

time-frame between replacing FDR in April 1945 and confronting a mid-term election in November 1946.

President Eisenhower was also divested of the opportunities of unified party control after only two years in office. Like President Clinton, he had been elected after an extensive period when the presidency had been controlled by the opposition party. But unlike Clinton, Eisenhower was the leader of the minority party which had controlled the House of Representatives for only one Congress in the previous 22 years. Eisenhower had helped the Republicans to achieve a marginal but unsustainable majority of eight seats in the House in the presidential election year of 1952. Eisenhower could not, therefore, be regarded as culpable for the reversal of party control in 1954 (losing 18 seats in the House and one in the Senate) which assumed the appearance of normality after the atypical result of 1952. Other presidents have suffered mid-term losses, but none – including both Truman and Eisenhower – underwent what President Clinton experienced in 1994. Because his party lost control of both houses of Congress, he was suddenly placed in a position of operating in a condition of split-party control where the split had been inverted from the customary position of Republican presidents operating alongside a Democratic-controlled House of Representatives (with the probability of a Democratic Senate) to that of a Democratic president coexisting with triumphant Republican majorities in both houses. Moreover, the transformation had occurred within the minimum period of two years. During the modern era, the recurrence of split-party control had until 1994 always followed at least a four-year spell of unified party control, which was invariably provided by Democratic presidents coexisting with Democratic Congresses. The mid-term elections of 1994 led to the biggest reduction of House Democrats (52 seats lost) since 1946 in political conditions that made it difficult for Clinton to argue that the results were something other than a personal indictment of his presidency. To make matters worse, he would now be confronted by a Republican leadership that had acquired a national prominence in the election and which was able to stake a claim to a popular mandate in opposing the policy direction of the incumbent president. For President Clinton and observers of the presidency, therefore, the 104th Congress represented uncharted territory. The volatility of party politics which had led to such a rapid and unconventional return of split-party control, with a Democratic president engaging with a Republican Congress for the first time in a nearly half a century, raised the prospect of new insights into the nature of contemporary institutional relationships and in particular into the properties of the presidency in postmodern conditions.

The strategies and calculations of executive–legislative relations had suddenly shifted and, as a consequence, the sample of available political contexts for presidential analysis was enlarged to include a thoroughly unexpected and revealing set of dynamics. The interaction of the Republican Congress with the Clinton administration has supplied a new store of experiences with which to re-examine the validity of some of the established categories and boundary lines of presidential inquiry. The contention in this analysis is that President Clinton's relationship with the 104th Congress provides an exceptional insight into the problematic nature both of contemporary presidential leadership and contemporary presidential analysis. Three dimensions in particular are illustrated by President Clinton's relationship with the 104th Congress. The first relates to the identity and exclusiveness of the presidency's role in government; the second examines the potential and limits of the presidency's position in an issue environment of declining expectations, diminishing government and volatile public opinion; and the third pertains to the changing character of partisan interaction within the parameters of a single Congress.

ROLE INCURSION

The first theme to be addressed is that of role incursion by the House Speaker, Newt Gingrich, following the Republican Party's sweeping success in the 1994 congressional elections. The precarious nature of presidential authority, especially compared to the norms of the modern presidency, were dramatically underlined by Gingrich's ability to galvanise his party on a national basis, to provide it with a common electoral identity and to make the Congress responsive to a declared programme of reform. Between 1994 and 1995 Gingrich effectively challenged Bill Clinton's presidential credentials by essentially laying claim to the characteristically executive mantle of national leadership and governmental co-ordination. Gingrich demonstrated the extent to which it had become possible for a congressional leader not merely to become a nationally recognised party leader in a non-presidential year, but to use the position to supplant the presidency's role in setting the agenda and pace of legislative action and in moulding the configuration of political debate. In leading such a formidable political and electoral organisation, committed to a conspicuous manifesto, Gingrich openly wrested the central initiative from the president and prompted Bill Clinton to issue the forlorn assurance to the American public that he was still relevant to the political process. Gingrich posed the threat of becoming an alternative or counter-president by illustrating the potential for the boundaries of traditional roles to melt under contemporary conditions and for legislative leadership functions once thought indigenous to the presidency to be in effect transferable to a congressional leader.

A key element of the conventional modern presidency model has always been the recognition that a president should 'regularly initiate and seek to win support for legislative action as part of his continuing responsibilities'.[2] It is now recognised that presidents are not and never have been in the position of being exclusive policy providers. And yet, the expectation remains that the presidency will assume primary responsibility for guiding the nation's response to problems and for protecting the public interest by sponsoring a range of strongly supported and closely supervised policy initiatives. Even if such policies do not originate in the White House, the presidency is still obliged to assume responsibility for giving them the kind of prominence and momentum to transform them into legislative measures. The rationale of the presidency in the modern system was largely defined by the need for the vigorous executive to provide a benevolent counterweight to the fragmented legislature. Congress's decentralised and disjointed organisation was thought to match the pluralistic nature of its multiple constituencies and the politics of particularised benefits that went hand in hand with subnational representation and local electoral strategies. In the development of the modern presidency, Congress was almost invariably seen as the deadweight of immobilism and insularity that the presidency was responsible for shifting in order to secure unity and movement within an otherwise chronically divided system. This was a view made explicit by Clinton Rossiter:

> The president alone is in a political, constitutional, and practical position to provide such leadership, and he is therefore expected ... to guide Congress in much of its lawmaking activity. Indeed, since Congress is no longer organised to guide itself, not even under ... tough-minded leaders ... the refusal or inability of the president to point out the way results in weak or, at best, stalemated government.[3]

Just as presidential leadership became equated with agenda-setting and management of Congress, so in the light of this conventional perspective the passage of major legislation through the system was closely associated with energetic presidential activism motivating change and policy accomplishment.

The 104th Congress witnessed an explicit challenge to the presidency's legitimacy as an expression of democratic consent, national sovereignty and social need. The Republicans had not only taken control of Congress, they had done so on the basis of a national programme of radical right measures for change and a leadership zealously committed to driving change through an institution which had been firmly established in the public mind as being the defining centre of Washington's multiple negativism. 'Rarely, it seemed, had a movement united so large a constituency so unequivocally.'[4] Gingrich and his followers claimed a clear national mandate on the basis that after having publicly endorsed the Contract With America (CWA), enough Republican candidates had subsequently achieved electoral success to assume control of Congress. The Contract not only included public policy commitments but incorporated a set of pledges to reform Congress, thereby linking the need for political change with structural transformation.

However problematic the Republican mandate may actually have been, it was no more problematic than any presidential mandate. The latter have often been conspicuous by the way they were devised subsequent to, rather than prior to, an election. Presidential mandates have invariably been interpretive constructions of the popular will and the national interest, based upon the exigencies of aggregated preferences within an electoral context. A president prevailing over his competitors is taken to be the expression of democratic choice. Newt Gingrich's mandate was in the same vein in that the CWA was employed after the election to rationalise the variety of separate Republican victories. The Contract was reconstituted as a collective embodiment of electoral achievement, an ascribed *ex post facto* cause of the Republican victory and, as a consequence, a motivating *raison d'être* of the new Republican majority. By the end of November 1994, the CWA had become an integral component of American political discourse with clear public approval given to eight out of the ten pledges.[5] In defining a majority in terms of such a programme, Gingrich convincingly demonstrated Congress' potential to become a collective entity with a genuine claim to represent the American people.

Gingrich's very success in asserting the existence of a national mandate was itself a sign of his authority within the party and the institution, and an illustration of his access to the general public and to its frustration with government in particular. The populist insurgency against government was assisted by Gingrich himself who, between 1993 and 1994, had been instrumental in blocking many of President Clinton's key reforms. Gingrich helped to define the terms of political success and failure in relation to the presidency. It was claimed that the reputed failure of the

Clinton presidency in 1993–4 could be corrected by a Republican Congress which would satisfy the public's need for innovative action and pass its litmus test of securing radical change. Gingrich's party was to be a *de facto* presidency with the collective force to change the political agenda and to occupy the centre stage in Washington. Gingrich's national prominence was warranted by his centrality to a Republican campaign that was not only nationally organised but had progressively acquired a national character following the election. Given the raw materials of such an election and given the creative and coercive skills of the Republican leader in the House, it was not implausible to conclude that Gingrich had encroached upon the presidency's role of national leader, popular tribune and central activist in a system requiring signs of responsive action and discernible change.

This was certainly a conclusion that was widely shared by analysts and opinion-formers during 1995. Richard Fleischer, for example, observed that the 104th Congress had 'shown us that the conventional wisdom that Congress is dependent on leadership from the president is overstated.'[6] William Connelly believed the Republicans under Gingrich had 'wrested control of the political agenda away from the president and raised new questions about the political system and the role of government'.[7] When Gingrich had first entered the House in 1979, he made the following claim: 'The Congress in the long run can change the country more dramatically than the president. One of my goals is to make the House the co-equal of the White House.'[8] In 1995, it was widely conceded that Gingrich had indeed transformed the Speaker's office not just into 'a bully pulpit like that of the presidency',[9] but one that would 'continue to displace Bill Clinton as the primary source of ideas and vision about where the country should be heading'.[10]

It is true that Gingrich was unable to sustain the momentum behind the Republican revolution and that within months he had acquired a lower approval rating than Clinton. The Speaker's political decline may reflect the inherent difficulties of holding together not merely a congressional party but an insurgency movement. The Speaker's fall from grace may reveal the existence of limitations upon any leader's capacity both to counteract the fissionable properties of congressional politics and to give the institution a conscious and positive collective identity instead of its customarily ambiguous and externally imposed corporate image. Gingrich's abrasive and strident personality may also have been instrumental in his rapid descent within a public arena into which he propelled the office of Speaker. All these factors may be relevant, but they do not invalidate the point of central significance which is that Gingrich demonstrated conclusively the extent to which a congressional leader in contemporary conditions can take the initiative not just from a sitting president, but a president from the majority party and one who had been in office for only two years after an extended period of Republican hegemony in the White House. The Republican radicals and especially the phalanx of 73 newly elected members, convinced that they had been swept to Washington on Gingrich's ideological, organisational and financial coat tails, had been led by the Speaker and his lieutenants into a position where President Clinton's role in the formulation of national policy and the articulation of a public philosophy was largely eclipsed. The CWA largely achieved its political and legislative objectives and, in doing so, it shifted the parameters of public debate and political action decisively in favour of Gingrich's position – if not towards him as a political leader.

Irrespective of the misjudgements and miscalculations that marked Gingrich's first year as Speaker, Gingrich clearly revealed an ability to set the agenda of national politics. He and his supporters made their priorities the main issues upon which political attention was centred. The achievement was palpable at the time:

> Astonishingly, Mr Gingrich is doing all this from Capitol Hill rather than from the White House, which is ... like steering a canoe from the front. With few exceptions, the Republicans' discipline in Congress has been iron, as though Mr Gingrich were the head of a parliamentary government. The onslaught has relegated the president himself to the sidelines. He can do little but watch and threaten to use his veto, and wait for Mr Gingrich to stumble.[11]

President Clinton let the Republicans run with the ball because it was so evident that Gingrich had it in his possession. The president was contrite. He had 'heard America shouting' and acknowledged his own failings: 'I have made my mistakes and I have learned again the importance of humility in all human endeavour.'[12] Clinton conceded the need to listen because he had been marginalised from the centre of the policy-making process. The period 1994–5 showed not merely that Newt Gingrich regarded himself, and behaved as if he were, a chief executive, but that the functional difference between himself and the president had in essence become one of degree rather than of kind.

THE POPULISM OF 'TRIANGULATION'

The second theme relates to the mechanics and strategies of the politics of a separated system in an era of diminishing government when the

near-conventional stimulus–response model of Republican presidencies
and Democratic Congresses was inverted. The classic configuration of
'divided government' or 'split-party government' had until this period
been one in which Republican presidents could engage in ideological
stances against big government, taxes and deficits secure in the knowledge
that congressional Democrats would ensure that the expenditure cuts to
the positive and regulatory state would remain within the bounds of social
tolerance. This pattern of relationships was not merely one between two
institutions or two parties. It was a combination of public rhetorical
licence and a residual private pragmatism reserving the security of state
provision. It related to a highly complex amalgam of different levels and
dimensions of political conviction that generally coexist with one another,
but which can be separated out to produce logically contradictory yet
socially inclusive dualities. The impulse to demand more government
service and lower taxation is a common disjunction. Others are less cognitive anomalies and more the intuitive attachment to two fundamental and
ideological outlooks that can be separately activated by different issues.
According to the classic inquiry by Lloyd Free and Hadley Cantril,[13]
American political values can be differentiated between abstract general-
isation and practical application. According to their survey of public attitudes, Americans do not differentiate between liberalism and conservatism
by means of a single evaluative criterion. At the abstract ideological level,
a majority of respondents possessed conservative beliefs in favour of a
minimal state. Nevertheless, when enquiries were shifted to the level of
tangible and immediate government programmes, the study elicited strong
support for this type of practical liberalism. What Free and Cantril concluded was the existence of two simultaneous dimensions of meaning,
value and attachment based upon (i) ideological and (ii) operational
frames of reference. When an amalgam of social thought like this is mixed
with the enriched symbolism of 'the state' or 'big government' as a com-
pelling catalyst of political rhetoric and debate, the consequences can be a
volatile mix of shifting positions and commitments.

President Clinton found that in the first two years of his administration,
he constantly had to live down the reputation for being a tax-and-spend
liberal, which he had acquired by association with the Democratic Party,
by his introduction of reforms like health care and by the black propaganda of the Republican Party whose interests were served by identifying
Clinton with the worst excesses of American liberalism. Clinton sought to
distance himself from the social pathology of government by drawing
attention to the achievements of the National Performance Review in eliminating 16,000 pages of federal regulations and in cutting federal employ-

ment by over 200,000 jobs, thereby reducing the bureaucracy to the smallest percentage of the civilian work force since 1933.[14] Nevertheless, he was continually confronted by the mobilisation of fear, on the part of both economic and cultural conservatives, that a unified party government threatened the dislocation of society by new forms of liberal engineering or the continued stagnation of society through the inertial force of government expenditures on the welfare state. Both change and the status quo under the Democrats were condemned by the Republicans. Unified government gave them a unified target to inflate the *bête noir* of government into a catch-all issue of voter frustration and campaigning rage in 1994. As has already been noted in earlier chapters, the mid-term election result gave a far from simple message. When its complexity was conflated with the bargaining and gaming culture of the separated powers system, especially under split-party control, not only were the opportunities for positional manoeuvring rife, but the symbolic permutations of the government issue became more evident.

The Republican Party in Congress threatened to change the scale and priorities of the federal government in American society. Its presumptive mandate was one of a populist licence to attack the state. Bill Clinton was placed in the unconventional position of a president seeking to use the office to curtail the Republican programme of administrative and budgetary reform, to limit the inventiveness of the Republican agenda and to steer the Republican engine of change away from the social dangers of its own indiscriminate appetite for cuts. As a 'new Democrat', President Clinton was well aware of the symbolic force of the big government issue and the corresponding need to rationalise the organisation of the federal government. He also knew that the voters' demand for change was a rallying cry but also a call for change, conditioned by the need to discriminate against sweeping change. Just as there was beneficial government and detrimental government, so there was good change and bad change. Newt Gingrich acknowledged the distinction but found it difficult to convey it, given both the fundamentalist nature of the revolution and the mobilising capacity of the government issue to the Republicans' radical-right power base. As a result, the Republicans became vulnerable to Democratic charges that they were intent upon dismantling the federal government's structure of social provision. Bill Clinton, on the other other hand, could acknowledge the abstract legitimacy of the issue but then attach himself to the deeper public interest dimension by defending the practical merit of publicly valued individual programmes in such fields as social security, education, health and environmental protection.

President Clinton knew the potential but also the limits of the government issue. The theme had practical considerations, but it was heavily impregnated with the symbolism of therapeutic complaint and measured invective. Even though Gingrich and the House Republicans knew that anti-government rhetoric was not the same as a mandate for moving indiscriminately against government, the very symbolism of their insurrectionist movement succeeded in swamping the actual substance of the programme. President Clinton by comparison was astute in realising the symbolic character of the government issue. He identified with it, but he was also aware of the point at which the outer margins of rhetoric merged into the real anxieties of actual cuts in the government's social provision. Even though an extensive programme of reform was no longer a politically feasible option for the president, the protection of established government programmes in the face of radical congressional action soon became a viable public interest defence of the president's role in the new politics of extreme budget discipline. President Clinton was adept at riding the two horses of ideological commitment and practical management at the same time. His style reflected the popular misgivings about the exact implications of Republican fervour. Polls showed that in January 1995, 12 per cent believed that welfare was the nation's most pressing problem.[15] This was the first time that the issue had reached double figures in such rankings. In another poll taken in the weeks following the 1994 elections when the CWA was receiving maximum publicity,[16] 78 per cent thought that the welfare system required fundamental change. Furthermore, a majority (52 per cent) believed that there needed to be a reduction in the support offered by government. And yet, when the issues raised by polls became more specific, the responses were noticeably more humanitarian in tone. Over half the people questioned (52 per cent) thought it would be unfair to cut off payments to those who had been on welfare for two years. Majorities also opposed denying welfare benefits to single teenage mothers or to children whose fathers could not be identified.

Bill Clinton followed a strategy of 'triangulation' devised by Dick Morris and designed to place the president in the centre ground of political argument in which the president would 'take a position that not only blended the best of each party's views but also transcended them to constitute a third force in the debate.'[17] It also helped to define and publicise the centre by creating distance between the president and the liberal Democrats in Congress on the one hand, and by the dramatisation of Republican threats to social security, Medicare and environmental protection on the other. The president's advantages in this role were recognised at the time:

Under the new circumstances, Mr Clinton's natural inclination to seek out the middle ground becomes an asset rather than a liability. When he was the initiator of policy, his constant compromising smacked of weakness or worse, slipperiness. Now that he is in the main reacting to Republican policy – in some cases highly unpopular policy – the search for the centre looks much more convincingly presidential.[18]

In the most immediate sense of legislation achieved, however, there was a price to pay. In the most partisan session of Congress (1995) yet to be recorded by the *Congressional Quarterly*, President Clinton had a 'presidential success' rate of only 36.2 per cent (compared to rates of 86.4 per cent in both 1993 and 1994), which was lowest score for any president in their third year of office during the modern era.[19] Even allowing for the insensitivity of such an aggregate measure, the relative decline in presidential support was evident. It is true that the congressional Democrats did close ranks in the face of the Republican assault with an average of 80 per cent of Democrats in the House and 81 per cent in the Senate supporting the party in the *Congressional Quarterly's* 'party unity' votes.[20] It was these record levels of unity[21] that provided Clinton with the base from which to engage in defensive strategies. Nevertheless, party unity is a double-edged sword, especially for a minority party president, and as 'party-line voting reached extraordinary proportions' in 1995,[22] the Congress acquired a record for 'never [having] been as active, as partisan or as willing to defy a president'.[23] The presidential support and party unity scores reflected the political configuration of the first session of the 104th Congress: 'The Republican leadership's initiative completely eclipsed Clinton, a president whose legislative ambitions once had threatened to overwhelm Capitol Hill ... Republicans simply owned the agenda, making Clinton far less of a force in Congress than GOP Presidents Ronald Reagan and Bush had been during Democratic majorities.'[24]

And yet the president's stock increased in this period. His defensive posture of appealing to the middle ground and relying upon obstructionist minority methods (e.g. filibuster, cloture and veto) to place pressure on the Republicans in both the House and Senate to diminish their zeal paid political dividends in the second half of the year. Initially, the Clinton White House found it difficult to adjust to the new political landscape of the 104th Congress. In particular, the legislative liaison team experienced problems in transferring from collaboration with an established Democratic leadership on a Democratic agenda to working with a highly disciplined and self assertive Republican Party intent upon ignoring the White House. When it became clear that the potential for driving wedges into the House Republican battalions was minimal and that there was no prospect of a cooperative partnership between Democrats and moderate Republicans in the House, the Clinton White House recognised that its posture would have to be mainly one of defence rather than construction. With the assistance of a number of senior Republican moderates in the Senate who were alarmed over the Contract With America, Clinton delayed or blocked a large segment of the Republican agenda (e.g. federal regulation reform, tax reduction, welfare restriction, the expansion of property owners' rights, the criminalisation of flag desecration, the reduction of federal benefits schemes). When he could not rely upon Senate Republicans, the president resorted to vetoes which were so successful that only one of the 11 was overturned. The net effect was that only 88 bills were signed into law by the end of the session – the lowest number since 1933.

The most dramatic example of this strategy came with the protracted struggle over the fiscal 1996 budget reconciliation bill into which a large part of the Republicans' legislative programme was packaged. It set out a series of integrated taxation and deficit reduction measures that would fundamentally alter the entire profile and role of the federal government in American society. After a coalition of Democrats and moderate Republicans in the Senate had ensured the failure of the constitutional amendment designed to establish a balanced budget, the Budget Reconciliation Act assumed even greater significance as the organising instrument of the Republican revolution. It aimed to eliminate the deficit by 2002. Each chamber adopted its own version of the measure on 29 June 1995. President Clinton was immediately placed on the defensive and criticised the legislation for seeking to balance the budget on the backs of children, the poor and the elderly. The president threatened to veto the bill if it was not softened to meet White House concerns. In response, the House Republican leadership felt that President Clinton was so politically weakened following the 1994 electoral rout that he would not veto such a pivotal measure as a budget reconciliation bill. No president had ever vetoed such a large budget enactment before.

To keep the pressure on Clinton, the Republican leadership threatened to use, and eventually did use, the device of attaching key items of their agenda to legislation either raising the federal debt limit, or providing temporary funding cover for the government's activities. If the president vetoed the Republican riders, he would also have had to veto the debt servicing or funding items, thereby putting the nation into a position of defaulting on its debts, or shutting down selected parts of the government. Gingrich and his colleagues did not think that the president had the political or personal backbone to risk a confrontation with such high stakes. But the president had the advantage of political time and public access. The process for such a major restructuring of the federal budget had fallen behind schedule and the president was able to play upon the Republicans' need to make rapid progress while party unity held. The Republican leadership became increasingly frustrated with a president who seemed intent upon intransigence. The budget process began to lose pace and became dependent upon a series of last-minute stop-gap measures to keep the nation and the government solvent until the conflict between the White House and the Republican Congress could be resolved. House Republican leaders, however, were so confident that the president would ultimately submit to their priorities that in November 1995 they decided to pre-empt the reconciliation process and attach a number of key substantive demands to two short-term funding resolutions. Clinton emphatically vetoed the measures and immediately precipitated a partial shutdown of the federal government. Republicans believed that the president would have wanted to avoid such a damaging outcome at all costs. But it was the Republican Congress whom the public blamed for the precipitous action of 'closing the government'. The president had taken his case directly to the public with two veto messages crafted to appeal to the middle ground and to the positive element of government provision: 'If America must close down access to quality education, a clean environment and affordable health care for our seniors in order to keep the government open then that price is too high.'[25] The president objected to the Republican strategy of blackmail and responded in kind:

> Republicans in the Congress have resorted to extraordinary tactics to try to force their extreme budget and priorities into law. In essence, they have said that they will not pass legislation to let the government pay its bills unless I accept their extreme, misguided priorities. This is an unacceptable choice and I must veto the legislation.[26]

The shutdown distracted attention away from the Republicans' central achievement in establishing agreement in both the House and Senate for the budget reconciliation bill and with it the largest expenditure cuts in the nation's history. The measure would have reduced projected federal spending by $894 billion over seven years (including cuts of $270 billion to Medicare, $163 billion to Medicaid and $175 billion to entitlement programmes) and cut taxes by $245 billion over the same period. It had taken ten months for the congressional Republicans to translate the 1994 victory into a coherent and integrated programme of deficit and taxation reduction.

The Republican show-piece was passed on 17 November 1995. Clinton immediately hit back with his own plan for a more moderate route to a balanced budget with fewer expenditure cuts and less tax reduction. On 6 December came the *coup de grâce* when the president vetoed the entire measure evoking again the centrist objections to what he regarded as an extreme and punitive response to the country's budgetary problems. Although the Republican leadership was able to salvage elements of their programme from the ensuing wreckage, it was unable to withstand the president's veto or the threat of a veto in the protracted budgetary negotiations which ultimately extended half way into the financial year of 1996. After 14 stopgap spending measures, the process ended with the president's anticipated or actual vetoes having restored and even increased funding in such areas as education, job training and environmental protection. Although the Republicans could claim that they had reduced spending by $43 billion (i.e. the largest one-year cut since 1945), most of the cuts lay in the projected rate of increase rather than in actual expenditure. Furthermore, no meaningful cuts had been made in the fastest growing programmes (i.e. Medicare, Medicaid, welfare), which had been targeted for economies by the Republican leadership and for protection by the president.

   The legislative history of the budget reconciliation bill demonstrated the way in which split-party control had produced a different type of gridlock in which a Democratic president fought a rearguard action to prevent Republican majorities from fulfilling their party's agenda. Bill Clinton subverted the normal political and analytical categories of policy-making by adopting a reactive and preventative role in the process of legislation – i.e. the use of negative techniques usually associated with anti-government stances to challenge and nullify the active mobilisation of congressional forces to reduce government. David Mayhew observed that 'not only [was] the president not taking a major part' in the process of legislative initiation, he was 'largely on other other side'.[27] The dynamics of the legislative–executive dialectic had apparently been reversed. To Charles O. Jones, before Clinton 'it had never been the case ... that a president [could] do well by preventing things from happening.'[28] But it was increasingly recognised that with Bill Clinton it was possible for a president to be both protectionist and responsible; to be effective by being benevolently obstructive.

   President Clinton essentially employed separation of powers politics to engage in a form of inverted populism against the insurgency of Gingrich's Republican revolutionaries. At the very point at which such a movement threatened to harness governmental power to reduce the remit of its services and responsibilities, President Clinton succeeded in playing upon the cognitive and affective disjunction between ideological conservatism and practical liberalism to issue a public warning of the consequences likely to be incurred by *real* change. He turned the Democratic Party to a position of populist reaction to the prospect of a government animated by Republican action. Conscious of the subtleties and nuances of the big government issue, Clinton ensured that while moving to the right in response to the shift in public opinion he claimed the conspicuous role of public protector against the alleged excesses of a movement committed to the imperative of ideological and political maximisation. Clinton exploited Gingrich's problems in holding both his party's radicalism and its rank and file together, not merely by delaying tactics within Congress, but by using the public prominence of his office to associate the Republican programme with anti-social extremes and irresponsibility. Like any effective counter-puncher, Clinton allowed his opponent the space to come on to the shots; and there were many such body blows as Clinton identified himself with the public's private anxieties by equating the Republican revolution with the populist demonology of America's 'special interests'. For example, on 11 April 1995, Clinton used his weekly radio address to warn the nation of the effects of the Republicans' proposed policy changes in the environmental and health sectors:

> In the last few months, a small army of lobbyists for polluters has descended on Capitol Hill, mounting a full-scale assault on our environmental and public health protections. And this Congress has actually allowed these lobbyists to sit down and rewrite important environmental laws to weaken our safeguards ... This budget will mean dirtier water, more smog, more illness and a diminished quality of life ... Well, I've got bad news for the lobbyists and their allies. We don't want more pollution to balance the budget. As president, it is my duty to protect the environment, and on my watch, America will not be for sale.[29]

The president returned to the theme in August of the same year when at an impromptu news conference, Clinton referred to the House of Representatives' action in the same field of environmental and public health protection as 'a remarkable exercise of special interest power' because of the way in which '17 special interest provisions' had been added to the bill. He continued: 'This is Washington's special interest politics at its most effective and at its worst ... In the past few days, a battalion of lobbyists has swarmed Capitol Hill, exerting enormous pressure to save these loopholes. I said I would use the power of my office to help people, not polluters.' The president went on to observe 'that while

Congress [had] been taking care of the special interests, it [was] also taking care of itself ... [Y]ou can see who's in control in this Congress ... and it's not good.' Clinton reminded the Congress that 'all the special interests have to be subordinated to the broader, public interest'.[30] On 7 June 1995, the president widened the attack when he vetoed a rescissions bill:

> HR 1158 slashes needed investments for education, national service, and the environment, in order to avoid cutting wasteful projects and other unnecessary expenditures. There are billions of dollars in pork – unnecessary highway demonstration projects, courthouses, and other federal buildings – that could have been cut instead of these critical investments ... In the end, the Congress chose courthouses over education, pork-barrel highway projects over national service, government travel over clean water.[31]

In the wake of attacks like these, and of plunging poll ratings for both Gingrich and the Congress, President Clinton was able to attach public culpability for governmental failings and policy fears to the Republicans. Clinton's barbed self-effacement left Gingrich conspicuously exposed in a position of public accountability of his own making. As more Republican measures became bogged down, Gingrich was increasingly left as the person who 'did more than anyone or anybody else to make Clinton look good'.[32] Clinton had come to rely on the bombastic irascibility and aggression of Gingrich for his own survival. By early 1996, the dynamic between president and congressional leader had been set: 'The Speaker has given the long beleaguered commander in chief his first effective foil since George Bush left the stage three years ago. Compared with Newt, Clinton can appear measured, careful with his words, disciplined in his behaviour ... Newt is Clinton's redemption, the man who made the president "relevant" again.'[33] Gingrich's struggle to precipitate a revolution in American politics and society was hampered by the lack of a critical catalyst and by the problematic nature of attaching crusading zeal at the centre to the relative nullity of governmental reduction. Clinton reminded voters of the provision of the state that feeds the security of dissent.

PARTISANSHIP AND PRESIDENTIAL STRATEGIES

In *The Presidency in a Separated System*,[34] Charles O. Jones refers to presidents needing to engage in different governing strategies with

Congress depending upon the circumstances of their arrival in office and the contextual conditions of their political position. Employing Jones' terminology, President Clinton in 1993–4 had a 'mixed mandate' and sought to pursue an active programme within the system's 'agenda orientation' or 'policy-setting'[35] that was basically a composite of the 'consolidative', 'contractive' and 'fiscal' categories of policy dimension.[36] The level of consensus over the agenda was correspondingly low and accompanied a balanced institutional interaction between the Congress and the presidency over policy objectives and priorities. The president's attempts to counteract both his electoral weakness and his inexperience of Washington politics led to a 'compensatory' leadership strategy by which he devised 'supplementary means for authenticating his leadership'.[37] The ideological and institutional parameters of the 104th Congress forced Clinton to adapt his governing strategy to accommodate the sudden insurgency of the 'Republican revolution'. His 'compensatory leadership' had even more deficiencies to compensate for and as a result Clinton deployed the resources of the public presidency to launch a campaign of presidential reinstatement by taking appeals to the public interest directly to the people. His dramatisation of the Republican threat in such sensitive areas as Medicare, social security and environmental protection helped to polarise the parties and inflate the level of partisanship between the presidency and Congress in 1995. Vetoes, threats of vetoes, government shutdowns and budgetary intransigence characterised the first session of the 104th Congress.

The second session was different in character, not least because of the influence of presidential politics upon Congress. Apart from the implications of the forthcoming presidential election in which Bob Dole (R.KS), the Senate Majority Leader, was the likely nominee of the Republican Party, Clinton's performance in 1995 had succeeded in moulding the rhetorical and evaluative context within which the Republicans would be competing for re-election. In effect the Republican Party had become closely identified with the strident and very public zeal of the House Republicans and especially Gingrich's vanguard of freshman irreconcilables. The congressional Republicans were perceived as having been responsible for the government closures in 1995 and for generally having overreached themselves in their absolutist approach to government management. The danger for the Republicans was that the 1996 elections would be a referendum on the first joint Republican majorities in Congress for 40 years and that with President Clinton's capacity to point up Congress' excesses to national audiences, the effect might be to end the Republican control of Congress after just two years. In the same way that

2nd session

the Republicans could not afford any repetition of the prolonged budget battle of 1995, the president also needed to avoid the impression of negativism. The consequence was a general amelioration of partisanship in which a small group of Republican moderates and Democratic conservatives acted as brokers and helped to bring about a sufficient level of cooperation to achieve a significant quantity of legislation (see the chapter by John Owens in this volume). Even if compromise was reluctant, the political need for accommodation was evident in the flow of enactments during 1996. In the field of environmental protection, for example, the Republicans found that they 'were most successful when they took the time to craft bipartisan compromises and run the political traps suggesting a strategy that would work regardless of who controls Congress'.[38] After being publicly vilified by President Clinton in 1995 for its plans to deregulate key sectors of environmental management, the Republican leadership acknowledged the need for a more moderate approach to such a sensitive issue in an election year. As a consequence, the second session of the Congress was much more constructive than the first, with legislation passed to provide comprehensive revisions of government regulation in such areas as pesticides, fisheries and drinking water.

Cross-party accommodation was also in evidence in the fight to increase the minimum wage. Strongly supported by President Clinton, such a traditional Democratic issue aroused strong ideological opposition from the House Republicans who sought to link the proposal to a 'deal breaking' revision of the welfare and Medicaid system. The 'deal breaker' in the Senate was Bob Dole's repeal of the 1993 4.3 per cent increase in gasoline tax. The latter was dropped after a Democratic filibuster on the repeal, while in the House 'pressure from about two dozen Republican moderates forced House leaders to act against their ideological inclinations'.[39] The traditional Democratic agenda, however, suffered a substantial blow when President Clinton agreed to sign legislation reforming the federal government's organisation of welfare policy. Although the president had objections to the bill, he was aware that welfare reform had bipartisan and public support, that he had already vetoed two previous GOP reform plans, and that to veto a third attempt at revision in a presidential election year would undermine his public standing as a president committed to welfare reform. His Republican opponent, Bob Dole, wanted his party to present a measure that the president would find unacceptable and that would therefore lead to an electorally damaging veto. After Dole's departure from the Senate, the level of partisanship diminished as each party became less inhibited over making concessions that might advantage or disadvantage the Republicans' prospective presidential candidate. The threat of President Clinton's veto, which had proved such a potent influence in the confrontations over budget legislation, was also a constant factor in the political calculations surrounding this issue. As both parties became more aware of a mutual interest in facing the electorate with the achievement of welfare reform behind them, the House Republicans dropped the Medicaid overhaul from the bill and incorporated enough of the more moderate Senate bill to increase the legislation's appeal to the president. The historic measure replacing the structure and provision of welfare provision which had been in place for 60 years was accepted by Clinton because Congress had largely met his earlier objections and because to have vetoed it would have benefited Dole more than Clinton. The president was markedly conciliatory towards what he saw as a more accommodating measure:

> The bipartisan legislation before the Congress today is significantly better than the bills I vetoed. Many of the worst elements I objected to are out of it ... [E]ven though serious problems remain in the non-welfare reform provisions of the bill, this is the best chance we will have for a long, long time to complete the work of ending welfare as we know it.[40]

The pressures and incentives towards a more co-partisan approach within Congress and in legislative–executive relations was reflected in the number of bills enacted climbing from 88 in 1995 to 150 in 1996. *Congressional Quarterly* listed only five pieces of significant legislation in 1995. In 1996, the list of significant enactments contained 15 items.[41] The 1994 mid-term elections had raised the stakes in partisanship on both sides but especially amongst the House Republicans, who sought to close ranks against a Democratic president portrayed as an ideological enemy of the 'revolution'. The public reaction against the consequences of excessive partisanship, the congressional Democrats' assimilation of their new minority status and role (see the chapter by Dean McSweeney in this volume), the time constraints of an election year and a politically vulnerable president – all shifted the relationship between the White House and Congress from one of partisan intransigence and veto threats to one of co-partisan negotiation and competitive credit claiming of legislative achievement.

CONCLUSION

The 104th Congress demonstrated the extent to which balanced participation between the president and the Congress, together with inter-party negotiation and pragmatic accommodation, can produce significant legislation in split-party conditions – even in circumstances when party positions are ideologically entrenched and ostensibly supported by recent mandates. The 104th Congress also revealed the way in which the ideological coherence of a controlling party attracted public culpability for evidence of governmental incoherence. The individuated prominence of President Clinton allowed him to adapt positions more readily and more conspicuously than the collective and institutional character of Congress. Neither President Clinton nor the Republican congressional leadership wished to be held accountable for legislative failure and as a consequence each side became more amenable to constructive incremental engagement. Just as the president's public rhetoric and negotiating stance became more conciliatory in tone, so the Republican leadership moved to restore its public esteem by marginalising the Contract With America and by conceding ground to Clinton's spending priorities. The governing strategy of partisanship significantly altered within a single Congress indicating that the conditions which determine presidential relationships with Congress are so fluid in nature that a president has to review and adjust his strategic principles on a continual basis. Moreover, as Bill Clinton showed in the 104th Congress, the president can influence the configuration of congressional attitudes and the matrix of political calculations with which he has to engage as a policy participant through his access to the channels of public contact and popular anxiety.

Even though the congressional Republicans had succeeded in shifting Clinton to the right (e.g. on welfare reform, tax cuts and a commitment to a balanced budget by 2002), it was the president who emerged with his political reputation enhanced and with his reselection prospects secure. Clinton had demonstrated that it was possible for a Democratic president to succeed within the unconventional context of a newly and highly ambitious Republican Congress set upon a revolution in public values. Democratic Congresses had been closely associated in past constructions of 'divided government' with the practical dimension of liberalism which offset the ideological conservatism of a Nixon or Reagan. The dynamics of the 104th Congress revealed the problems of congressional activists in trying to engage in an ideological crusade against 'big government' while being confronted by a president who was highly adept at mixing the two dimensions into one familiarly inconsistent and yet intuitively acceptable composite.

President Clinton demonstrated not only the capacity to adapt his presidency's governing strategy but the need to change rapidly and dramatically to new conditions and to altered perspectives of more settled circumstances. Clinton's position in the 104th Congress was quite exceptional in nature. He was forced to adopt a rearguard preventive strategy only two years after a party-changing presidential election. Whatever mandate or authority he could claim in 1993 had been undermined by the end of 1994. The situation was further compounded by the confused and discordant policy agenda and by the unprecedented degree of ambiguity surrounding a Democrat in the White House. The volatile swings in public allegiance and electoral behaviour that had produced both Clinton's victory in 1992 and the reversal of Democratic Party fortunes in 1994 left the president with little in the way of a definable Democratic agenda with which to give his presidency a positive identity. In the context of a highly constrained budget, the ominous presence of Ross Perot's pool of politically alienated voters, the rapid development of a politics of personal ethics charges and counter-charges, and an established political discourse of a diminishing state, Clinton found that even a Democratic president could only expect to deal in marginal changes and limited objectives. Although he may have been more politically astute and professionally self-aware than President Bush, the 104th Congress revealed President Clinton to be as reactive and circumscribed a leader as his predecessor. Contrary to the traditional norms of the modern presidency that conflate policy formulation, congressional mobilisation and legislative achievement, Bill Clinton, like George Bush, sent very few major agenda-setting bills to Congress for consideration. The Republican Congress, and Clinton's relationship with it, epitomised the current state of the presidency which is characterised by an ever deepening disjunction between the increasingly high public profile of the office and the pervasive continuity of its limitations irrespective of party change, reform cycles or public calls for national leadership. Clinton was compelled to defer to a consolidatory rather than a innovatory role and to accept that even for a Democratic administration the emphasis was necessarily one of realistic minimalism. As Clinton himself acknowledged shortly before the end of his first term: 'We're in an era when people don't want promises to be high flown and unrealistic … I've learned that the system simply won't accommodate big changes even when in theory you think they're warranted'.[42] For a Democratic president to have accepted such a premise about government constitutes the real 'revolution' of the 104th Congress.

NOTES

1. Charles O. Jones, *The Presidency in a Separated System* (Washington, D.C.: The Brookings Institution, 1994), pp. 48–51.
2. Fred I. Greenstein, 'Change and Continuity in the Modern Presidency', in Anthony King, ed., *The New American Political System* (Washington, D.C.: American Enterprise Institute, 1978), p. 46.

3. Clinton Rossiter, *The American Presidency*, rev. edn (New York: Mentor, 1960), p. 26. On this theme see also Greenstein, 'Change and Continuity in the Modern Presidency', pp. 45–61; Stephen J. Wayne, *The Legislative Presidency* (New York: Harper and Row, 1978); Paul C. Light, *The President's Agenda: Domestic Policy Choice from Kennedy to Reagan*, rev. edn (Baltimore: The Johns Hopkins University Press, 1991); James L. Sundquist, *The Decline and Resurgence of Congress* (Washington, D.C.: The Brookings Institution, 1981), ch. 6.

4. Garry Wills, 'What Happened to the Revolution?', *New York Review of Books*, 3 June 1996, p. 11.

5. Michael Golay and Carl Rollyson, *Where America Stands 1996* (New York: John Wiley, 1996), p. xxxiii.

6. Quoted in Donna Cassata, 'Swift Progress of "Contract" Inspires Awe and Concern', *Congressional Quarterly Weekly Report*, 1 April 1995, p. 909.

7. Quoted in Cassata, 'Swift Progress of "Contract"', p. 909.

8. David S. Cloud, 'Speaker Wants His Platform to Rival the Presidency', *Congressional Quarterly Guide to Current American Government*, Fall 1995, p. 69.

9. Ronald D. Elving, 'The Media Whirlwind of Speaker Gingrich', *Congressional Quarterly Weekly Report*, 9 December 1995, p. 3774.

10. Cloud, 'Speaker Wants His Platform to Rival the Presidency', p. 67.

11. 'The Evolution of a Revolution', *The Economist*, 25 March 1995.

12. Bill Clinton, State of the Union Address, 24 January 1995, *Congressional Quarterly Weekly Report*, 28 January 1995, p. 300.

13. Lloyd A. Free and Hadley Cantril, *The Political Beliefs of Americans: A Study of Public Opinion* (New Brunswick, NJ: Rutgers University Press, 1967).

14. Donald F. Kettl and John J. DiIulio, Jr, eds., *Inside the Reinvention Machine: Appraising Governmental Reform* (Washington D.C.: The Brookings Institution, 1995).

15. Golay and Rollyson, *Where America Stands 1996*, p. 70.

16. Time/CNN poll quoted in Richard Lacayo, 'Down On the Downtrodden', *Time*, 19 December 1994.

17. Dick Morris, *Behind The Oval Office. Winning the Presidency in the Nineties* (New York: Random House, 1997), p. 80.

18. 'Bill Flings it Back', *The Economist*, 25 March 1995.

19. Jon Healey, 'Clinton Success Rate Declined to a Record Low in 1995', *Congressional Quarterly Weekly Report*, 27 January 1996, p. 194.

20. 'Party unity votes' are defined by *Congressional Quarterly* as 'the percentage of recorded floor votes in each chamber on which a majority of one party voted against a majority of the other party'.

21. In the House, 73.2 per cent of recorded votes featured a majority of Republicans voting against a majority of Democrats; the equivalent figure for the Senate was 68.8 per cent. Such levels of party voting had not been registered before by the *Congressional Quarterly* measure since the organisation began compiling data in 1954.

22. Dan Carney, 'As Hostilities Rage on the Hill, Partisan Vote Rate Soars', *Congressional Quarterly Weekly Report*, 27 January 1996, p. 199.

23. Jeffrey L. Katz, 'A Record-Setting Year', *Congressional Quarterly Weekly Report*, 27 January, 1996, p. 195.
24. Healey, 'Clinton Success Rate Declined to a Record Low in 1995', p. 193.
25. President Clinton's veto of a second temporary continuing appropriations resolution (13 November 1995), 'President Clinton Vetoes Continuing Resolution', *Congressional Quarterly Weekly Report*, 18 November 1995, p. 3559.
26. President Clinton's veto of the temporary extension of the federal debt limit, 'Temporary Rise in Debt Limit is Vetoed by President', *Congressional Quarterly Weekly Report*, 18 November 1995, p. 3559.
27. Quoted in Cassata, 'Swift Progress of "Contract" Inspires Awe and Concern', *Congressional Quarterly Weekly Report*, 1 April 1995, p. 911.
28. Quoted in Healey, 'Clinton Success Rate Declined to a Record Low in 1995', p. 193.
29. Bill Clinton, 'Radio Address by the President to the Nation', November 4, 1995 (White House Electronic Publications, The White House <Publications-Admin@WhiteHouse.Gov>, 4 November 1995).
30. News conference given President Clinton (1 August 1995), 'Clinton Says Congress is on "Wrong Track"', *Congressional Quarterly Weekly Report*, 5 August 1995, p. 2391.
31. 'President Clinton's Veto of Rescissions Bill', *Congressional Quarterly Weekly Report*, 10 June 1995, p. 1669.
32. Wills, 'What Happened to the Revolution?'
33. Nancy Gibbs and Karen Tumulty, 'Master of the House', *Time*, 19 December 1995/1 January 1996, p. 51.
34. Jones, *The Presidency in a Separated System*.
35. Jones, *The Presidency in a Separated System*, pp. 164–81.
36. 'Consolidative' refers to that agenda orientation in which the emphasis is upon entrenching the policy reforms and budgetary commitment of a pre-ceding period of government expansion. 'Contractive' refers to an agenda orientation of scepticism towards the role of government in society and an intention to reduce the rate of increase in government intervention and expenditure. A 'fiscal' policy agenda provides a more defined focus upon the failure to control the growth in government spending and with it a commensurate emphasis upon tax cuts and deficit reduction. See Jones, *The Presidency in a Separated System*, pp. 167–78.
37. Jones, *The Presidency in a Separated System*, p. 49.
38. Alan Freedman, 'Accomplishments, Missteps Mark Congress' Record', *Congressional Quarterly Weekly Report*, 12 October 1996, p. 2918.
39. Jonathan Weisman, 'House Untangles Gridlock on Minimum Wage Deal', *Congressional Quarterly Weekly Report*, 18 May 1996, p. 1390.
40. 'Statement by the President: Remarks by President on Welfare Reform' 31 July 1996 (White House Electronic Publications, The White House <Publications-Admin@WhiteHouse.Gov>, 1 August 1996).
41. See The Editors, 'Assessing the 104th Congress. What Passed and What Didn't', *Congressional Quarterly Weekly Report*, 2 November 1996, pp. 3120–1.
42. Quoted in transcript of interview with President Clinton in E. Pooley and J. F. O. McAllister, 'If You Try it All at Once ...', *Time*, 2 September 1996.

7 Minority Power? Democratic Defeat and Recovery

Dean McSweeney

Political scientists have shown little interest in the minority party in Congress. A monograph, written a quarter of a century ago by Charles O. Jones, specified the options available to and pursued by the minority parties during the twentieth century.[1] Other contributions to a sparse literature have provided case studies, all dealing with the Republican Party.[2] As the Republicans set new records for longevity as the minority so their factional alignments, leadership strategies and internal discontents substituted for discussion of minority politics in general. Even the Democrats' loss of the Senate majority in the early 1980s generated no new studies of minority party behaviour.

In depriving the Democrats of majorities in both chambers for the first time in 40 years, the 1994 elections provide an opportunity to return to the study of minority politics, escaping dependence on the Republicans as the sole available case. More than this: in the 104th Congress, minority Democrats exhibited many distinctive features, adding to the value of studying them. As the most durable House majority in history, it was to be expected that adjustment to minority status would create stresses greater than for any previous minority. We assume that a new minority will operate differently from an old one and 1995 provided the first opportunity in 40 years to study a new House minority. Only one House Democrat in 1995 had ever served in the minority. Democratic representatives were required to adapt to new conditions. Second, House Democrats were confronting the most programmatic majority in history. No previous majority had ever come to power cohering around such an extensive set of legislative commitments as the House Republicans in the 104th Congress. The new majority not only had a programme but also a self-proclaimed electoral mandate to implement it. At least in the twentieth century, it is difficult to think of another congressional party so publicly committed to its own programme prior to taking office. Third, the

140

Democrats encountered a novel form of split-party control in the 104th Congress. As Michael Foley showed in the previous chapter, the president ceded control over the congressional agenda to the majority to a degree unprecedented in the post-Roosevelt era. By surrendering legislative initiative and distancing himself from his own party, Clinton deprived the minority of a working alliance with the White House. Unlike the Republicans in most of the preceding 40 years, Clinton offered his party in 1995 neither a programme to rally around nor the resources of the White House in resisting the majority. To the contrary, the triangulation strategy Clinton adopted advertised his divorce from congressional Democrats, forcing the party into an independence in devising legislation and executing strategy untypical for the minority. Fourth, Democrats in the House were confronting procedures which they had devised to protect majority legislation. Since the 1970s innovations in the use of special rules had cramped the scope for the minority to participate in legislation.[3] In the 1980s Democratic Speaker Tip O'Neill had summarised the imbalance of influence between majority and minority in his observation, 'Republicans are just going to have to get it through their heads that they are not going to write legislation.'[4] This dismissive attitude echoed Czar Thomas Reed's observation that the role of the minority was 'to draw its check and make up a quorum, nothing more.'[5] Procedural domination now had to be withstood by the minority which had accentuated majority rule.

STRATEGIC OPTIONS

Jones identifies a six-point range of minority strategies, extending from severely restricted under inhospitable conditions to unrestricted in auspicious circumstances. The formative influences defining strategic options are political conditions both outside and inside Congress. The temper of the times, relative political strength of the minority, the degree to which the two parties are internally unified and the power of the president constitute the relevant external variables. Determining influences inside Congress are procedure, the size of the majority's margin over the minority, the leadership and organisation of the two parties, the duration of minority status and the relations between the minority party leaderships in the two chambers.

Five conditions were favourable to the Democrats in 1995–6. Outside Congress they exhibited considerable if receding political strength. Democratic identifiers continued to outnumber Republicans. Suffering defeats at all electoral levels in 1994, especially in the South where the frequently predicted realignment finally arrived, Democrats were on the brink of minority status. However, the party's hold on elective office at all levels of government was greater than for most minority parties. In this respect the Democrats were dissimilar to the apparent permanence of the Republican minority from the New Deal.

Inside Congress, minority Democrats had four assets. Some procedures changed in the House to minority advantage in 1995. The incoming Republican majority relaxed the use of restrictive rules insulating legislation from minority amendments (see the chapter in this volume by John Owens). Without returning to the predominance of open rules common prior to the late 1970s, restrictive rules became less common, reducing the procedural obstacles to minority participation in legislation. Proxy voting in committee, used by the majority to assert control in members' absence, was prohibited. Committee ratios were altered to reflect the closer numerical balance in the House between majority and minority. However, its value to the minority was offset by the diminished autonomy afforded to committees in a Congress characterised by centralised control from party leaders.

Democrats were aided by being a large minority. Constituting 47 per cent of the membership of each chamber, the party was the largest congressional minority since the 85th Congress (1957–8). Virtually anything less than Republican unanimity required Democratic participation to make a majority. A unanimous Democratic Party required only four Republican senators or 16 representatives for a floor majority. For defensive actions, Democratic numbers were more than sufficient. Only a substantial majority of Democrats in either chamber was necessary to preclude the extraordinary majorities necessary to pass constitutional amendments or override presidential vetoes. In the Senate a united Democratic Party was sufficient to prevent the invoking of cloture. Democrats were not handicapped by a minority mentality. Such a mentality acts as a self-denying curb on minority ambition. To the contrary, Democrats in 1995 struggled to adapt to minority status. Journalist Elizabeth Drew described House Democrats at the opening of the 104th Congress as 'still in shock' and their Senate counterparts as 'still in a daze'.[6] Though adjustment took time, Democrats were intent on regaining a majority, widening the strategic options available to them. Unable to control the legislative agenda, the minority party leadership of the two houses had few incentives for liaison. But coordination did develop in the 104th Congress as leadership teams worked on strategies to recapture majorities. The chairs of the two Steering Committees, Representative Vic Fazio (D.CA) and Senator John Kerry

(D.MA), coordinated their activities through regular contacts. House Minority Leader Richard Gephardt (D.MO) met regularly with his Senate counterpart Tom Daschle (D.SD). Both participated in the monthly meetings inaugurated in April 1995, bringing together the congressional leadership, congressional campaign committees, the Democratic National Committee and White House staff working to promote Democratic success in the 1996 elections.

Three unfavourable external conditions limited the Democrats strategic options. The temper of the times discouraged both obstruction in Congress and liberalism. Negative public attitudes towards government institutions, especially Congress, remained prevalent. Probably a mix of disapproval of individual improprieties and institutional failure, the 1994 election signified a desire for the end of 'business as usual'. Unified government in the first years of the Clinton presidency had not enhanced public confidence. The restoration of divided control, intensifying the risk of gridlock, was potentially even more corrosive of public morale. Democratic obstructionism, frustrating the House Republican 'mandate', appeared an electorally unpromising strategy for a party seeking to recapture popular support. The 1994 elections also registered the unpopularity of liberalism. The electorate exhibited a closer connection between ideology and partisan preference than in any previous mid-term election which enabled the Republicans to convert the preponderance of conservatives over liberals to electoral advantage.[7] Defence of past liberal achievements appeared an electorally unrewarding option in 1995.

The parties' policy positions exhibited the internal ideological homogeneity and differentiation from each other which had developed since the 1960s. The social and foreign policy divisions of that past had lost their intensity. Democratic identifiers, though more diverse than their numerically fewer Republican counterparts, were less fragmented on issues than they had been in the late 1960s or early 1970s.[8] Democratic activists – who staff campaigns, serve as party officials and attend national conventions – were concentrated to the left of public opinion on most issues; sympathetic to labour, minorities and environmental interests. On economic, welfare, foreign and socio-cultural policy the Democrats were a predominantly liberal party.[9] However, defeat divides. Tensions in the party, contained by electoral success, intensified in defeat. The conflicts over appropriate vote-winning strategies, so long concentrated at the presidential level where victories had proved so elusive, spread to the Congress when the party lost its majority. Defeats in the South, which reduced the party to controlling a minority of seats in the region for the first time since Reconstruction, amplified calls for the party to modify its liberalism to revive public support. Republicans, in contrast, were unified in and by victory. For a generation Republican activists and identifiers had cohered around conservative positions. In 1994 Republican identifiers cast 93 per cent of their votes for the party's candidates. The election had also produced an unprecedented coherence of conservative support around Republican candidates. Moreover, the primarily economic emphasis of the Contract With America maximised Republicans unity, eschewing the potentially more divisive and electorally unpopular socio-cultural issues such as abortion.

Following the 1994 elections Clinton was a politically vulnerable president, lacking the resources to set the congressional agenda, mobilise public opinion or aid his party. His first two years in office had yielded a succession of strategic failures, exemplified in the collapse of health care reform; inconsistency, repeatedly evident in foreign policy; and recurrent scandal – all of which combined to sully the president's reputation. Clinton's initial response to the Republican takeover was to retreat from legislative initiatives, surrendering what little control over the agenda he might have exerted. This was not a president seeking to maximise his power resources. Rather, it was a president seeking electoral capital from an American version of French *cohabitation* in which the chief executive presides over government, aloof from the making of domestic policy but uses public forums to denigrate the work of the legislative majority. Such a presidency deprived the minority of a source of influence within Congress. David Truman argued that the president provides the minority party with an alternative source of legitimacy to the majority,

> provided that it has not been temporarily discredited and that its occupant does not entirely neglect the opportunity to set the legislative programme, the presidency should be a source of leverage to the minority's leaders.[10]

Both conditions Truman specifies for the president to assist the minority were absent in 1995: Clinton was discredited and he declined even to attempt to set the legislative agenda.

Inside Congress the Democrats were initially handicapped by the inexperience and disunity around the leadership in each chamber. The 1994 elections left the principal Democratic leadership positions vacant in both the House and the Senate. Tom Foley (D.WA) was the first Speaker defeated for re-election since 1862, symbolising public repudiation of Democratic control. Among House Democrats, only Sidney Yates of Illinois, a survivor from the 83rd Congress, had experience of serving in the minority. The election to replace Foley ended the sequence of uncontested successions of the next in line to the principal party leadership position. Charlie Rose's challenge to the outgoing Majority Leader Gephardt produced the first contested ballot since 1971. In the minority Democrats encountered the contests for leadership which had recurred amongst Republicans during the previous 40 years. The minority's discontent and weaker leadership resources yielded greater divisiveness. Rose (D.NC), belying his own liberal voting record, presented himself as a southern voice for moderation. A similar southern versus heir apparent contest took place for the post of minority whip when Charlie Stenholm of Texas opposed the outgoing majority whip, David Bonior (D.MI). In both contests a quarter of the Democratic Caucus registered dissatisfaction with the existing leadership by voting for their opponents.

In the Senate the retirement of George Mitchell (D.ME) required the selection of a minority leader. The contest between Tom Daschle and Christopher Dodd revealed no ideological fault-lines. Rather, voting alignments were defined more by regional and generational differences, and preferences over leadership style. Daschle drew support primarily from non-eastern and less experienced senators. Dodd's support included most eastern senators and committee chairs. Daschle, unlike most of his colleagues, had not served in the Senate minority in the first six years of the Reagan presidency. His one-vote margin hardly demonstrated overwhelming support. *conditional party leadership*

Congressional leaders are agents of the membership. The power they exercise is ceded to them by members. Lacking the support of significant minorities in their parties, Gephardt, Bonior and Daschle took over with very circumscribed authority. Assertive leadership, always constricted in the minority by the shortage of formal powers and informal resources, was improbable under such conditions.

Though also dependent upon members for grants of authority, the Republican leadership possessed greater personal resources to deploy on their party's behalf. In both chambers the outgoing minority leaders moved into the parallel majority party positions without a contest. In the Senate Robert Dole (R.KS) was leading his party for the tenth year, resuming the majority leadership post he had held in 1985–6. His presidential aspirations generated conflicting demands on time and brought him into competition with fellow senators with similar ambitions. But as the favourite to compete against Clinton, most other Republicans had a vested interest in his attempts to convert the Senate leadership into an electoral asset.

As the first Republican Speaker in 40 years, Newt Gingrich lacked governing experience, but he also embodied the party's ambition to escape from its prolonged minority status. Constructing a durable Republican majority in the electorate required legislative accomplishments which would depend upon skilful leadership. Gingrich entered office commanding the allegiance of his colleagues for his role in winning a majority for his party. Instrumental in mobilising the party behind the Contract With America, he had recruited candidates, raised funds and campaigned for a Republican Congress. Many in the large freshmen class were indebted to Gingrich for their election. (For a more detailed discussion of Gingrich's position within his party see the chapters by Owens and Sinclair in this volume.)

DEVISING STRATEGY

Jones identifies eight possible minority party strategies: support (of the majority), inconsequential opposition, withdrawal, cooperation (with the majority), innovation, consequential partisan opposition, consequential constructive opposition and participation (with the president).[11] A ninth strategy can be added to Jones's list, inaugurated after he wrote: 'bomb throwing'. Designed to harass, embarrass and discredit the majority, 'bomb throwing' was originated in the early 1980s by Gingrich and others in the Conservative Opportunity Society (COS). Little concerned with legislative substance, bomb throwing was aimed at the C-SPAN television audience and influencing their future voting behaviour.[12] Though bomb throwing was originated by junior members, it continued to be used by COS members when they were incorporated into the leadership suggesting that it had the sanction of a *party* strategy.

Conditions beyond the Democrats' control foreclosed two strategies. Clinton's retreat from legislative initiative and conspicuous displays of distance from congressional Democrats precluded a participation strategy. Secondly, cooperation was forestalled, at least in the House, by Republican cohesion which pre-empted the need for bipartisanship in majority-building. The ideological gap between the two parties rendered such an alliance politically impossible on many issues.

More assertive strategies require independence from the president and the congressional majority; they also require party unity to execute. For innovation the minority defines alternative priorities to the majority. For

consequential partisan opposition the minority resists the majority programme. For consequential constructive opposition the minority accepts
the majority's priorities but offers alternative solutions. At the inception of
the 104th Congress Democrats lacked the cohesion to pursue any of these
strategies. House Democrats differed over the appropriate response to the
Contract With America. Liberals, seeing the Contract as an onslaught on
the party's heritage, advocated all-out resistance. More moderate members
argued for a selective approach to the Contract, supporting some measures. They viewed resistance as undesirable on some issues, and unwise as
a strategy which might reinforce the party's image as an anachronism.
Either strategy risked deepening divisions. The former carried the risk of
stimulating conservative defections. Alabama Senator Richard Shelby had
already switched to the Republicans immediately following the elections.
Up to a dozen defections from the House Democratic Caucus were
rumoured at the opening of the 104th Congress. Though no defections
took place at the beginning of the session, five Democratic representatives
and one senator became Republican converts during 1995, providing the
leaderships with persistent reminders of the party's vulnerability in the
minority. Amid these tensions, reconciling Democrats to each other
assumed primacy over developing an immediate response to Republican
initiatives.

In both chambers Democratic leadership groups were enlarged to incor-
porate the losing side in the leadership elections. Daschle added seven senators to his leadership team, including several Dodd supporters. In the
House southern representation was strengthened in the minority leadership. Chet Edwards of Texas was appointed deputy chief whip. Stenholm,
the defeated candidate for minority whip, was one of two southerners
added to the leadership group.

Unifying efforts in the House involved frequent meetings to bring
Democrats together to find bases of agreement. Caucus meetings were
held once or twice a week. Twelve task forces were organised on subject
including welfare reform and immigration. Gephardt observed,

> We meet all day and all night – we're trying to get people to think not
> so much that they're legislating but that they are creating a message or
> an alternative that can be expressed to people over time, so that we
> can define Democrats and the Democratic Party in a positive and con-
> structive way.[13]

On one occasion when the House adjourned over Democratic objections,
instead of dispersing, Democrats staged an impromptu caucus. Other party

gatherings became foci for forging unity. Party retreats, which had been
in use for more than a decade, were transformed into forums for policy
discussion. Policy, previously devolved to committee fiefdoms, was
opened for discussion. Personal relations became less structured once
control was lost over committee and subcommittee leadership positions. In
these settings members found scope for defining what the Democrats stood
for, deprived of what had become the party's *raison d'être*: control of
Congress. Preoccupied with exercising power the party's programmatic
purpose had been obscured. Forced to discuss what the party represented,
members rediscovered why they shared a party identity which enhanced
their ability to work together in the future.

But this interaction within the party was still being developed whilst
much of the Contract passed the House. The unity which would permit
support for a common programme or strategy was lacking. Speaking in
January 1995, Gephardt anticipated it would take 4–6 months to formulate
an alternative. Some Republican initiatives solidified Democrats into
opposition, defending Medicare, Social Security and education against
cuts. For liberals a defensive response was sufficient when cherished programmes were under attack. According to Bill Clay of Missouri, 'We're
not offering any new initiatives. We're just trying to protect what is
there.'[4] Months later – after Gephardt's deadline for the formulation of an
alternative had passed – some liberals remained content with a negative
strategy. Pete Stark (D.CA) argued, 'The reason we don't have an alternative is we don't need one.'[15]

Moderates exhibited less sympathy for a purely defensive strategy.
Believing that Republicans had captured voter support by offering reform
to a discontented electorate, a negative Democratic response risked
confirming the party's image as defenders of a discredited status quo.
The conservative Blue Dog group, consisting of two dozen representatives
committed to moderating the party's liberal image, sought to develop constructive alternatives to Republican initiatives. According to Blue Dog
Gary Condit of California, 'We cannot consistently get away with just
criticising ... We have to be solution-oriented.'[16]

On occasions in 1995, Blue Dog proposals filled the vacuum left by
the absence of an alternative programme emanating from the leadership.
A conspicuous success in unifying the party behind a Blue Dog programme was the version of welfare reform developed by Nathan Deal
(D.GA). Unlike Republican reform, Deal's plan preserved entitlements
to public assistance for the poor. It was supported on the floor by a
unanimous Democratic party, falling 13 votes short of passing in March
1995.

Unable to concert a partisan response to Republican proposals, the House Democratic leadership deployed bomb throwing methods in an effort to undermine the majority leadership. Undertaken by individuals, its effectiveness does not depend upon backing from a united party. Thus bomb throwing allowed liberals to use aggressive tactics which neither required the support of moderates nor alienated them by opposing the substance of the majority's programme. Attacks were made on the conduct of the Republican leadership rather than its reformist agenda. Focus of these needling tactics was Speaker Newt Gingrich. Charging ethics violations in the use of campaign funds and income from publishing royalties, Gingrich was subjected to the hectoring methods he had deployed in his ultimately successful campaign to depose Speaker Jim Wright in the late 1980s. Some Democrats envisaged disruption of the Republican legislative programme if Gingrich could be politically disabled. According to George Miller of California, 'Newt is the nerve center and energy source. Going after him is like trying to take out command and control.'[17]

Consensus-building efforts during 1995 yielded alternative Democratic agendas in each house in 1996. *Expanding America's Greatness*, issued by Senate Democrats, recommended initiatives on workers' rights, education, health care, crime and the environment. Legislative commitments derived from the document included increasing the minimum wage and providing for pensions' portability. Daschle rationalised the programme in terms which define a consequential constructive opposition strategy: 'Our sole purpose is not to oppose the Republican agenda, but to propose one ourselves.'[18]

House Democrats devised the *Families First* programme. A 21-point programme promised enhanced assistance through the tax system to finance child care, medical insurance portability, tax incentives to invest in education and job training. Like its Senate counterpart, *Families First* evinced a focus on the economic security of working Americans. Both plans were designed to differentiate Democrats from their previous concerns with minorities and the underprivileged. Campaigning on *Families First* issues in the 1996 elections, Gephardt conceded, 'We're all New Democrats now.'[19] Notwithstanding the party's clear intention to reposition itself towards the centre, both plans sought to distinguish Democrats from Republicans, using rather than reducing government, and attending to the concerns of middle-class Americans rather than the wealthy and businesses, who were regarded as the principal beneficiaries of Contract programmes. Both programmes served primarily electoral objectives. Polling evidence informed their preparation in the search for vote-winning commitments. They were not intended as a guide to Democratic action during the 104th Congress, which was more than half-way through by the time the plans were released. Rather, they were intended to win votes to regain the majority which would then enable the programmes to be enacted.

So, by the spring of 1996 the minority Democrats in each chamber had devised platforms. This programmatic strategy contrasts sharply with customary minority practice which had rarely made a constructive contribution to policy-making.[20] In the past constructive contributions had rarely been attempted. Where they were, they were usually confined to particular issues rather than entire platforms. The inception of a strategy of innovation by the minority gave the Democrats the appearance of a British-style Opposition, deploying an alternative programme both inside and outside Congress, to distinguish itself from the majority and cultivate popular support. The parallels are imperfect in that without the party controls over candidate selection or campaign finance, the congressional party cannot enforce use of the platform in elections or adherence to it in office. But the development of congressional platforms signalled efforts to nationalise elections, aimed at modifying the parochial, candidate-centred character of modern electioneering. Tip O'Neill's maxim that 'All politics is local' is losing its validity.

MEDIA AND MESSAGE

Like bomb throwing, platforms demonstrated the sensitivity of the minority Democrats to their public image. Deprived of control over legislation, the Democratic leadership sensed that it was more feasible to influence the public rather than legislation. Caucus chair Vic Fazio articulated the shift of emphasis necessitated by the loss of majority status: '[As the minority] we don't control the agenda. We don't control the votes. We're not able to write legislation ... We have to do the best we can and focus on what message we're sending out.'[21]

On becoming the minority the Democratic leadership increased the emphasis on public communication. Daschle established the Technology and Communications Committee to coordinate the Senate Democratic leadership's public relations effort. In the House, Gephardt founded a message group designed to relate tactics on the floor to the image the party wished to transmit to the public. Existing organisations, such as the whip operation, assumed more responsibility for external relations. Task forces, previously used only to mobilise votes on the floor, became responsible for devising policy ideas. Minority Whip Bonior's responsibility for mobilising votes switched from the floor to the electorate: 'My role will be to emphasise the message which we are trying to convey to the American people.'[22]

In order to counteract conservative bias in radio talk shows, House Democrats sought opportunities to give interviews. A team of 30 House Democrats, trained in presentation, was deployed by the leadership to offer a Democratic interpretation of events. The House floor was used to score party political points for public consumption. One-minute speeches and Special Orders were used for bomb throwing opportunities, scandalising Gingrich's finances and Republican extremism. Like their predecessors in the minority, amendments were offered on subjects such as the overhaul of environmental regulation, less in the expectation that they would be adopted, more to expose the majority's resistance to popular causes. These methods, revealing the Democrats' change of role from controlling legislative output to acting as a public watchdog, were summarised by James McDermott (D.WA):

'You have to come to understand your role as a minority, which is to point out what the majority's up to rather than to spend hours and hours trying to carefully draft what you want to have passed.[23]

Media events were staged outside Congress to expose the majority's unpopular legislation. When Republicans voted for cuts in the school lunch programme, House Democratic leaders urged members to visit their local schools at meal times to draw media attention to the effect of Republican initiatives. After House Democrats walked out of Medicare hearings, complaining that insufficient discussion was being allowed, they subsequently convened their own hearing on the Capitol lawn to publicise their support for the programme.[24]

NEITHER LEGISLATING NOR TOGETHER

As the previous chapter has shown, the bilateral responsibility for legislating shared between president and Congress was untypically lopsided in 1995–6. Clinton ceded influence over the congressional agenda to the Republican majority. Moreover, the White House reduced its attempts to affect legislative output, particularly in the House where throughout 1995 Republican unity precluded presidential influence. Clinton's abdication of legislative agenda-setting depleted his party's influence in Congress. The president denied his party a programme to rally around to influence the legislative process. Clinton's retreat created the programmatic vacuum which his party struggled for a year to fill. When Democrats did offer an alternative, such as the Deal welfare reform bill, the White House did not lobby for its passage.

To reaffirm his credentials as a New Democrat in time for the 1996 election, Clinton needed a public divorce from the 'Old' Democrats on Capitol Hill. None of the congressional party was informed prior to Clinton's announcement of his commitment to a balanced budget in June 1995. His admission that Medicare spending could be cut without reducing benefits effectively disrupted congressional Democrats' campaign to defend the programme against Republican attacks. The strategic gap between Clinton and his party was evinced in the comment of the chair of the Democratic Congressional Campaign Committee, Martin Frost (D.TX): 'The Democratic Leadership will proceed as if the president's speech never occurred.'[25] Others perceived intent in the outcry his announcement provoked within his own party. George Miller of California observed, 'I think Clinton *wanted* a pretty sound chorus of Democratic anger.'[26] The antagonisms between Clinton and the congressional party eased during the protracted struggle over the FY 1996 budget. Daschle and Gephardt were recruited to the White House team negotiating with Gingrich, Dole and others. Whilst some Democrats were never reconciled to a balanced budget, most congressional Democrats applauded Clinton's resistance to the severity of proposed Republican cuts in social and environmental programmes. Senate Democratic leaders collaborated with the White House in devising a balanced budget which made smaller cuts in taxes and social programmes. As relations between Clinton and the Republican leadership polarised during the budget *impasse*, so the president's liberal credentials were restored. A White House aide observed:

> The need or ability to triangulate has lessened. You can't easily triangulate on Medicare. The more this became up or down on specific issues, the more the president took traditional Democratic positions.[27]

Reconciliation between the president and his party was also eased by the revival in their popularity whilst that of Republicans declined. Clinton's re-election prospects rose. Association with him became an electoral asset to his party in Congress. Election pressures stimulated

Democrats to back compromises negotiated between the president and the Republican majority. Welfare reform, twice passed against Democratic opposition and vetoed by Clinton, won the support of most of Democratic senators and half of House Democrats when passed at the third time of asking. Clinton's support provided protective cover for Democrats needing a legislative record while avoiding the antipathy of the party's traditional constituency.

Roll calls, posing stark 'yes' or 'no' alternatives, do not show triangulation at work. We hypothesise that a roll call strategy of triangulation could consist of: fluctuations in the president's support across different votes, revealing no consistent alliances; support from majorities in both parties; opposition from majorities of both parties. Any of these outcomes would blur the president's partisan and ideological identity. In fact, Clinton's support *was* partisan. Democratic majorities rarely opposed him, Republican majorities rarely supported him (see Table 7.1). Presidential support scores calculated by *Congressional Quarterly* show Clinton in 1995 to have stronger partisan identity than most post-war presidents. Compared to most of his predecessors, Clinton enjoyed higher than average support from his own party; support from the opposition party was abnormally low. Triangulation, therefore, did not reverse the intensified partisanship originating under Reagan.

interesting

Table 7.1   Congressional majorities supporting President Clinton, 104th Congress

| | Percentage of roll call votes on which | | | | |
	Only majority of Democrats supported Clinton	Majorities of both parties supported Clinton	Only majority of Republicans supported Clinton	Minorities of both parties supported Clinton	All roll call votes on which Clinton took a position
House	74.3	17.3	3.6	4.7	100.0
Senate	69.8	23.5	4.7	2.9	100.0

Notes: Includes only roll calls on which the president took a position.
Source: *Congressional Quarterly Weekly Report*, various dates.

This operationalizat. of 'triangulation' is flawed. a better measure: to those used that Clint. compromi., struck deals w/ Repub., that maj. of Dem. then opposed?

MINORITY INFLUENCE

In a period of consensus politics and stable partisanship amongst the electorate, like the 1950s, the congressional minority may both accept its fate
and cooperate with the majority on legislation. Such conditions were
absent from the 104th Congress. Embittered partisanship, and a possible
watershed in electoral preferences in congressional elections, contributed
to a hostile minority, aggrieved and intolerant of its new status, alienated
by much of the House Republican programme. When Democrats mustered
the unity to define a party response the objective was to block, modify or
displace the Republican agenda. Combining these insider strategies with
external attempts to mobilise campaign resources and influence public
opinion, the Democrats aimed to recapture a majority at the first attempt.
Our measures of minority success therefore employ an internal standard of
resistance to Republican legislation and an external standard of
Democratic electoral performance in 1996.

Internal Unity

The capacity for resisting the majority's legislation is facilitated by
minority unity. But, as discussed above, that unity was lacking at the
opening of the 104th Congress. House Democrats' disarray precluded a
united response to the Contract in the first 100 days. In time greater
cohesion developed as many Republican measures challenged
Democratic priorities and past achievements. On roll calls which, by
posing stark 'yea' or 'nay' alternatives, tend to funnel diversity into an
appearance of cohesion, party unity votes were more common in 1995
than at any time since *Congressional Quarterly* began compiling records
in 1954. Compared to previous minorities, the Democrats demonstrated
higher than average cohesion. On *Congressional Quarterly*'s measure of
party unity for 1995, Democratic senators averaged 81 per cent and their
party's representatives 80 per cent. Both figures show a fall in unity of
only 3 per cent compared to 1994, when the party was in the majority.
However, the effectiveness of such unity in resisting majority legislation was constrained by the even greater cohesion amongst Republicans.
The Senate majority averaged 89 per cent party unity while that of
House Republicans averaged 91 per cent. The Democrats displayed
above-average cohesion for a minority but, inferior in both numbers and
unity compared with the Republican majority, the party was usually
defeated on roll calls (Table 7.2).

Table 7.2 Democratic victories on party unity votes, 104th Congress

| | Percentage of party unity votes won by Democrats | |
	House	Senate
1995	11.6	18.2
1996	18.8	30.9

Source: *Congressional Quarterly Weekly Report*, 21 December 1996; *Congressional Roll Call 1995* (Washington, D.C.: Congressional Quarterly, 1996).

Influencing Legislation

Floor defeats of Republican measures were confined to the uncommon occurrence of greater minority than majority cohesion or votes requiring exceptional majorities for passage where minority cohesion was sufficient to ensure defeat. The most prominent example of the former occurred in the 1996 House vote on campaign finance reform when a unanimous Democratic Party allied with a minority of Republicans to defeat the bill on final passage. More common was Democratic success on constitutional amendments, veto overrides and cloture motions, where a united minority frequently deprived the Republicans of the extraordinary majorities needed to prevail. Constitutional amendments on flag desecration and balanced budgets (where a single Republican defection was crucial) were defeated with most Democrats in opposition. Clinton first used the veto during the 104th Congress, seeking to negate 17 bills passed with predominantly Republican support. The magnitude of Democratic opposition on final passage deterred efforts to override most vetoes. Of six attempts put to a vote Democratic majorities opposed five, prevailing on each occasion. In the Senate, Democratic cohesion was usually sufficient to be cloture-proof. More attempts to invoke cloture were made in the 104th Congress than at any time since the procedure was adopted in 1917. Of 50 attempts, only six succeeded, the lowest success rate in more than a quarter of a century. Confronted by concerted minority obstruction the Republican leadership withdrew bills on term limits and regulatory overhaul after the attempts to terminate debate failed.

The more deliberative pace of Senate business, the pivotal votes of Republican moderates, the limited enthusiasm of some in the majority for the *House* Republican Contract, norms of bipartisanship and mutual *tries to estab. influence of Democ. minority on legislat. But methodolog. problems vitiate*

accommodation and greater procedural opportunities for minority resistance assisted Democratic senators in attempts to block conservative measures. In addition to filibusters, Democrats in the second session procrastinated over the appointment of conferees. Such tactics not only obstructed enactment of bills which had passed both houses, but also pressured House Republicans into concessions to enable conferences to proceed. One such success was the removal of House-passed caps on medical liability claims from the conference report on the Kassebaum–Kennedy revisions to medical insurance. The dilatory proceedings of the Senate outraged the dedicated conservatives in the House. Frustrated Representative Mark Souder of Indiana condemned the upper house as 'the biggest graveyard in America'.

To assess Democratic influence on legislation three measures are employed. A qualitative analysis is pursued though the examination of the content of 14 major bills which passed both houses. Two quantitative measures are adopted to gauge the minority impact. The first counts Democratic support for House amendments. The second counts Democratic support in each chamber for bills on final passage.

typo /h

poor measures

The 14 bills chosen for detailed examination passed both houses and proposed substantial changes in policy. Democratic influence was classed as 'minor', 'moderate' or 'dominant' on the basis of information obtained from reports in *Congressional Quarterly Weekly Report*. 'Minor' registers the minority's inability to shape bills' objectives and the costs of proposed policy. Minority influence is confined to detail. The final outcomes were expressions of majority will. A Democratic majority would not have produced such bills. For 'moderate' influence to be exerted the individual Democrats or the party collectively modified the objectives or costs of the policy as defined by the majority. The minority succeeded in limiting majority will. For the minority to be the 'dominant' influence requires Democrats to have shaped the objectives and costs of proposed policy. Such a bill would not have passed if the Republican majority had been dominant (see Table 7.3).

Marginal more appropr. than minor

The seven instances of *minor* Democratic influence *marginal* were characterised by Republican unity, Senate deference to House initiatives, passage through both houses during 1995 and, with one exception, derivation from or consistency with the commitments in the Contract With America. The ending of unfunded mandates, inauguration of a line-item veto and the reform of welfare were express Contract commitments, evoking House Republican solidarity around manifesto commitments. Many Democrats were sympathetic to the ending of unfunded mandates, though liberals feared the depletion of public health and environmental services which they

These 2 measures do not measure minority party's impact on content of legislation

were votes partisan or not ?

Table 7.3 Democratic party influence on the content of selected legislation, 104th Congress

Legislation and degree of Democratic influence	Percentage of Democrats Voting for Final Passage		
	House	Senate	Clinton Veto
Minor Influence *Marginal/no influence*			
Unfunded mandates	64%	78%	No
Line-item veto/enhanced rescissions	35	41	No
7-year balanced budget	4	0	NA
Reconciliation FY 1996	2	0	Yes
Debt limit extention	2	0	Yes
Late-term abortions	37	25	Yes
Welfare reform I	3	76	Yes
Moderate Influence			
Bosnia troop deployment	33	98	NA
Product liability	23	33	Yes
Telecommunications deregulation	50	65	No
Farm bill — *Rep. were divided*	29	43	No
Welfare reform II	15	30	No
Health insurance portability	20	100	No
Dominant Influence			
Minimum wage increase	97	100	No

Source: *Congressional Quarterly Weekly Reports*, various dates.

sought, with little success, to insulate from coverage under the legislation. Both the principle and form of the line-item veto divided congressional Democrats. Senator Robert Byrd (D.WV) engaged in a failed attempt to preserve the constitutional authority of Congress over the budget by a filibuster. Of the two forms of line-item veto that were passed it was the House-passed expedited rescisions, less attractive to Democrats than the Senate's separate enrollment of Appropriations provisions, which emerged from conference. A private conference which excluded Democrats exemplified the majority's monopoly over the final version of the bill.

On welfare reform Democrats in each chamber introduced alternative versions of reform. Both sought to retain the entitlement to assistance and were defeated on near-perfect party-line votes. Both bills that passed ended guaranteed aid. The House bill's more austere provisions for ending aid to legal immigrants and allowing the states to proscribe aid to unmarried mothers under 18, emerged from conference. The bill was vetoed by Clinton.

Budget reconciliation, raising the debt limit and eliminating the deficit by 2002 were weapons in the Republican armoury in the confrontation with Clinton over the budget for FY 1996. These mechanisms became alternative means to realising the Contract aim of a balanced budget once the constitutional amendment promised in the Contract failed in the Senate. Opposed to Republican budgetary priorities, Democrats achieved near-unanimity in their failed attempts to defeat the proposals on regular passage.

Alternative budgets offered by Democrats moderating the severity of the cuts to social spending in the Republican bills were defeated. Both debt limit extension and reconciliation were vetoed by the president. (The requirement that the budget be balanced in seven years, framed as a resolution, was not presented to the president.)

The ban on late-term abortions provides the only example of minor influence which was unconnected to the Contract With America. Republicans were more united in favour of the ban than Democrats were in opposition. Democratic opponents of the ban worked to insert amendments creating exemptions from the ban but were regularly defeated. The bill was vetoed by the president.

Democrats exerted moderate influence on six items. They were distinguishable from the minor category in eliciting less intense partisanship, and only one derived from the Contract. They also registered a stronger influence from the more bipartisan, less conservative Senate. Legislative work on most of the bills was concentrated in 1996 after the uncompromising assertiveness of House Republicans had peaked.

On the farm bill and telecommunications overhaul both parties were divided by constituency interests, producing alliances across party lines. Members of both parties opposed the House Republican leadership Freedom to Farm plan to phase out many subsidies within seven years. A Democratic filibuster extracted concessions in the Senate to retain subsidies for conservation, nutrition and rural development. Support from a minority of House Democrats was crucial to provide majorities to preserve sugar and peanut subsidies.

Telecommunications reform had been attempted by the Democratic Congress, indicating that the issue enjoyed bipartisan support. Both in the Senate and in conference Ernest Hollings (D.SC) succeeded in tempering the legislation's deregulatory thrust. Democrats succeeded in pressing for the introduction of the V-chip to allow parents to regulate the type of cable television programmes accessible to their children. The timing of entry of the regional Bell companies into the long-distance market was a compromise between Republican senators' preferences for setting a deadline and Democrats' demand for regulation by the Justice Department. The final version provided for control by the Federal Communications Commission with advice from the Justice Department.

On the other four items, Senate Democrats moderated the radicalism of House Republicans. The Senate version of health insurance portability was a bipartisan effort, known after its co-sponsors as Kassebaum–Kennedy, chair and ranking minority member of the Labour and Human Resources Committee. The bill passed the Senate with unanimous support, whereas the House version divided members along party lines. In conference, measures objectionable to Democrats in the House bill were removed or muted. Caps on medical malpractice lawsuits were dropped and medical savings accounts confined to a pilot programme.

In the 1996 version of welfare reform, Democrats pressed unsuccessfully to preserve guarantees of assistance. But on other aspects Democrats gained bargaining power from the White House threats of vetoes (two versions of reform having already failed when opposed by the president). Under Democratic pressure Medicaid was dropped from the House bill. In the Senate an amendment proposed by Kent Conrad (D.ND) was adopted, excluding food stamps from state control. In conference Democratic demands won concessions on vouchers for children of parents removed from welfare and a requirement that states opt into (rather than out of) the 'family cap', denying increased aid for children born to mothers on welfare.

Product liability reform, like telecommunications reform, had died in Democratic congresses. Several Democrats were proponents of reform, notably Senator Jay Rockefeller (D.WV) who co-sponsored a narrow version of liability restriction with Slade Gorton (R.WA). House Republicans backed a broader bill, restricting a wider range of consumer and client rights than Rockefeller–Gorton. Attempts to pass a broader bill in the Senate encountered a Democratic filibuster. In the face of Democratic opposition the Senate passed, and the conference adopted, a narrow version of reform. Clinton subsequently vetoed the bill.

The use of US troops in Bosnia enjoyed little support in Congress. But Democrats pressed to preserve the president's discretion in foreign policy. Many House Republicans sought to exclude American forces from peacekeeping or implementing the peace accords in Bosnia by denying the funds for such a mission. In the Senate a bipartisan alliance defeated a funding ban. In the House Democrats provided four-fifths of the votes which defeated a funding ban by eight votes. The resolutions which passed expressed the concern of Congress at the participation of American troops (some units were already in Bosnia), but did not prohibit their involvement.

Democrats were dominant only on legislation to raise the minimum wage. The minority temporarily gained control over the congressional agenda, enabling Democrats to initiate legislation rather than react to majority proposals. Senate Democrats exploited a lapse in majority control in filling the amendment 'tree' to introduce the minimum wage increase as an amendment to an unrelated bill. Support for the measure from 80 per cent of the public weighed on Republicans facing re-election in 1996. Sympathetic moderate Republicans, presidential support and a lobbying campaign by organised labour increased the pressures for passage. Faced by a filibuster, Senate Democrats retaliated by blocking the progress of gas tax repeal and adding minimum wage amendments to a succession of unrelated bills. When Republican blocking efforts were abandoned bills passed in both houses on a measure described by House Majority Leader Armey as 'the dread minimum wage increase'.

The success of minority-backed amendments on roll calls can be used as a quantitative measure of Democratic influence in the House. Duplicating Rohde's methodology in an earlier study provides a comparative measure of success between the Democrats in 1995–6 and their Republican predecessors in the minority in earlier congresses. It examines first-order amendments adopted in the House by non-consensual votes (at least 10 per cent of the vote cast in opposition). Democratic-favoured amendments are defined as those supported by a larger majority of Democrats than Republicans. Democratic-favoured amendments accounted for 41 per cent of the total in the 104th Congress. In the period 1971–88, Republican minorities favoured 40 per cent of amendments in just two Houses. The Democrats were then an untypically successful minority in the 104th House,[28] although Democratic influence on bills rarely penetrated the core of the Republican programme, the Contract With America.

A second quantitative measure provides an indirect gauge of minority influence in shaping legislation. The assumption is that the greater the support from the minority on final passage, the more legislation reflects their demands. In the 104th House only 7.3 per cent of votes on final passage were Democratic-favoured in that they commanded wider support amongst the minority than the majority. Whilst broader majority support is unsurprising, the rarity of minority favoured bills in the House was low measured against earlier congresses for which Rohde's work provides a comparison. For the 17 congresses between 1955 and 1988 minority-favoured bills on final passage fell below 10 per cent on only four occasions.

Most bills passed by non-consensual votes in the 104th Congress were opposed by a majority of Democrats. Only 33 per cent of bills coming to a vote in the House and 40 per cent of those in the Senate were passed with

a Democratic majority in favour. Reflecting the partisanship of the contemporary Congress, such figures reveal the inability of the minority to
block or modify most bills to command the support of the minority party.

Winning the Next Election

The second form of measurement for Democratic success is based on
what Jones identifies as the objective of the minority: becoming the
majority. The Democratic leadership in both houses appreciated from
early in 1995 the potential for using Congress as a public relations platform to revive the party's election prospects. By 1996 congressional
Democrats' popularity had recovered sufficiently to threaten Republican
control after just two years, as in 1948 and 1954. Democrats thrived upon
conditions not of their own making, benefiting from the public's reproach
of the majority for government shutdowns and the revival of Clinton's
popularity. Government closures confirmed the Democratic message of
an extremist majority. In the middle of 1996, generic polls showed
Democrats with a 10 per cent lead in congressional voting intentions.
Democratic campaign efforts were assisted by the AFL-CIO, which
invested more heavily in the congressional elections than ever before, and
by environmental groups alienated by the deregulatory majority.

In the House campaigns Democratic efforts focused on Republican
freshmen and women. Their zeal in support of the Contract and confrontation with Clinton over the budget helped to portray them as extremists.
They were also vulnerable as marginal winners in 1994. Almost two-thirds
of the Republican freshmen had been elected with under 55 per cent of the
vote. Disadvantaging the Democratic campaign for both chambers was the
preponderance of Democrats amongst the retiring incumbents. In the
Senate incumbent retirements exposed four seats in the South where victories for the party in open seats have been rare over the last two decades.

Most Republicans proved adept in exploiting the advantages of incumbency, campaigning with funding advantages over their Democratic opponents. During 1996 some members moderated their conservative records,
supporting popular causes like the minimum wage increase, pursuing pork
barrel projects instead of radical budget cuts and distancing themselves from
the unpopular Gingrich. They also ran constituency-oriented campaigns,
ignoring the Contract. Democrats were hampered by the majority's incumbent advantages, the exposure of Democratic open seats, the limits to
Clinton's appeal in the presidential contest despite a divided and unattractive
opposition, and a grudging public contentment with the status quo, militating
against a desire for change. That nearly half of Republican House freshmen

experienced a decline in their share of the vote, quelling the 'sophomore surge', registers success for Democratic campaign efforts. That only a fifth of the freshmen/women were defeated demonstrates its limitations.

CONCLUSION

Since Democrats had last served in the minority, majority cohesion and control had intensified. Largely denied participation in the legislative process, House Democrats borrowed opposition methods patented by their Republican predecessors. Bomb throwing, and the cultivation of public opinion through an expanded media operation – the search for power in the future where influence in the present was inaccessible – resemble Gingrich's practice of minority politics prior to 1995. Even a large minority like the House Democrats in the 104th Congress struggled to affect legislation against a cohesive majority utilising its controls over procedure. Although House Democrats had some successes in winning adoption of their amendments they were usually achieved with the support of most Republicans. In the Senate, Democrats were still able to constrain what the majority could attain. Bicameralism was reinforced by party politics as Senate Democrats enforced moderation or defeat on House Republican initiatives.

Both on the floor and in their public relations campaigns Democrats adopted a confrontational approach towards the Republican agenda. But Democrats made their accommodations with the majority's conservatism. The principle of a balanced budget was accepted. Though federal mandates proliferated under Democratic congresses many in the party supported their curtailment. One of the legacies of the New Deal, the guarantee of aid to poor mothers and children, was abandoned with backing from nearly half the congressional party.

Having failed to regain control at the first attempt, Democrats have to experience their most extended period in the minority since the 1920s. The probability of mid-term setbacks for the president's party in 1998, and the exposure of a majority of Democratic-controlled Senate seats, may well prolong the party's minority status into the twenty-first century. But the context of minority politics is likely to change in the party's favour in that time. The cohesion of the majority is unlikely to persist at the levels obtaining during the 104th Congress – in the absence of a platform to unite the party and the leadership resources Gingrich commanded in 1995. Democrats will remain the minority for several years but strategic opportunities are likely to change during that time allowing different styles of minority politics to develop.

NOTES

1. Charles O. Jones, *The Minority Party in Congress* (Boston: Little, Brown, 1970).
2. David B. Truman, *The Congressional Party. A Case Study* (New York: Wiley, 1959); David W. Rohde, *Parties and Leaders in the Postreform House* (Chicago and London: The University of Chicago Press, 1991); William Connolly, Jr and John J. Pitney, *Congress's Permanent Minority. Republicans in the US House* (Lanham, MD: Rowman and Littlefield, 1994).
3. Rohde, *Parties and Leaders*; Steven S. Smith, *Call to Order: Floor Politics in the House and Senate* (Washington, D.C.: The Brookings Institution, 1989); Barbara Sinclair, *Legislators, Leaders, and Lawmaking: The U.S. House of Representatives in the Postreform Era* (Baltimore and London: Johns Hopkins University Press, 1995).
4. Rohde, *Parties and Leaders*, p. 128.
5. Quoted in George Hager, 'Furor Over Spending Bill Promises a Stormy Summer', *Congressional Quarterly Weekly Report*, 15 July 1995, p. 2043.
6. Elizabeth Drew, *Showdown: The Struggle Between the Gingrich Congress and the Clinton White House* (New York: Simon and Schuster, 1996), pp. 18–19.
7. Alan I. Abramowitz and Suzie Ishikawa, 'Explaining the Republican Takeover of the House of Representatives: Evidence from the 1992–94 NES Panel Survey'. Paper presented to the annual meeting of the American Political Science Association, Chicago, 31 August–3 September 1995.
8. William G. Mayer, *The Divided Democrats: Ideological Unity, Party Reform, and Presidential Elections* (Boulder, CO and Oxford: Westview Press, 1996), ch. 5.
9. Mayer, *The Divided Democrats*, pp. 87–9; Byron E. Shafer and William J. M. Claggett, *The Two Majorities: The Issue Context of Modern American Politics* (Baltimore and London: Johns Hopkins University Press, 1995).
10. Truman, *The Congressional Party*, p. 312.
11. Jones, *The Minority Party in Congress*, ch. 2.
12. Connolly and Pitney, *Congress' Permanent Minority*, pp. 27–30.
13. Drew, *Showdown*, p. 74.
14. Eliza Newlin Carney, 'Don't Count Us Out', *National Journal*, 29 April 1995, pp. 1022–7.
15. Jackie Koszczuk, 'Democrats Find Strength, Unity in Anger over Medicare Plans', *Congressional Quarterly Weekly Report*, 23 September 1995, pp. 1899–2900.
16. Richard E. Cohen, 'On the Mend?', *National Journal*, 9 September 1995, p. 2211.
17. Drew, *Showdown*, p. 74.
18. *The Hill*, 6 March 1996.
19. Quoted in Martin Fletcher, 'President Tells Party Strategists to Focus Campaign on Congress Fight', *The Times*, 21 September 1996, p. 17.
20. Jones, *The Minority Party in Congress*, ch. 9.
21. Carney, 'Don't Count Us Out', p. 1024.

22. Gabriel Kahn, 'Bonior Overhauls His Whip Operation', *Roll Call*, 16 January 1995, p. 16.
23. Carney, 'Don't Count Us Out', p. 1027.
24. Paul S. Herrnson, 'Directing 535 Leading Men and Leading Ladies: Party Leadership in the Modern Congress', in Herbert Weisberg and Samuel C. Patterson, eds., *Great Theatre: The U.S. Congress* (forthcoming).
25. William Schneider, 'Political Pulse', *National Journal*, 13 June 1995, p. 1686.
26. Drew, *Showdown*, p. 236. Original emphasis.
27. Drew, *Showdown*, pp. 358–9.
28. Rohde, *Parties and Leaders*, pp. 156–8.

8 Republican Rule in the 80th Congress
Anthony Badger

'And so died the New Deal! ... For more than thirteen years it has regimented and restricted the country, but now it passes.' In such triumphal and confident terms on 7 November 1946, the *Detroit News* celebrated the mid-term election results. Republicans had taken over control of Congress, by a margin of 246 to 188 in the House and 51 to 45 in the Senate.

In January 1995 veteran New York liberal and former ambassador to the United Nations, William vanden Heuvel was asked to address the Mid-Year Institute of Oklahoma City University on the 1994 elections. He started:

A beleaguered president looks over the election results and wonders about his future – and what precisely was the message the electorate was delivering. The Senate falling to the Republican party was an anticipated possibility, but for the Republicans to take 55 seats from the Democrats – thereby taking control of the House of Representatives was a shock – unexpected, undesired, and unanticipated. The president would now have not only the Republicans in control of the Congress but – even worse – the archenemies of his legislative objectives taking control of the congressional committees. The election was hardly over before leaders in his own party began calling for him to step aside. Other leaders in the Democratic party began talking openly of supporting the country's most famous military hero – although the general's political identification was far from certain. With the decline of his popularity confirmed by the election results and the falling polls, with his party defeated and defeatist, with fellow Democrats avoiding him and many calling for him not to run again, with the Republicans well-financed and supremely confident of their growing power, what course would the president take?[1]

Vanden Heuvel, of course, had to explain to his young audience that he was talking about 1946, Harry Truman and Dwight Eisenhower not 1994, Bill Clinton and Colin Powell,

THE 1946 ELECTIONS

There was no doubting Harry Truman's political unpopularity in November 1946. The Gallup Poll showed that his approval ratings had sunk from 82 per cent in January to 32 per cent. Democratic candidates and party officials warned him to stay out of sight in the 1946 campaign. Rather than have Truman address the electorate, party leaders preferred to have Roosevelt speak. In one of a series of 9-minute radio commercials, a discussion of the meat shortage, a voice said, 'Here's what President Roosevelt had to say about it' – even though the beef shortage had developed after Roosevelt died. Truman had singularly failed to extend the New Deal reforms. His imperious demands for virtually the full programme of Roosevelt's unfinished business from the Economic Bill of Rights, demands unsustained by detailed or serious congressional liaison, foundered, as his predecessor's reform demands had done since 1938, on the rock of the bipartisan conservative coalition of Republicans and southern Democrats. More important, Truman had been undone by the politics of inflation. In the deflationary conditions of the 1930s, New Deal policies had been politically popular because economic necessity demanded rewarding powerful interest groups.

In the inflationary climate of the Second World War restraints could be imposed on those groups by appealing to patriotism and invoking emergency powers. The end of the war unleashed pent-up consumer demand, but industry struggled to reconvert to domestic production sufficiently quickly to satisfy that demand. The politics of inflation demanded that the government restrain, not reward, powerful interest groups, thus the Administration soon fell foul of key elements of the Democratic coalition most notably and personally in Truman's case, organised labour.[2]

In January 1995, vanden Heuvel told students: 'Tonight, I predict Bill Clinton will be re-elected as president in November 1996.' In January 1947, statistician Louis Bean outlined the conditions in which the Democrats could win in 1948. Bean laid the blame for the Democratic failure firmly at the door of rising living costs. He noted that pre-election polls for the American Institute of Public Opinion gave no hint that the electorate wanted to dismantle the New Deal. The most important issue for voters was the issue of control of inflation, followed in descending order of importance by peace, and labour and strikes. He noted that the Republican share of the vote in 1946 only modestly rose in farm states such as Kansas and Nebraska. It rose dramatically and accounted for most of the 55 House seat gains in the heavy goods industry states such as Ohio and Michigan where workers found their purchasing power eroded most by increased prices. Voters had not switched to the Republicans in large numbers, rather they had refused to cast their ballots. Even allowing for the customary fall-off in voter turnout in mid-term elections, voters had stayed away in probably the largest numbers, both absolutely and relatively, since the First World War. Bean estimated that nine million voters stayed away – seven million Democrats and two million Republicans. Comparing the Democratic losses to losses sustained in 1938 and 1920 at times of recession, he predicted that a pick-up in the economy would lead to the return of the stay-away Democrats in 1948.[3]

Louis Bean's predictions were substantially correct. As for the Republicans, they certainly failed to dismantle the New Deal during the 80th Congress. They did secure, of course, a major revision of the country's basic industrial relations law, balancing the anti-employer thrust of the Wagner Act with the anti-labour thrust of Taft–Hartley, and they did engineer a tax cut. But what they did not do was more interesting. They resisted increases in the minimum wage but did not seek to repeal the Fair Labor Standards Act. They excluded newspaper and magazine vendors from social security coverage, but did not attempt to dismantle the Social Security Act. They resisted increased appropriations for soil conservation and for the purchase of increased storage bins by the Commodity Credit Corporation, but passed a farm act that perpetuated fixed price supports until 1950. They prevented the TVA building a steam plant, but made no effort to privatise it. In doing so, they made the 80th Congress in Harry Truman's words his 'Exhibit A' and the 'Do-Nothing Congress'. Republican Herbert Brownell was in no doubt that 'the 80th Congress defeated Dewey, not the Democrats ... the congressional leadership deserves credit for the 1948 Republican defeat.'[4]

Why did the Republican Congress fail to fulfil the high hopes of the *Detroit News*? Why was Harry Truman able to revive his political fortunes at its expense? The answers lie in the experience of the 80th Congress *and* the efforts of Truman.

THE 80TH REPUBLICAN CONGRESS

The Republicans had fought the 1946 election on the issue of 'Had Enough?' Government surveys during the war had indicated that the American people's post-war aspirations were 'compounded largely of 1929 values and the economics of the 1920, leavened with a hangover from the makeshift controls of the war.' What Republicans were able to exploit was the fact that a year after final victory in the war, Americans were still living under wartime controls, which had been nevertheless unable to stem inflationary pressures. The Republicans ran a relentless campaign against controls, in favour of tax cuts and against the excessive influence of communists in government. Paying federal income taxes was a relatively new experience for Americans: in the 1930s less than 5 per cent of the population paid them, but during the war the figure rose to 74 per cent. From early in the New Deal, conservatives had argued that the New Deal was 'communistic' and that the New Deal ideology was alien. In the late 1930s that charge was extended to the more specific one that many New Dealers were actually communists, owing their prime loyalty to a foreign power. The Republican campaign about the dangers of communism inherent in the New Deal were given much greater force by the international situation in 1946 as relations with Russia deteriorated. The Democrats' espousal of controls and taxes, according to the Republican message, reflected their totalitarian tendencies. As Senator Robert A. Taft (R.OH) alleged in the election, Truman wanted a Congress 'dominated by a policy of appeasing the Russians abroad and fostering Communism at home'.[5]

Leadership and the Committee System

The dominant Republican in the new 80th Congress was Taft ('Mr. Republican') although he did not occupy the politically perilous position of Senate Majority Leader. Taft was the son of former Republican president and Supreme Court Chief Justice William Howard Taft, and a former mayor of Cincinnati. His political career epitomised the revival of the Republican Party after Roosevelt's and the Democratic Party's landslide successes of 1936. After that election, Democrats controlled both Senate seats, the governorship, and 22 of the 24 Ohio congressional seats. The Republican revival started in 1938 when Taft was elected to the Senate and John Bricker (a future US senator) to the statehouse. After the 1946 election, Republicans controlled both Senate seats and 19 of the 23 House seats from Ohio. Taft believed that the New Deal was economic heresy, he deplored excessive government spending but he also opposed the New Deal for constitutional and moral reasons. It promoted excessive centralisation, giving the executive unwarranted power over the Congress, and Washington over the states. He particularly disliked the quasi-judicial status of regulatory agencies which he believed infringed the liberty of individual Americans. Taft did accept social security, the right to collective bargaining and the idea of a minimum wage, and he positively endorsed the idea of federal involvement in low-cost housing and federal assistance to education. But, in general, his Senate career had been built around his apparently limitless capacity for hard work, his partisan combativeness and his reputation for unrelenting opposition to the New Deal. 'There is only one way to beat the New Deal', he declared, 'and that is head on. You can't outdeal them.'[6]

In January 1947 Taft, at last, seemed to be in a position to beat the New Deal head on. He appeared to radiate confidence. The *New Republic* complained that Congress consisted of the House, the Senate and Bob Taft. Cabel Phillips reported that the Republicans in Congress were operating like a well-oiled machine. Taft dominated his party intellectually, but he owed his power base to more prosaic institutional considerations as well. He had been chair of the Senate Republican Policy Committee since 1944 and he was steadily building up both its staff and its budget. By allowing the self-important Arthur Vandenberg (R.MI) to take the lead in foreign policy on the committee, Taft retained virtually absolute control of the committee in domestic policy. The Legislative Reorganisation Act of 1946 also gave the Republican leadership room for manoeuvre in the allocation of committee chairmanships. The Act restricted both the number of committee assignments and the number of chairmanships individual members could hold. Taft was ranking Republican on both the Senate Finance and Labor and Public Welfare committees. Under the Act, he could choose just one committee to chair. He chose Labor and Public Welfare because otherwise George Aiken (R.VT) would have taken over and Taft rightly suspected that he would not be so uncompromising in revising the Wagner Act. He could rest easy on Finance because the chair there was taken by conservative ally, Eugene Milliken (R.CO). In the House, Speaker Joe Martin (R.MA) and Majority Leader Charlie Halleck (R.IN), in combination with Rules Committee chairman, Leo Allen (R.IL), ensured conservative control. Fiercely anti-union Fred Hartley (R.NJ) took over the Education and Labor Committee, and the more liberal Richard Welch (R.CA) was sidelined to Public Lands. At Appropriations, 'Meat-Axe' John Taber (R.NY) became chairman. Fierce critic of price and credit controls Jesse Wolcott (R.MI) controlled the House Banking and Currency Committee.[7]

Taft exercised great care in sorting out committee chairmanships because committees continued to be the key to congressional government. Through the 1940s and 1950s, as Jim Wright who went to Congress a few years later noted, 'the committee structure is perhaps the most vital organ in the lawmaking body. It is like the heart which by continuing to pump keeps the blood flowing in the human body.'[8] Committee chairmen could bottle up legislation they did not like. In turn, the Rules

Committee, dominated by conservative Republicans and southern Democrats, could prevent legislation from those committees reaching the floor. Committee chairmen who had acquired the positions through the seniority system had an independent power base: junior members of the committee relied on their goodwill for the success of legislative proposals they favoured. Even when the chair lost a vote in committee, he could go to the Rules Committee, as Jesse Wolcott did, and testify against a housing bill reported by his own committee. The Rules Committee backed Wolcott, not the committee, and killed the bill.[9]

The committee structure was a formidable weapon for those who wanted to block new initiatives. On the whole, the Republicans aimed more to curb Democratic and presidential excesses than to formulate their own dramatic changes. There was little need to change the institutional structure of the House and Senate. House Republicans in 1946 had rejected the creation of a Republican Policy Committee to complement the Senate Committee. The experience of the 80th Congress led some liberal Republicans to advocate a Policy Committee to provide a greater national party input into congressional Republican activities.[10]

Party Discipline

The liberals could scarcely dispute the degree of party control exercised in the 80th Congress. Using *Congressional Quarterly*'s definition of party votes as those on which the majority of Republicans voted against the majority of Democrats, over 60 per cent of Republican representatives (147) supported the party in over 90 per cent of such votes. Only 8 per cent voted with the party less than 80 per cent of the time. The small group of 20 dissenters came almost entirely from outside the great Republican Plains states and the north-eastern industrial Republican strongholds of Michigan, Indiana, Ohio, Illinois, New Jersey and Pennsylvania. They came instead from Border, Western and New England states. Party control was slightly less evident in the Senate where 18 per cent of the Republicans voted with the party in less than 80 per cent of the votes. But the party control exercised in the House was a good deal more conservative than in the Senate.[11] The trio of Martin, Halleck and Allen, together with chairmen like Hartley and Wolcott, gave a formidable conservative slant to the overall Republican stance in the House. This orientation reflected the fact that, even in industrial states, House Republicans tended to represent rural and small town constituencies. Their Senate Republican counterparts inevitably had to pay more attention to the needs of their states' urban centres. House Republican constituencies had much in common, except for race, with the rural, small town homes of southern Democrats. As Susan Hartmann has commented, 'the conservatism of the House leadership made Taft seem a middle of the roader.'[12]

The Republicans' Legislative Agenda

The Republicans' main agenda was to secure a tax cut, slash government spending and enact a labour law to restrict the powers unions enjoyed under the Wagner Act. They succeeded in passing tax cuts in both 1947 and 1948, not overriding Truman's veto on the first occasion, but succeeding the second time. They slashed appropriations for Interior and Agriculture. They passed the Taft–Hartley Act which has effectively determined the parameters of industrial relations ever since. The political consequences of these legislative successes were not unambiguous. Nevertheless, they effected significant changes in America's policy directions and blocked Truman's efforts to extend New Deal measures incrementally or extend the regulatory and interventionist role of government into new areas of public policy like health and education. Also, in a bid to control excessive presidential power and to stop another Roosevelt, they secured passage of the 22nd Amendment to the Constitution restricting a president to two elected terms.

These successes, however, scarcely amounted to tackling the New Deal head on. Back in 1943 astute Senate observer Allen Drury noted that 'Taft, perhaps more than any other, is the leader of the powerful coalition of Republicans and southern Democrats.'[13] Given that that alliance had been so successful in stymieing both Roosevelt and Truman between 1938 and 1946 when the Democrats controlled Congress, surely the Republicans, now that they were in charge, could enact their conservative alternative to the New Deal.[14] That they found it difficult to do so reflected both the divisions within the Republican Party, particularly the presence of liberal Republicans, and the absence of a monolithic southern conservative Democratic bloc.

Republican Difficulties

Recently, Nicol Rae has given us a salutary reminder of that almost forgotten animal, the liberal Republican. Republicans from the start had been divided over the correct response to the New Deal. Western progressives were broadly in sympathy with many of the aspirations and programmes of the early New Deal, especially its measures for financial regulation, relief and agricultural recovery. Eastern conservatives were resolute in their opposition to virtually all that the New Deal stood for. As Rae and Barbara Sinclair have pointed out, western progressives had largely turned away from the statist policies of the New Deal in the late 1930s. Once agricultural recovery had been achieved, these western progressives were suspicious of the growth of federal bureaucracy and hostile to non-emergency New Deal measures which seemed increasingly to favour urban residents and organised labour. Eastern Republicans, by contrast, responded increasingly to the welfare needs and demands of urban liberalism and to an increasing corporate awareness that New Deal reforms not only could be lived with but might promote economic stability.[15]

By the 80th Congress, it is possible to detect an alignment among Republicans in Congress that approaches the topology of James Reichley: progressives, moderates, stalwarts and fundamentalists.[16] The progressives on the left and the fundamentalists on the right displayed a purist, ideological approach to politics. The moderates and the stalwarts in the middle displayed a pragmatic professional approach to congressional action. In the Senate, Wayne Morse (R.OR), George Aiken (R.VT) and William Langer (R.ND) represented the purist progressive wing of the party. Morse, for example, denounced demands for party unity as a 'brazen demand for reactionary control of the Republican party'. In the House, a new member like Jacob Javits (R.NY) deferred to what he perceived to be the Democratic character of his constituency, saw himself tongue-lashed by established rural Republican conservatives, voted to sustain Truman's veto of Taft–Hartley and found himself working in a liberal bipartisan coalition to build up support for veterans' housing.[17]

More moderate liberals included the two senators from Massachusetts, Salstonstall and Lodge, Bill Knowland from California, John Sherman Cooper from Kentucky, Roger Baldwin from Connecticut and Ralph Flanders from Vermont. The fundamentalists included senators like Kenneth Wherry from Nebraska and John Bricker from Ohio. The House with its greater imposition of party control contained more of the conservative stalwarts and fundamentalists. The dominant figure in domestic politics in the Senate, Taft, and House leaders like Speaker Joe Martin and Majority Leader Charlie Halleck could be characterised as professionals and stalwarts. Martin was conservative but also pragmatic. As he told Javits, 'As long as you vote Republican for the organisation of the House, from then on it is your job to get reelected and to do whatever it takes to get reelected.'[18]

As Henry Cabot Lodge said, he and other moderate Republicans did not want the party to be one 'which said no to all proposals for change'. They joined a party which was 'evolutionary and idealistic' characterised by 'sacrifice and generosity'. They saw no need to take a meat-axe to appropriations for New Deal programmes. They found it difficult to see such programmes as 'socialistic, New Deal, communistic schemes ... obnoxious, if not wholly un-American' as some of their colleagues did. They could see no reason to oppose the confirmation of David Lilienthal as chairman of the Atomic Energy Commission. They saw the need for government programmes to develop the nation's infrastructure, most especially housing and education and public power. They toned down, especially in the Senate, the anti-labour provisions of the Taft–Hartley Act, and resisted efforts to take people out of the social security system. Their moderating influence on both Taft–Hartley and the 1948 tax cut enabled those measures to attract enough Democratic support to override presidential vetoes.[19]

Crucially, however, they were unable to secure passage of housing legislation, despite the fact that Republican senators like Taft, conscious of their urban constituents, saw the need for low-cost housing and were prepared to work with Democrats to sponsor legislation. They were stymied by opposition in the House. Jesse Wolcott, chair of the Banking and Currency Committee, was determined to halt public housing legislation. Rural and small town representatives had little sympathy with the housing needs of big cities and were particularly susceptible to the lobbying activities of the National Real Estate Association. Nor were the moderates able to protect appropriations for public power, natural resources and soil conservation. Finally, in the special session called by Truman to dare Congress to enact the genuinely moderate Republican platform, they were unable to persuade the fundamentalists, including this time Taft, to enact 'responsible' legislation and thus call Truman's bluff. In 1948, the Republican platform listed the accomplishments of the 80th Congress but also called for measures which Congress had rejected: anti-monopoly action, slum clearance, housing and education legislation and civil rights legislation. Herbert Brownell was sent by presidential candidate Thomas Dewey to plead with congressional Republican leaders to enact some of the platform's recommendation's. 'They refused to do so,' he recalled. 'For years they had opposed the New Deal on the basis of a very conservative alternative.'[20]

Could the Republicans expect support from southern Democrats? In 1949, V.O. Key Jr cast doubts on the conservatism of southern Democrats in Congress on the basis of the analysis of roll call votes from 1933 to 1945. In both the House and the Senate he found no more than just over 10 per cent of roll call votes demonstrated what he described as the 'classic' pattern of southern Democrats and Republicans uniting against non-southern Democrats. Race and race-related issues were the main ones which saw southern solidarity.[21] Most recently, Katznelson, Geiger and Kryder have basically confirmed Key's findings and related them more specifically to the 80th Congress by examining a greater number of roll call votes and extending the analysis through to 1950. In the 1940s they see three coalitions at work: a bipartisan alliance of non-southern Democrats and Republicans and Democrats on civil rights, a party-based liberal coalition of non-southern and southern Democrats on welfare state, fiscal, regulatory and planning issues, and the 'classic' cross-party working of Democrats and Republicans in the single area of labour policy. If Key saw the southern reactionary veto as one applied primarily to race, Katznelson *et al.* add in a southern veto on labour. But, unlike Barbara Sinclair who sees a lessening of southern support for social welfare and non-labour legislation, they identify a certain southern Democratic liberalism.

> Apart from labor questions, southern representatives did more than reject conservative Republican positions: they joined their non-southern colleagues to support much of the party's social democratic agenda with a level of enthusiasm appropriate to a poor region with a heritage of opposition to big business and a history of support for regulation and redistribution.[22]

There were, of course, southern conservatives who routinely voted with the Republicans – the Virginia senators, Byrd and Robertson, Hoey and Umstead from North Carolina, McKellar and Stewart from Tennessee. But for every McClellan of Arkansas there was a Fulbright (D.AR), for every Walter George of Georgia, there was a Russell (D.GA), for every Eastland of Mississippi, a Stennis (D.MS), for every Holland of Florida, a Claude Pepper (D.FL). In February 1948, Truman spoke warmly of John Sparkman of Alabama, Richard Russell, Allan Ellender of Louisiana and Stennis. Stennis had been elected in a special election to succeed the notorious Theodore 'The Man' Bilbo. He had campaigned as a self-confessed moderate – almost the last time in Mississippi a political candidate would admit to that designation. Truman described him as 'the best man to have come from the state in a long time'. In Alabama, Lister Hill and John Sparkman headed a congressional delegation that had the most liberal voting record of all southern delegations. Robert Jones and Albert Rains in Alabama were matched by representatives like Kefauver and Gore in Tennessee, Lyndon Johnson and Lindley Beckworth in Texas, Charles Deane in North Carolina.[23]

Most southerners did follow the Katznelson model and vote to support Taft–Hartley and to override the presidential veto. But they also indicated a substantial support for liberal Administration economic measures. In part, this reflected little more than a simple need to secure farm price supports – bringing into play the wheat–cotton coalition, which was, for example, largely responsible for the passage of the Hope–Aiken Farm Act of 1948. In part, it reflected residual loyalty by older politicians and congressional leaders to the New Deal which had rescued the region in 1933. But the South had also seen the emergence of what James Sundquist identified in the North as 'issue-' rather than 'patronage-' oriented politicians, men like John Sparkman and Lister Hill in Alabama who saw federal assistance as the key to modernising the region. They saw themselves as TVA liberals and supported a New Deal strategy for modernising the region from the bottom up by raising mass purchasing power, getting federal assistance for welfare programmes, and securing federal investment in the region's infrastructure – notably cheap power, credit and education. Indeed, from South Carolina Olin Johnston could complain in 1948 that Truman was not liberal enough in economic policy: he 'seems to have finally succeeded in getting himself tied hand and foot by the ultra-conservatives – except for the race issue.' In most states these liberals were involved in an intense post-war factional struggle against traditional conservative elites in an effort to shape the economic future of their states and to bring a sort of time-lagged New Deal to their localities as they experienced unprecedented prosperity but still lagged far behind the rest of the country. Time and again it was southern votes that sustained presidential vetoes of Republican measures or forced moderating concessions from the majority party.[24]

Of course, the stultifying effect of the race issue was already in evidence. Lister Hill stood down as party whip in the Senate because he feared he would be in conflict with the president over civil rights. At the local level, southern liberals lost the local battles in the long run over economic and racial policy. At the national level, too, the constant need to satisfy the racial conservatism of their constituents remorselessly drove the southern congressmen into the arms of economic conservatives. But in the 80th Congress that die was not yet cast.[25] But the record of Congress in a divided government is as much determined by the attitude of the president as by the desires of congressional leaders.

THE 80TH CONGRESS AND TRUMAN

Alonzo Hamby has consistently pointed out that Truman's handling of Congress was judged at the time by liberals and later by historians by inappropriate standards. Critics blamed him for failing to exercise charis-matic national authority, for his inability to appeal over the heads of Congress to the people who would then exert constituency pressure to bring Congress in line with presidential wishes. Inevitably he was com-pared unfavorably with his predecessor, even though Roosevelt himself had been unable to exercise that sort of leadership over Congress since 1936.[26]

Truman's record with the 79th Democratic Congress did little to inspire confidence. Impulsiveness masqueraded as decisiveness. Imperious demands for the full panoply of liberal measures were rarely accompanied by careful preparation or the cultivation of congressional leaders who in any case were ineffectual. Bold initiatives were followed by embarrassing climb-downs. Liberal policies were frequently undercut by conservative subordinates appointed by the president itself, such as Treasury Secretary, John Snyder or White House aide, John Steelman. Far from the buck stop-ping here, the buck frequently did not get as far as the White House. In most domestic policies, the description applied by Phileo Nash to civil rights policies could equally well be applied: the backtrack after the bang.[27]

Truman was a more effective in dealing with a Republican Congress, at least in political, if not policy, terms because the weaknesses that plagued his handling of congressional relations throughout his presidency were much less relevant when Congress was controlled by the opposition party. Indeed, the bluster and contradiction served his purpose well.

In part, Truman positioned himself effectively on the right to pre-empt traditional Republican issues. On labour, no sooner than the elections were over than he won a major confrontation with United Mine Workers' leader John Lewis, utilising the courts to force Lewis to back down. His State of the Union message in 1947 contained at least some proposals that would form part of the Taft–Hartley Act. On controls, Truman moved immedi-ately to end virtually all remaining wartime price and allocation controls. He had little alternative, but it did remove a potent Republican issue. On the budget, Truman reduced the federal budget by almost two-thirds from its wartime levels. Only eight times since 1933 has the federal budget been balanced, Truman managed the feat four times. Above all, he planned to balance the budget for fiscal year 1948. He could appear as the exponent of sound finance, seeking revenue to reduce the national debt, vetoing tax cuts as inflationary, as well as inequitable.[28]

Above all, Truman temporarily outmanoeuvred the Republicans on the issue of domestic anti-communism. Republicans had hammered home at the issue of communists in government in both the 1944 and 1946 election campaigns. In setting up the Loyalty Review Board in 1947, Truman took the initiative in policies designed to clear the federal government of subversives. His tough anti-communist foreign policy, his disavowal of support from 'Henry Wallace and his communists', indeed the very presence of Wallace and the Progressive Party as domestic and foreign policy critics, enabled Truman to control the anti-communist issue through the 1948 elections. Such control was, of course, vulnerable to external developments, as the events of 1949 were to demonstrate. There was a considerable cost as well. Careless administration rhetoric could fuel, rather than dampen, the fires of anti-communist hysteria. The incompetent and casual administration of the Loyalty Review Board was not only careless of civil liberties but in the long run failed to satisfy anti-communist critics.[29]

In general, however, Truman's congressional strategy has been interpreted in the light of two apparently crucial memoranda. The first by James Rowe to Clark Clifford in December 1946 laid out a strategy for cooperation with Congress. The second in November 1947 was also by Rowe, but Clifford himself forwarded it to the president as his own effort because Rowe was out of favour. Entitled 'The Politics of 1948', the second memo laid out a programme of confrontation with Congress designed to establish a record on which to revitalise the Democrats' electoral coalition and fight the 1948 election. The first called for a spirit of conciliation and cooperation with the Republican Congress, the careful cultivation of Democratic congressional leaders, the avoidance of specific detailed legislative demands, and the sparing use of the veto. The second advocated tactics that 'must be entirely different than if there were any real point to bargaining and compromise'. Its recommendations must be tailored for the voters, not Congress: they must display a 'label' which reads 'no compromise'. With this strategy, Truman could reach out to the key elements of the Democratic coalition whose support he needed in 1948: western progressives, farmers, the professional liberals whom Truman despised, labour, African-Americans and urban ethnic groups. According to Susan Hartmann, Truman attempted to follow a conciliatory approach to Congress until May 1947. His vetoes of the 1947 tax cut and the Taft–Hartley Act signalled a shift towards a policy designed to label the Congress as reactionary and an enemy of the common man, a shift that became an integral part of Truman's electoral strategy.[30]

In foreign policy, Truman consistently followed a bipartisan conciliatory approach. As Hamby notes, Truman's success with the 80th Congress was especially remarkable. Given the widespread reluctance to commit American military and economic resources to an internationalist foreign

policy, especially in the Republican Party, it was indeed extraordinary for
Truman to secure support and appropriations for the Truman Doctrine, for
interim aid to Europe for the winter of 1947–8, for the long-term Marshall
Plan, for a temporary draft and for the preliminary steps towards NATO.
To secure bipartisan support, Truman and his advisers did what they sig-
nally failed to do in domestic policy. They devoted great energy to culti-
vating Republican leaders, notably Senator Vandenberg; they made a
serious effort to prepare public opinion and take their case to the people;
they made essential concessions to Republicans to safeguard their support.
Of course, they benefited from the real sense of crisis in US–Soviet relations and did little to dampen down fears of Soviet expansion. Not only
could they rely on the support of eastern internationalist Republicans, they
could also hope that the anti-communism of many midwestern
Republicans might outweigh their suspicious isolationism.[31]

Truman was reluctant to invest such political capital in his congressional relations over domestic policy. He got on well enough with many
congressional Republican leaders. As Truman noted in his diary on 1
January 1947:

Called [Speaker] Joe Martin. He assured me that cooperation was at the
top of his consideration. And that he wanted very much to help run the
country for the general welfare. He told me that he would be most
happy to talk with me at any time on any subject. I am inclined to
believe that he meant what he said.

But that tolerance did not extend to all Republicans. In February 1947, he
wrote to his sister:

Most of the senators and congressmen I was glad to see, but there were
half a dozen I'd rather have punched in the nose. I told Bess if she'd trip
[Senator John] Bricker up so he'd sprawl on the floor in front of us, I'd
give her the big diamond out of the scimitar the Crown Prince of Arabia
gave me. It is about five carats. But she didn't have the nerve to do it. If
she had, he'd have been out sure enough. Then there was Taft and old
Taber of New York.

Meaningful liaison with Republican leaders, or indeed with sympathetic
moderate Republicans, was not seriously entertained. No help was given
to National Labor Relations Board officials when they attempted to work
with Senator Irving Ives (R.NY) to develop bipartisan support for a moderate alternative to Taft–Hartley. Little was done to sustain the very real

bipartisan cooperation in the Senate on the Taft–Ellender–Wagner housing legislation, which provided a rare opportunity for enacting social welfare legislation, since northern Republicans like Taft and southern senators were both acutely aware of post-war urban housing needs in their constituencies.[32]

Not that collaboration with Democratic congressional leaders was much closer. In vain, Administration loyalists in Congress tried to find out where the Administration stood on portal to portal minimum wage legislation, tax cuts or Taft–Hartley. Draft bills prepared by the Administration were often not ready in time to be any use to minority party members. Meetings with House Minority Leader Sam Rayburn (D.TX) and Senate Minority Leader Alben Barkley (D.KY) were rare. Presidential and congressional Democratic strategy were rarely coordinated until late in the 1948 session. As Barkley memorably complained at the time of the 1948 tax cut proposals:

> This is like playing a night ball game. I'm supposed to be the catcher and I should get the signals. I not only am not getting the signals but someone actually turns out the lights when the ball is tossed.[33]

Rather than painstakingly work to build up support for feasible legislation, it was far easier, and seemingly more congenial for Truman, to use his veto accompanied by harsh denunciations of the opposition as tools of the special interests, even if there was no chance of it being sustained. He vetoed 32 measures in 1947; 43 in 1948. It was easier to summon Congress into Special Session and demand legislation that had no chance of passage[34] or to send special messages to Congress on a whole raft of measures of interest to vital groups in the Democratic coalition that would serve to expose divisions among congressional Republicans.

It did not appear to matter that the legislation vetoed might, like Taft–Hartley, contain elements that the Administration itself had earlier espoused and which the president would be only too happy to utilize in the future. It did not matter if the legislation demanded was not actually wanted by the administration. Not only did the anti-inflation controls on which Truman demanded action in the Special Sessions in November 1947 and July 1948 have no chance of passage, there is also no evidence that the administration wanted to use them if they had passed. In November 1947, administration officials were so alarmed that Congress might actually pass some of their demands, that they deliberately made them so extreme as to be absolutely unpalatable to the Republicans. The Council of Economic Advisers in July 1947 did not think that any anti-inflation legislation would actually make much difference to economic performance or check inflationary pressures.[35]

The strategy also enabled Truman to advocate measures that he knew that his own party would not support. He needed, Clark Clifford asserted, to take bold action on civil rights to safeguard the support not only of crucial African-American voters in northern cities but also of northern liberals generally. Clifford's advice was posited on the mistaken assumption that whatever Truman did the South would not defect. When southerners reacted so angrily to his special message endorsing his own Commission's Report *To Secure These Rights*, Truman rapidly backtracked and remained as silent as possible on the issue of civil rights right through the election. His caution explained his anger at the liberals for successfully inserting a ringing endorsement of his own policies in the 1948 party platform. Truman raged against the 'crackpot Biemiller' (a former House Democrat from Wisconsin) and his 'crackpot amendment'. He was angry because the amendment promoted a southern walkout at the Convention and the formation of the States Rights or Dixiecrat Party, which nominated South Carolina Governor Strom Thurmond for the presidency. In the 1948 presidential elections, the Dixiecrat revolt only took four Deep South states out of the Democratic column. In the July 1948 special session which Truman had called to highlight Republican divisions and the basic conservative thrust of Republican policy,[36] the Republicans cleverly insisted in considering anti-poll tax legislation as the first item of business.

Truman's confrontation strategy also enabled him to send messages to Congress and demand legislation on measures on which he had neither party backing, nor any discernible popular majority support. Federal aid to education and national health insurance were the most obvious examples of measures that would go beyond incremental improvements of New Deal policies and would, indeed, be part of the Democratic agenda until versions of them were enacted in 1965. But as the 81st Congress demonstrated, Truman did not have a majority of his own party in the late 1940s behind these measures.[37]

Thus, Truman could cheerfully lambast the Republicans in the 80th Congress for failing to enact legislation that his administration did not want. He could demand Republican action on measures for which he could not deliver the support of his own party. He could identify the Republicans as tools of 'the special interests' and enemies of the common man when they passed measures with substantial backing from his own party. He could interpret the failure of the Republicans incrementally to improve New Deal measures as indicative of their desire to 'do a real hatchet job on the New Deal'.

The strategy appeared to work. The Republicans in vain protested their innocence but the outraged fundamentalists in their own ranks were unable to devise a successful strategy to counteract the propaganda barrage launched at the 80th Congress in the summer of 1948. Truman's policy did appear to mobilise the support of the traditional elements of the Democratic coalition. The attack on Republican cuts in agriculture, interior and natural resource appropriations and programmes appeared to win over enough western progressives and midwestern farmers. The veto of Taft–Hartley and the attacks on Republican failures to increase the minimum wage or extend social security appeared to secure the support on labour and northern urban working-class voters. Pioneering civil rights proposals won the support of northern African-American voters. Right up to the convention discontented liberals, as well as southerners, had been looking to replace Truman as the presidential nominee, yet in the end Truman won liberal endorsements as he portrayed himself as the defender of the New Deal against Republican assault.[38]

AN ASSESSMENT OF THE 80TH CONGRESS

The 80th Congress controlled by the Republicans was not, as the president alleged, a 'Do-Nothing Congress'. Congress had given him what he needed on foreign aid and foreign policy. It had passed a makeshift farm programme, extended modified rent controls and the authority to alter tariffs. The Republicans authorised the establishment of a Department of Defense to unify the armed forces and provided for the civilian control of atomic energy. From the Republican agenda set by Taft and his allies, Congress had also cut taxes and passed a major law to regulate labour unions. It had defeated the president on universal military training, civil rights legislation, public housing, aid to education, more extensive social security benefits and higher minimum wages. For all the anti-New Deal rhetoric, the Republicans had not set out to destroy the New Deal social and farm programmes. If their aim was primarily to halt the extension of the New Deal, to reverse the statist drive of the Democrats, they could rely on the traditional institutional and committee structures of Congress. Theirs was not a revolutionary strategy. The record of the 80th Congress was a source of pride to many congressional Republicans, but, in the way that Truman was able to portray it, it was not an electoral asset.[39]

Louis Bean's predictions appeared to be right. Truman's strategy and prosperity brought back to the polls in 1948 enough Democrats who had stayed away in 1946 to win what is commonly described as a 'maintaining election'. Polls suggested that many of those Democrats made up their minds to return only in the last weeks of the campaign. But Truman did not bring back all those Democratic stay-aways and Truman trailed behind many local Democratic candidates. What the 81st Congress would show was that Truman could misread an electoral mandate just as comprehensively as the most fundamentalist anti-New Deal Republican. The 81st Congress would also demonstrate that the skills and tactics that Truman had deployed in handling the 80th Republican Congress were of little use in winning the legislative support of House members and senators of his own party, and that the lack of presidential skills in congressional relations which had been obscured by divided government would be fully exposed by a Congress controlled by the president's own party.[40]

NOTES

1. William J. vanden Heuvel, 'Address to the Mid-Year Institute', Oklahoma City University, 4 January 1995.
2. Donald R. McCoy, *The Presidency of Harry S. Truman* (Lawrence, KS: University of Kansas Press, 1984), pp. 65–6; William E. Leuchtenburg, *In the Shadow of FDR: From Harry Truman to Bill Clinton* (Ithaca, NY: Cornell University Press, 1993), p. 23.
3. *New York Times Magazine*, 19 January 1947.
4. Nicol Rae, *The Decline and Fall of the Liberal Republicans from 1952 to the Present* (New York: Oxford University Press, 1989), p. 35.
5. Anthony J. Badger, *The New Deal: The Depression Years, 1933–1940* (London: Macmillan, 1989), pp. 104, 301. James T. Patterson, *Mr Republican: A Biography of Robert A. Taft* (Boston Houghton Mifflin, 1972), p. 313.
6. Patterson, *Mr Republican*, pp. 315–34; James T. Patterson, 'Robert A. Taft', in Donald C. Bacon, Roger H. Davidson, and Morton Keller, eds., *The Encyclopaedia of Congress*, Vol. 4 (New York and London: Simon and Schuster, 1995), p. 1905.
7. Patterson, *Taft*, pp. 335–51. Susan Hartmann, *Truman and the 80th Congress* (Columbia, MO: University of Missouri Press, 1971), pp. 11–4. George Goodwin, Jr, *The Little Legislatures: Committees of Congress* (Amherst, MA: University of Massachusetts Press, 1970), pp. 18–25.
8. Jim Wright, *You and Your Congressman* (New York: Putnam's, rev. edn, 1976), p. 132.
9. Hartmann, *Truman and the 80th Congress*, p. 150.
10. Charles O. Jones, *Party and Policy-Making: The House Republican Policy Committee* (New Brunswick, NJ: Rutgers University Press, 1964), pp. 21–7.

11. *Congressional Quarterly Almanac* (Washington D.C.: Congressional Quarterly, 1948), pp. 37–43.
12. Hartmann, *Truman and the 80th Congress*, p. 14.
13. Allen Drury, *A Senate Journal, 1943–1945* (New York: McGraw Hill, 1963), p. 30.
14. Patterson, *Mr. Republican*, p. 265.
15. Rae, *The Decline and Fall of the Liberal Republicans*, pp. 25–40. Barbara Sinclair, *Congressional Realignment, 1925–78* (Austin, TX: University of Texas Press, 1982), p. 59.
16. A. James Reichley, *Conservatives in an Age of Change: The Nixon and Ford Administrations* (Washington, D.C.: The Brookings Institution, 1981), chapter 2; see also; Rae, *The Decline and Fall of the Liberal Republicans*, pp. 163–73, especially Table 5.4
17. Hartmann, *Truman and the 80th Congress*, p. 133; Jacob K. Javits, *Javits: The Autobiography of a Public Man* (Boston MA: Houghton Mifflin, 1981), pp. 98–100.
18. Hartmann, *Truman and the 80th Congress*, p. 136; Javits, *Javits*, pp. 98–100.
19. Rae, *The Decline and Fall of the Liberal Republicans*, p. 30. Hartmann, *Truman and the 80th Congress*, pp. 3, 35–6, 79–80, 132–7.
20. Hartmann, *Truman and the 80th Congress*, pp. 149, 191; Rae, *The Decline and Fall of the Liberal Republicans*, p. 35.
21. V.O Key Jr, *Southern Politics in State and Nation* (New York: Alfred Knopf, 1950), pp. 355–9, 374.
22. Ira Katznelson, Kim Geiger and Daniel Kryder, 'Limiting Liberalism: The Southern Vote in Congress; *Political Science Quarterly* 108/2 (1993), pp. 283–306; Sinclair, *Congressional Realignment*, p. 57.
23. Robert H. Ferrell, ed., *Truman in the White House: The Diary of Eben A. Ayers* (Columbia, MO: University of Missouri Press, 1991), p. 244.
24. Anthony J. Badger, 'Fatalism, Not Gradualism: Race and the Crisis of Southern Liberalism, 1945–1965', in Brian Ward and Anthony J. Badger, eds., *The Making of Martin Luther King and the Civil Rights Movement* (London Macmillan, 1996), p. 75; Numan Bartley, *The New South: 1945–1980* (Baton Rouge, LA: Louisiana State University Press, 1995), p. 71.
25. Bartley, *The New South*, pp. 71–3.
26. Alonzo Hamby, *Liberalism and Its Challengers: From F.D.R. to Bush* (New York Oxford University Press, 1982), pp. 67–68; Alonzo Hamby, *Man of the People: A Life of Harry S. Truman* (New York: Oxford University Press: New York, 1995), pp. 363–4, 493.
27. Hamby, *Man of the People*, pp. 361–86.
28. Hamby, *Man of the People*, pp. 419–20, 423; Robert H. Ferrell, *Harry S. Truman: A Life* (Columbia, MO: University of Missouri Press, 1994), pp. 230–2; Iwan W. Morgan, *Deficit Government: Taxing and Spending in Modern America* (Chicago: Ivan Dee, 1994), pp. 55–60.
29. Alan D. Harper, *The Politics of Loyalty: The White House and the Communist Issue, 1946–1952* (Westport, CT: Greenwood, 1969), *passim*.
30. Ferrell, *Harry S. Truman*, pp. 274–7; Hartmann, *Truman and the 80th Congress*, pp. 16–7, 45–6, 128–9.
31. Hamby, *Man of the People*, pp. 387–403.

32.   Robert H. Ferrell, ed., *Off the Record: The Private Papers of Harry S. Truman* (New York: Harper and Row, 1980), pp. 107–9; Hartmann, *Truman and the 80th Congress*, pp. 81, 149–50.
33.   Hartmann, *Truman and the 80th Congress*, pp. 17, 133.
34.   R. Alton Lee, 'The Turnip Session of the Do-Nothing Congress: Presidential Campaign Strategy', *Southwestern Social Science Quarterly*, 44 (1963), pp. 256–67.
35.   Hartmann, *Truman and the 80th Congress*, pp. 115–6, 194–5.
36.   Ferrell, *Off the Record*, p. 143; Hamby, *Man of the People*, pp. 433–5, 445–6, 448.
37.   Hartmann, *Truman and the 80th Congress*, p. 147.
38.   Ferrell, *Harry S. Truman*, pp. 280–4.
39.   Patterson, *Mr. Republican*, pp. 393–4.
40.   Hamby, *Man of the People*, pp. 464–6, 488–508.

9 The 104th Congress in Perspective

Dean McSweeney

The 104th Congress presented opportunities to the political science profession which had been absent for a generation. Since the transformation of social science research methodology by the behavioural revolution political scientists have been limited by the absence of Republican Congresses. Since 1955 – virtually the lifetime of modern political science – there have been no Republican congresses to study. For 40 years the writing on Congress has been about a Democratic Congress. The institution was largely shaped by the demands, objectives and internal tensions of the Democratic Party. So much of what was written about Congress – its internal power structure, electoral stability, the tendencies towards policy gridlock – reflected how power was won and used by the same majority party. Changes in election technique, power within the institution and its legislative products were usually the work of the Democratic majority.

At the outset of the Democrats' long period of dominance in 1955, factional divisions prevented centralised control of the party in Congress. Policy assertiveness by central party leaders was precluded. Institutions like the Caucus were unused. Creative leadership by the two Texans, Speaker Rayburn and Senate Majority Leader Johnson, consisted in brokering differences within and across party lines, simultaneously advancing legislation and preserving Democratic unity. 'Committee government' decentralised power into nearly autonomous, specialised work groups, subject to meagre control (and rare attempts to exert control) by the Democratic leadership. The impetus for congressional reform came from the discontented liberal faction reacting against the obstructiveness of southern conservative Democrats centered in the committee systems in both chambers and the Senate filibuster. Reforms instituted in the 1960s and 1970s to enhance liberal influence within Congress were targeted at these conservative minority strongholds. The enlargement of the Rules Committee, the inception of the 21-day rule, the reduction in the votes needed to terminate filibusters, the election of committee chairs by the Caucus, all enhanced the influence of the majority within the majority party.

Use of the Caucus in the 1970s and assertive leadership in the 1980s were facilitated by the homogenisation of the party stimulated by the Voting Rights Act of 1965, ideological polarisation between the parties and the frequency of divided control. Leading from the front became possible when factional divisions waned, broadening the range of issues on which Democrats agreed beyond economic interventionism and social insurance which united the party from the New Deal. Instead of the bipartisan accommodation between centrists, Eisenhower, Johnson and Rayburn in the 1950s, by the 1970s conservative Republican presidents confronted liberal-leaning Democratic congresses. In this more conflictual era congressional Democratic leaders were encouraged by the majority rank and file to resist major components of presidential programmes and, on occasion, to substitute their own legislative initiatives. An active House Democratic Caucus enlarged leadership authority over the committee assignment process, and commanded greater responsiveness and accountability from committee chairs through control over their selection. Chairs insensitive to their own majorities were deposed – the fate of three in 1975. The Caucus also became an instrument of party discipline upon rank-and-file members. The removal in 1983 of Phil Gramm (another Texan) from the Budget Committee for assisting the first Reagan budget through the House provides an example of a party sanction imposed for disloyalty.

The legislative products of Congress reveal the ideological transition of the Democratic Party during their dominance of Congress. Gridlock centred on the issues which either divided the majority or united them in opposition to a Republican president. But the issues on which *impasse* developed altered. In the 1950s legislation was immobilised on issues like civil rights and federal aid to education which polarised the Democratic Party into northern and southern blocs. More recently, a mix of ideological and constituency conflicts stymied reform of welfare and health care. Differences between Democrats in the House and Senate baulked change in campaign finance law.

For 40 years Democrats were dominant in congressional elections. But that stability in election outcomes disguised the alteration in the sources of the party's electoral advantage. For at least the first decade of Democratic control the party profited from their lead in party identifiers amongst the electorate. As long as congressional elections approximated the 'normal vote', Democratic majorities were assured. Associations with popular domestic programmes central to the work of Congress (particularly the House), such as social security, welfare benefits, environmental protection and farm subsidies, assisted the party in winning elections.[1] Democratic dominance over state government permeated and reproduced an advantage in Congress, providing a plentiful supply of experienced, quality candidates to replace incumbents.[2]

When candidate-centred elections proliferated from the 1960s, and the impact of party allegiances on the vote declined, Democrats perpetuated their hold on Congress by exploiting the advantages of incumbency. The growth of perquisites – increases in staffing, district offices, use of the franking privilege – were inaugurated and used by the predominantly Democratic membership. It was a Democratic Congress which enacted the Federal Election Campaign Act in 1971 and its subsequent amendments which exaggerated incumbents' advantages in funding. Repeated attempts at campaign finance reform failed, perpetuating the advantages which accrued to the Democratic majority. These increases in resources allowed individualism to flourish as members adapted to their particular electoral environments, communicating with, responding to and servicing their constituents. Incumbent security was predominantly Democratic security.

The first Republican Congress in 40 years changed internal power structures, public policy and congressional reelection strategy. House Republicans' commitment to congressional reform was unsurprising for a former minority whose grievances had accumulated as majority Democratic control tightened. Institutional reform was part of the 1994 Republican election campaign, melding the party's and the public's discontent over the running of (the Democratic) Congress. Alleged waste and corruption were attacked by economies in staffing and the abolition of 'special interest' committees. Within the new majority, leadership controls were strengthened to expedite the Republican programme. Committee autonomy was constricted by the Speaker's appointment of all chairs. Particularly in early 1995 task forces were employed to police the committees' handling of Contract legislation to ensure they were reliable instruments of majority will. (The more detailed discussion of these changes appears in the chapters by Sinclair and Owens.)

Gingrich's control over committees exemplified the Speaker's dominance over the legislative process unseen since the Republican Czars Cannon and Reed prior to the First World War. But the sources of his powers differed from theirs. Their hierarchical controls were facilitated by the partisanship of the electorate which encouraged partisan behaviour in Congress. The Czars benefited from electoral conditions they had done nothing to create. Gingrich, in contrast, derived leadership resources from the debts he had acquired in helping to elect a Republican Congress. He had encouraged candidates to run and campaigned on their behalf. He was the author of the Contract to which most Republican candidates had committed themselves. His strategy of uncompromising denunciation of the Democratic majority appeared to work in 1994.

Relations between congressional party leaders and members have been likened to those between agents and their principals.[3] Leaders have resources afforded them by their principals. Gingrich was different. For many members he was the agent of the Republican victory. They believed they owed majority status to his efforts. Much of Gingrich's leverage derived from personal electoral debts. Previous academic treatments of electoral debts have seen them as a *presidential* resource in Congress, deference acquired through coat-tail effects. In the 104th Congress it was the Speaker who secured deference from his party members for his contribution to their electoral success. Gingrich also capitalised on the media focus on contemporary Speakers to project himself as an alternative, more electorally legitimate Chief Legislator and Party Leader than the president. As the centre of a network of interest groups and think tanks which supported the Contract, Gingrich could also mobilise lobbying efforts in Washington and members' districts to pressurise Congress to conform to the party's programme.

Previous party leaders have been pragmatists, adept in effecting compromises between different factions within their party, and in forging bipartisan coalitions. Gingrich, in contrast, was an ideologue, an aggressive exponent of the New Right ideas which had penetrated the Republican Party from the late 1970s. In the 104th Congress Gingrich had many like-minded allies amongst House Republicans, especially amongst first-and second-term members. They shared his uncompromising style and ideological consistency. He could lead because the members shared the goals towards which he was directing them.

Dependent upon so many personal, informal sources, Gingrich's power was highly vulnerable to changes in political conditions. When his public opinion ratings deteriorated, the former electoral asset became a liability. As the 1996 elections approached, members sought to advertise their distance from him and he retreated from the media spotlight. When he abandoned the confrontation with Clinton he betrayed the purists in his own party dedicated to the balancing the budget.

The House Republican approach to policy gridlock was to exploit the unprecedented claim of a new majority emerging from a twentieth-century mid-term election: an electoral mandate for a congressional party platform. As always, mandates are more the work of post-election analysts than of voters. Only a minority of voters had heard of the Contract. Few Republican candidates campaigned on it, though others used it selectively, publicising specific commitments such as term limits. Some Democrats exploited the Contract to deter potential Republican voters, and survey evidence shows its meagre effects on voters to be almost as much negative as positive.[4] (Note the absence of the Contract from Shafer's explanation for the Republican victory.) But the Republican leadership proclaimed a mandate, and most of the congressional party had signed the Contract creating a post-election obligation to act upon it.

House Republican cohesion on votes, untypically high for the twentieth century for a decade before the 1994 elections, reached record levels in 1995. Every Contract item was brought to a vote in the House within 100 days as promised (the commitment to vote rather than enact provided a note of caution in an otherwise messianic document). Republican agenda control and disciplined party-line voting excluded House Democrats from participation in legislation. Following precedents for minority strategy which Gingrich had established, the Democratic leadership redirected their efforts outside of Congress (see my chapter 7). If the legislative battle was unwinnable, Republicans could be beaten in the battle for public opinion. The Republican leadership's programme could not be resisted, but their reputations could be disparaged.

President Clinton's reaction to the election, abandoning legislative initiatives, ceded control of the congressional agenda to the new majority. No Congress since the inception of the modern presidency so challenged the assumption that the White House provides leadership on legislation and sets the policy agenda. This redistribution of power derived both from the assertiveness of the House but also the acquiescence of the president. Unlike Truman in 1946, Clinton interpreted the election as a repudiation of such liberalism as he had displayed since becoming president. Whereas Truman sought electoral profit by forcing Congress to respond to his liberal legislative demands, Clinton sought to reposition himself, embracing or moderating the conservative House programme. Needing some conservative legislative achievements for reelection, Clinton had a vested interest in ensuring a 'Do Something' rather than 'Do Nothing Congress'. (For more detailed discussion of Truman see Badger's chapter; Foley's chapter for a discussion of Clinton.)

Bicameralism persisted as a source of policy gridlock, for the Senate was a frequent impediment to legislation passed by the House. The mandate of the 1994 elections was confined to the lower house. No Republican senators had signed the Contract. Nor had the 1994 elections enhanced leadership resources in the Senate as they had in the House. No Republican senator owed their election to Majority Leader Robert Dole. Rather than being in the vanguard of a reinvigorated conservative movement, Dole was a traditional conservative, skilled in effecting legislative compromises, cool towards several Contract items. Nor did the new leadership seek to reform the institution. No new centralised controls were imposed; the scope for individual and minority obstruction was not curbed.

Senate Republican moderates were not constrained by the mandate which bound their House counterparts to party loyalty. Senate Democrats found minority protections such as the filibuster valuable in resisting or moderating legislation emanating from the House, and Clinton found the Senate more receptive to his lobbying efforts than the House. The Senate's resistance to a balanced budget constitutional amendment, tax cuts and regulatory overhaul were all supportive of the president's position. Similarly, the Senate's influence on the final versions of welfare reform, health insurance portability and telecommunications reform made the legislation acceptable to Clinton.

In seeking to found a new era of Republican-dominated electoral stability the new House majority adopted a partisan rather than individualistic strategy. Enacting the Contract became the test of the party's electoral credibility. The Contract had proclaimed that the party did not deserve re-election if it failed to fulfil its promises. On many Contract items a unanimous House Republican Party sought to carry out its perceived mandate. Party moderates rallied in support of the programme, acquiring more conservative voting records in the process. Speed was essential for the House majority to produce a legislative record which would help to consolidate their advantage in the 1996 election. But after the activism of the first 100 days, enactments were much slower to arrive.

Adverse public reaction to two government shutdowns, Gingrich's unpopularity and the risk of electoral defeat enforced a change of strategy in 1996. The leadership became more conciliatory. Individual members showed greater sensitivity towards constituency concerns, seeking to demonstrate their distance from the leadership to ensure electoral survival (a strategy Gingrich encouraged). The substantial Republican minority support for the minimum wage increase in 1996 exemplifies the triumph of electoral pragmatism over free market principle. Republicans did not so transform Congress that incumbent advantages were eradicated. Two of the legislative failures in the House – term limits and campaign finance reform – threatened incumbent security. In the 1996 elections Republicans' neglect of the Contract confirmed the reassertion of individualistic rather than partisan campaign styles.

Though some priority legislation was frustrated, the 104th Congress was productive. The magnitude of policy change, more than the number of bills passed, registers how much was accomplished. Welfare, agricultural subsidies and telecommunications were overhauled, the first two under-going the greatest transformation since their inception in the 1930s. The line-item veto added to the power of presidents to curb expenditure (assuming the Supreme Court upholds its constitutionality). The restrictions on unfunded mandates strengthen the deterrents against federal impositions on subnational government. Every one of these issues was addressed by the 103rd Congress without yielding legislative results. Some had been considered long before. Welfare overhaul has been on the congressional agenda since the failure of Nixon's Family Assistance Plan in 1970. Reagan had advocated a line-item veto in his 1985 State of the Union address before being obstructed by a Senate filibuster. Product liability (which Clinton vetoed) was a recurrent congressional issue from 1977. In the 1980s, five product liability bills emerged from committee, none passed either house. In the 104th Congress the barriers erected by intra-party divisions, bicameral conflicts, constituency and interest group pressures were overcome to produce far-reaching legislation.

The legislative products of the 104th Congress were not only substantial, they were also conservative. Economic deregulation, shrinkage of the federal government, the curtailment of welfare advanced on the fronts where Reagan had secured victories, extending and deepening the reaction against an active government taming market forces in pursuit of egalitarian aims. Reagan's welfare reforms whittled away at costs and eligibility not the eradication of the New Deal guarantee of assistance to poor families. Reagan's New Federalism sought to revive states' fiscal autonomy but did nothing to ease the burden of unfunded mandates. Studies of agenda-setting neglect congressional parties.[5] But the policy shifts which followed the 104th Congress suggest that future research should remedy this omission. The 103rd Congress debated universal health insurance. Its successor sought to preserve coverage for the already insured. Whereas its predecessor sought to guarantee access to abortion clinics, the 104th Congress voted to bar late-term abortions. The 103rd Congress debated the establishment of an Environmental Protection Department. The 104th Congress relaxed regulations on drinking water and pesticides.

The mix of an assertive House and a president on the defensive thus proved a productive form of legislative–executive relations. Divided government was again shown to be capable of producing a substantial legislative record.[6] Confirming the experience of the 100th Congress in Reagan's lame-duck years, the new Republican Congress demonstrated that the House could displace the president in legislative initiative. Armed with a programme, the House leadership imposed their priorities on Congress, forced the president to react and often to accept their legislation.

Substantial policy change is usually associated with presidential land-slides, unified government and large congressional majorities for the president's party.[7] In contrast, the mandate for the 104th Congress originated from a mid-term election which restored divided control. Electoral authority for action switched to Congress notwithstanding the fact that the Republicans were the smallest congressional majority since 1957. The productivity of the 104th Congress was thus achieved in the absence of all the 'right' conditions for policy innovation. Offsetting these unpropitious circumstance were the centralised control over a predominantly conservative party, an unprecedented mid-term mandate, massive voter disenchantment with 'politics as usual', and a repudiated president who saw his re-election dependent upon shifting towards the ideological terrain occupied by the new congressional majority.

In these conditions the Congress would inevitably be dominant over legislation and it would suit the president to allow them to be so. House Republicans wanted to establish a legislative record to perpetuate their majority beyond 1996; Clinton needed to re-establish his credentials as a New Democrat to earn a second term. Thus the 104th Congress provided the seventh post-war instance of what Jones has called congressional preponderance.[8] All have occurred under divided control. But in other respects the circumstances of 1995–6 diverged from the previous six cases. All previous cases followed elections which terminated six or more years of control of the presidency by the same party. All previous cases involved either lame ducks or former vice-presidents, who had either succeeded to or been elected to the presidency. Clinton was different in being his party's first president for 12 years, elected in his own right, only two years into his first term.

Like his predecessors in periods of congressional preponderance, Clinton had no electoral mandate. House Republicans did claim a mandate which, allied to the spectacular gains and the prolonged exclusion from power, fomented an assertiveness and cohesion untypical in congressional parties. A minority president (elected with the lowest share of the popular vote in 80 years), damaged by the mid-term rebuff, was strategically ill-equipped to pre-empt Congress' assertiveness. Moreover, reading the election as a victory for conservatism, Clinton's re-election strategy was designed to move towards the new majority whilst keeping sufficient distance from them to allow him to define himself as a moderate and his congressional opponents as extremists. During 1995–6 the president's domestic record consisted of a mix of compromises extracted from Congress and vetoes of radical attacks on existing programmes.

Although the 104th Congress proved a productive, workable form of presidential–congressional relations it is unlikely to recur often. Too many of the features of the 104th Congress were dependent upon political contingencies to provide a model of future Republican congresses. Heavy mid-term losses resulting in a transfer of congressional power are rare. The exceptional leverage Gingrich possessed within his own party partly derived from his role in producing the abnormal Republican victory. But in the absence of such untypical electoral conditions, the personal resources of the leadership equivalent to Gingrich's in 1995 may be unobtainable. An election mandate for a congressional platform drove the House majority but that is unique rather than rare. The subsequent electoral handicaps of a binding contract may deter rather than encourage imitation. Few first-term presidents are as electorally vulnerable as Clinton or likely to see political survival in effecting an ideological relocation in the direction of the congressional majority. For these reasons the 104th Congress may prove a unique form of *Republican* Congress.

NOTES

1. Gary C. Jacobson, *The Electoral Origins of Divided Government: Competition in U.S. House Elections, 1946–1988* (Boulder, CO: Westview Press, 1990), pp. 112–20; Byron E. Shafer, 'The Notion of an Electoral Order: The Structure of Electoral Politics at the Accession of George Bush', in Byron E. Shafer, ed., *The End of Realignment? Interpreting American Electoral Eras* (Madison, WI: University of Wisconsin Press, 1991), pp. 37–84.
2. Jacobson, *The Electoral Origins of Divided Government*, ch. 4.
3. Barbara Sinclair, *Legislators, Leaders, and Lawmaking: The U.S. House of Representatives in the Postreform Era* (Baltimore and London: The Johns Hopkins University Press, 1995).
4. James G. Gimpel, *Fulfilling the Contract: The First 100 Days* (Needham Heights, MA: Allyn and Bacon, 1996).
5. John Kingdon, *Agendas, Alternatives and Public Policy* (Boston: Little, Brown, 1984).
6. David R. Mayhew, *Divided We Govern. Party Control, Lawmaking, and Investigations, 1946–1990* (New Haven, CT: Yale University Press, 1991).
7. Leroy N. Rieselbach, 'Congress and Policy Change: Issues, Answers, and Prospects', in Gerald C. Wright, Jr, Leroy N. Rieselbach and Lawrence C. Dodd, eds., *Congress and Policy Change* (New York: Agathon Press, 1986), pp. 257–89.
8. Charles O. Jones, *The Presidency in a Separated System* (Washington, D.C.: The Brookings Institution, 1994).

Index

n indicates notes

abortion, 102, 115, 144, 191
abortions, late-term, 113, 144, 157, 158
Abraham, Spencer, 112
Abramowitz, Alan I., 163*n*
Abramson, Paul R., 31*n*
AFL-CIO, 161
agenda-setting, 119–23, 141, 151–2, 191
agricultural reform, 43, 63, 106, 112–13, 157, 158, 190–1
Agriculture Committee (House), 43
Aiken, George, 169, 172
Aldrich, John H., 31*n*
Allen, Leo, 169, 170
American Cause, 99
American Enterprise Institute, 97, 99
Americans for Tax Reform, 100
Anderson, Terry, 116*n*
anti-ballistic missile (ABM) system, 109–11
anti-communism, 176–7, 178
Appropriations Committee (House), 43
Archer, Bill, 39, 58
Armey, Dick, 3, 35, 39, 41, 46, 58, 81, 85, 86, 98, 102, 103, 115, 116*n*, 160
Ashford, Nigel, 3, 116*n*
assault weapons ban, 88
Atomic Energy Commission, 173

Babson, Jennifer, 68*n*, 116*n*
Bader, John B., 6*n*
Badger, Anthony, 5, 182*n*, 183*n*, 189
Baker, Richard, 68*n*
Baldwin, Roger, 172
Balz, Dan, 94*n*, 95*n*
Barkley, Alben, 179
Barr, Michael K., 6*n*
Barry, John M., 65*n*
Bartley, Robert, 116*n*

Bauer, Gary, 100
Baumer, David C., 66*n*
Bean, Louis, 166, 182
Beckworth, Lindley, 174
Bell Curve, The, 107, 116*n*
Bennett, Bill, 98
Bilbo, Theodore, 174
Bliley, Thomas, 39, 43
Blue Dogs, 148–9
  see also Democrats, conservative
Boehner, John, 3, 43, 85, 88
'bomb throwers', 75, 79, 84, 146, 149, 151, 162
Bonior, David, 145, 151
Bosnia, 110, 157, 159
Bricker, John, 172, 178
Brooks, Jack, 1
Brownell, Herbert, 167
Brownstein, Ronald, 94*n*, 95*n*
Buchanan, Pat, 99
budget
  balanced budget, 42, 48, 58, 90–1, 92, 104, 128, 136, 152, 162, 176
  Balanced Budget Amendment, 58, 91, 102–3, 155
  conflict 1996, 86, 90, 92, 128–9, 152, 157, 158
Burnham, Walter Dean, 6*n*, 31*n*
Bush, George, 2, 23, 47, 80, 96, 101, 102, 103, 114, 127, 132, 137
Byrd, Harry, 174
Byrd, Robert, 54, 157

Caldiera, Gregory A., 6*n*
California disaster relief, 84
campaign finance reform, 155, 190
Campbell, Angus, 31*n*
Campbell, James E., 31*n*
Cannon, Joseph, 33, 45, 187
Cantril, Hadley, 124, 138*n*

Index

SOCIÉTÉ ÉCONOMIQUE : L'AUTODESTRUCTION
THÉORISATION D'UNE MODERNITÉ ARCHAÏQUE

PSYCHANTHROPOLOGIE

TACK GUY ROSTIN

SOCIÉTÉ ÉCONOMIQUE : L'AUTODESTRUCTION
THÉORISATION D'UNE MODERNITÉ ARCHAÏQUE

Application n°4

Edition : Books on Demand,
12/14 rond-Point des Champs-Elysées, 75008 Paris
Impression : BoD - Books on Demand, Norderstedt, Allemagne
ISBN : 9782322012589
Dépôt légal : avril 2019

AVANT-PROPOS

En même temps que nous écrivons ce livre, aucune société de la planète ne peut revendiquer le statut entier de société économique. Mais depuis la fin de la seconde Guerre mondiale, en passant par le consensus de Washington et la chute du mur de Berlin, un paradigme spécifique s'évertue avec beaucoup de zèle à promouvoir la grande marche vers ce statut à l'échelle de la planète. C'est le paradigme néolibéral. Dès lors, en cette première moitié du 21e siècle, par rapport à cette grande marche, certaines nations sont plus avancées que d'autres.

Deux doctrines interdépendantes permettent la viabilité et la pérennité de la société économique. Ce sont le productivisme et le consumérisme. L'ensemble des sociétés de la planète qui, bon gré mal gré, tendent vers ce type de société adoptent tacitement ces deux doctrines. Le paradigme néolibéral déclenche leur concrétisation et leur extension. Bref, ce paradigme est un puissant levier de promotion de la société économique.

La transition vers la société économique entraîne progressivement une mutation profonde et structurelle des mécanismes sociétaux. Sont concernées, principalement, les structures sociopolitiques, socio-économiques et socioculturelles. Toutes ces mutations sédimentent ou colonisent au préalable les imaginaires[1] individuels et collectifs des populations dans les sociétés concernées et, dès lors, donnent un cap nouveau à chacun. A l'issue de ce processus, le statut de citoyen change en un autre très spécifique, celui d'homoeconomicus. A partir de ce moment, ce qui donne un sens à la vie d'homoeconomicus n'est que la conséquence de la structuration et du contenu de son imaginaire : le consumérisme. Ce dernier lie son existence à la consommation frénétique des Biens & Services. Mais cette nouvelle configuration spécifique se déploie avec de nouvelles formes d'interactions humaines, de nouvelles logiques culturelles et de nouvelles dynamiques initiées et pilotées principalement depuis la dynamique de l'inconscient humain. Par conséquent, elle heurte fondamentalement des valeurs revendiquées et espérées par la raison humaine telles, entre autres, la liberté, la démocratie, l'humanisme. Elle met en péril l'humanité, voire, l'ensemble des vies.

Pour sa compréhension globale, cet ouvrage

---

[1] Système cohérent psychique régissant une manière spécifique de concevoir et d'interagir avec le monde.

pourrait se suffire en soi. Mais, pour une meilleure fluidité, la lecture, au moins, du premier Livre de cette collection peut être utile. Idéalement, lire les cinq premiers livres est fortement suggéré.

INTRODUCTION

La société économique est un type particulier de société considérant l'économie et les institutions économiques comme plaque tournante du système sociétal. De par cette position, elle est dotée d'une structure, d'une organisation et de mécanismes spécifiques fondés sur l'économie. A ce titre, elle revendique une identité propre la distinguant de diverses autres formes spécifiques de sociétés : société religieuse, société politique, société de la connaissance, etc.

Puisque, littéralement, le cœur de l'économie est fondamentalement lié au diptyque production/consommation des Biens & Services, le système de la société économique tendra à maximiser ce diptyque. En d'autres termes, il faut produire et consommer toujours plus. Pour concrétiser et pérenniser ce diptyque, de manière structurelle, il faut influencer le comportement des consommateurs. Il faut mettre l'accent sur ce qui, en chacun d'eux, concourt à auto-entretenir le système. Dans les trois premiers Livres de la collection *Psychanthropologie*, nous avons distingué deux principales formes de motivations liées à la conservation (survie & bien-être) de tout Être humain. Chacune de ces deux motivations chapeautent divers manques potentiels spécifiques exprimables par le corps humain. La première forme est d'ordre physiologique, c'est le besoin. La seconde est d'ordre émotionnel, c'est le désir. Il existe une différence fondamentale entre ces deux formes de motivations. En fait, le potentiel d'expression, et donc de satisfaction, de la première connaît des limites. Celui de la seconde, stimulée via les organes de sens, semble illimité. Car l'ensemble des événements pouvant être captés par ces organes de sens sont incommensurables. Comme Platon, nous pouvons considérer que le désir humain est « *insatiable* »[2]. Donc seuls le désir et son caractère « insatiable » sont susceptibles de viabiliser et de pérenniser la société économique.

L'existence de la société économique étant tacitement indissociable de la stimulation du désir, il y a un impact structurel sur la configuration mentale des individus de ce type de société. Autrement dit, la pérennisation de la société économique dépend de la manière dont est structuré l'univers psychique de ces individus. Cette structuration doit lier leurs existences individuelles et collectives à la consommation des Biens & Services. C'est ce lien qui donne un sens à leur vie. En cela, la société économique se confond

---

[2] Platon, *La République*, Les Belles Lettres, 2002.

à la société de consommation. Dès lors, les individus de la société économique s'inscrivent ou s'enferment tous dans une doctrine tacite : le consumérisme. Leur statut de citoyens évolue vers un autre bien plus spécifique, celui d'homoeconomicus. Dans ce sillage, on définit le consumérisme comme étant une doctrine à partir de laquelle les homoeconomicus ne donnent un sens à leur vie qu'à travers la consommation des Biens & Services.

La liaison entre existence et consommation des Biens & Services n'est possible qu'à travers des dynamiques de conditionnement et d'endoctrinement. Elles aboutissent à une addiction consumériste régie exclusivement par la dynamique de l'inconscient. Les conséquences de cette liaison sont dévastatrices.

Dans la première partie de cet ouvrage, nous allons dresser un profil détaillé tant d'homoeconomicus que de la société économique. Nous démontrerons comment, à partir de la configuration psychique d'homoeconomicus, les fondements de ce type de société induisent mécaniquement l'individualisme et fondent, dans ce sillage, les interactions humaines exclusivement sur des rapports de force. Dès lors, à partir de ces fondements, nous montrerons comment ce type de société détient le niveau le plus élevé du potentiel de propension à la violence par rapport à tous les autres types de sociétés (société politique, société religieuse, société de la connaissance, etc.). Nous verrons aussi comment cette configuration induit systématiquement une servitude endogène en tous les homoeconomicus. En d'autres termes, nous démontrerons qu'homoeconomicus n'est absolument pas libre. A cause de l'immense pression de l'autorité de la dynamique de l'inconscient, cette servitude émerge avec le parasitage total et structurel de l'espace du libre arbitre[3] par les injonctions pressantes de cette dynamique primaire.

Dans la seconde partie, nous continuerons à mettre en lumière le profil de la société économique en analysant spécifiquement la dynamique du système de la société économique. Dans ce cadre, dans un premier temps, nous expliciterons toutes les interactions entre acteurs et composantes. Dans ce sillage, ensuite, une seconde forme de servitude, de champ exogène, d'homoeconomicus sera mise en exergue. Ce type de société produit structurellement de profondes inégalités ; elle neutralise les émotions de source sentimentale,

---

[3] Espace du conscient à partir duquel l'individu pose des choix et prend des décisions sans aucune forme de déterminisme. La construction de cet espace est analysée de manière exhaustive dans le Livre 4 (*Les origines de la liberté*) de la collection *Psychanthropologie*.

annihilant de la sorte l'altruisme et la compassion. A fortiori, contre toute idée acquise, nous démontrerons que la société économique est profondément totalitaire. Elle est donc absolument incompatible avec la démocratie.

D'une manière générale, nous démontrerons comment de par sa nature, ses fondements et sa dynamique, la société économique est une modernité ambiguë. Elle promeut en même temps le bien-être tout en détruisant la vie dans son ensemble dans une logique d'autodestruction. De par cette ambiguïté, la société économique connaît une profonde contradiction (modernité et archaïsme) qui la rend éphémère et caduque.

PARTIE 1

FONDEMENTS DE LA SOCIÉTÉ ÉCONOMIQUE

CHAPITRE 1

Du désir au consumérisme

Pour comprendre les fondements de l'émergence de la société économique, avant tout, il faut impérativement mettre en lumière et exposer les différences entre les deux principales motivations de l'Être humain dans le processus de sa conservation (survie et bien-être). Ce sont les besoins et les désirs. Ensuite, il faut analyser l'impact de chacune de ces motivations sur le comportement humain. Une partie de cette tâche est déjà réalisée dans les trois premiers Livres de cette collection. Nous allons rappeler l'essentiel de ce qu'il faut savoir sur ces deux motivations et continuer à approfondir les connaissances de leur impact tant sur les comportements que sur les systèmes sociétaux.

Section 1 : Les besoins et désirs humains

Les besoins et désirs sont les deux principales motivations de l'Être humain dans le processus de sa conservation. C'est à partir d'eux qu'il entre en contact tant avec ses congénères qu'avec l'ensemble des autres composantes de la nature. Ces besoins et désirs sont principalement régis par la dynamique de l'inconscient humain.

Sous-section 1 : Les besoins

Les besoins de l'Être humain, comme d'ailleurs de tous les Êtres vivants, sont précisément ceux de son corps (en tant qu'une de ses trois dimensions). C'est l'expression d'un ensemble de manques fondamentaux essentiels à la survie du corps. Ils expriment donc une nécessité tant physiologique qu'émotionnelle pour la survie. Les principaux besoins physiologiques, ou besoins primaires, du corps sont ceux de la nutrition, de la sécurité et de la reproduction. Alors que les principaux besoins émotionnels sont principalement d'ordre affectif. Bref, l'expression des besoins renvoie aux manques basiques garantissant la survie du corps. A ce titre, la satisfaction aux besoins ne produit pas spécialement le plaisir généré généralement à partir des organes de sens. Par exemple manger de la viande crue sans préparation quelconque peut suffire à satisfaire à un besoin de faim. Mais, l'Être humain n'en tire aucun plaisir. Au mieux, même si elle est cuite et sans aucun assaisonnement, le goût reste très basique mais suffit à satisfaire au besoin de survie. A travers l'assaisonnement, c'est la motivation par le désir qui intervient.

Au-delà de la qualité basique, la satisfaction au besoin se caractérise aussi par une limite quantitative de sollicitation de ressources. A ce titre, pour un besoin de réhydratation, s'il faut boire deux verres d'eau pour étancher votre soif, le troisième verre sera de trop. Les limites physiologiques dans le cadre de satisfaction à tout besoin sont atteintes rapidement. En d'autres termes, le potentiel de ressources nécessaires à la satisfaction à un besoin est très faible. Ce qui n'est pas le cas du désir.

Sous-section 2 : Les désirs

Tous les manques du corps, au-delà des besoins, sont des désirs. Avec le désir, l'Être humain n'est plus dans la nécessité mais dans le superflu. Dès lors, l'expression du désir commence là où s'arrête celle du besoin. Autant les besoins expriment des manques physiologiques et parfois émotionnels, autant les désirs n'expriment qu'exclusivement des manques émotionnels. A travers les désirs, l'Être humain recherche, au-delà de l'utile, l'agréable. Par conséquent, le désir a la particularité de repousser les limites physiologiques. A ce titre, Platon[4] considère qu'« *aucune possession sensible ne*

---

[4] Platon, *La République*, Les Belles Lettres, 2002.

saurait satisfaire le désir humain ». La satisfaction aux désirs serait donc semblable à un puits sans fond. En d'autres termes, le potentiel d'expression du désir est incommensurable et, par allégorie, ne semble pas connaître de limites. Comment étayer cette affirmation ?

L'expression du désir se fonde sur le plaisir que l'Être humain tire à vivre des événements spécifiques. Ces événements sont principalement captés par les organes de sens.

Les organes de sens et le désir

A travers tous les organes de sens, l'Être humain peut capter de multiples sensations agréables. Ces sensations lui procurent bien-être à travers des émotions positives. Suivant ce contexte, à travers divers événements, un plaisir chasse un autre dans l'espace et le temps.
Par exemple,
- Via le regard, il peut vivre divers événements impossibles à lister. Il peut aller regarder un match de football, aller au cinéma regarder un film, aller à la foire regarder de multiples attractions, aller dans divers musées, voyager et découvrir une multitude d'événements et de choses, etc.
- Via la langue, il peut découvrir de multiples

goûts, des plus basiques aux plus raffinés ; etc.

- Via l'ouïe, il peut entendre divers sons lui procurant des sensations agréables de niveaux variés ; etc.
- Etc.

Toutes ces sensations agréables qu'il peut vivre sont accessoires pour la survie.

Hormis les besoins physiologiques fondamentaux, il y a aussi le besoin vital de sécurité. L'intervention du désir permet, là aussi, de joindre l'agréable à l'utile.

Sécurité et désir

A travers la motivation par le désir, l'Être humain est capable d'aller au-delà du nécessaire en sophistiquant, à divers niveaux, tous les éléments qui assurent sa protection.

- Se loger

Les Êtres humains qui ne répondent qu'exclusivement aux motivations liées aux besoins peuvent se contenter de construire de simples huttes, igloos, etc. Ces formes d'habitats suffisent, de manière basique, à assurer leur protection dans leurs milieux de vie respectifs. C'est le strict nécessaire.

Comme, à travers ces formes d'habitats, les Êtres humains ne satisfont qu'au besoin, ils ne répondent donc qu'à la question de l'utile. Par contre, la question de l'agréable est motivée par le désir. Par exemple, des systèmes de chauffage, des systèmes de climatisation, des toilettes et douches internes, des systèmes d'isolation, divers gadgets de décoration, systèmes de sonnette, peinture de diverses couleurs pour murs et plafonds, installation de carrelages, etc. sont autant d'éléments qui permettent d'améliorer confort et bien-être.

- Se vêtir

Pour se vêtir, en fonction de leurs milieux de vie respectifs, les Êtres humains qui ne répondraient qu'exclusivement aux motivations liées aux besoins, pourraient se contenter d'une peau d'animal, etc. Malgré cet archaïsme vestimentaire, ils parviennent à s'adapter à leurs milieux de vie respectifs et, donc, à survivre. Suivant les raisonnements menés supra, le désir permettrait d'améliorer le confort et le bien-être des individus. Par conséquent, d'autres matériaux (laine, coton, soie, etc.) pour divers types et styles de vêtements (pull-overs, manteaux, vestes, chemises, etc.) verraient le jour.

- Etc.

A travers la motivation par le désir, on sort du basique ou de l'archaïsme pour tendre vers plus de sophistication.

Bref, la sophistication de tous les Biens consommables répond aux motivations humaines liées au désir. Les bénéfices que l'on tire de cette sophistication ne sont pas physiologiques et, donc, pas indispensables pour la survie du corps. A ce titre, par exemple, consommer des vers de terre vivants (et donc crus) et sans assaisonnement peut suffire à satisfaire au besoin physiologique de réalimentation. Par contre, considérons un plat spécifique proposé dans une ambiance feutrée, par un restaurant : steak-frites-salade, bien assaisonné, décoré et préparé selon un standard précis. Ce plat permet non seulement de satisfaire à un besoin physiologique (survie), mais aussi de faire vivre à celui qui le consomme diverses émotions captées par un ou plusieurs organes de sens spécifiques (la langue, les yeux, les oreilles).
Pour aller plus loin, on peut souligner une évolution intra-motivationnelle. C'est celle du désir basique au désir sophistiqué. Par exemple, avoir

une voiture basique répond à un désir de base. Mais avoir une voiture de grand luxe, full-option, permet d'en tirer des émotions toujours plus superflues par rapport à la survie. Etc.

C'est la satisfaction à divers désirs qui a permis progressivement l'émergence de la modernité. Car, dans le Livre 3 de la collection *Psychanthropologie* (*Les origines de l'intelligence*), nous démontrons que le désir est l'un des trois facteurs ayant concouru, à l'origine, à débrider progressivement le potentiel de l'intelligence humaine.

Etablir les différences entre les besoins et désirs humains est donc indispensable pour comprendre le passage d'une société archaïque vers une société moderne.

Section 2 : Le désir et les modernités

La modernité représente l'évolution d'une société archaïque vers une société plus élaborée. Les sociétés qui n'ont pas sophistiqué la partie matérielle de leur culture sont celles qui n'ont pas stimulé, de manière avancée, le potentiel du désir humain. Notamment, entre autres, nous démontrons (Livre 3) que le niveau d'exploitation du potentiel du désir est fonction de la nature du climat. Grâce à la Psychanthropologie, nous pouvons très aisément établir le lien entre climat et niveau de stimulation du désir, entre ce niveau de stimulation du désir et exploitation du potentiel intellectuel et donc, par transitivité, entre le climat et l'exploitation du potentiel intellectuel.

Cependant, les sociétés qui ne se modernisent exclusivement que sous l'impulsion du désir court un immense danger. Comme nous l'avons dit supra, c'est tel un train fou lancé à très vive allure et ayant atteint sa vitesse de croisière. Comme ce train, tôt ou tard ces sociétés rencontrent un obstacle de taille sur lequel elles se fracassent. Il faut anticiper cette éventualité en encadrant la libération du potentiel du désir. Deux facteurs sont susceptibles de remplir ce rôle d'anticipation. C'est l'adoption d'une autorité puissante de la morale, appartenant à l'instance du « surmoi », et l'amour. Nous traitons ces facteurs respectivement dans les Livres 4 & 5 de la collection *Psychanthropologie*. Ceci nous permet de mettre en exergue les différents types de modernités possibles.

Le niveau d'exploitation du potentiel du désir peut mettre en lumière trois types de modernités possibles. Pour les illustrer, appuyons-nous sur une des figures phares de la Psychanthropologie. C'est celle décrivant le processus complet de satisfaction équilibrée des manques exprimés par le corps à travers l'intelligence de l'inconscient. Précisément, exploitons son second bloc.

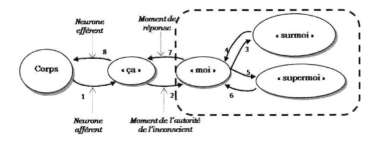

Figure n°1 : Les paramètres culturels

Description

Cette figure, dans son ensemble, est déjà largement explicitée tout le long de nos recherches sur la Psychanthropologie. Ici, ce qui nous intéresse c'est le second bloc (en encadré). Ce bloc concerne les principales instances à partir desquelles l'Être humain entre en contact avec les divers univers externes au corps afin d'y capter les ressources répondant aux divers manques (besoins et désirs) exprimés par son corps. Sont concernées l'instance du « moi » et ses deux sous-instances (le « surmoi » et le « supermoi »).

Les grandes lignes culturelles des sociétés peuvent être illustrées par les interactions entres les composantes de ce bloc. A titre de rappel, d'après la Psychanthropologie, la culture d'un peuple peut se définir comme étant le niveau d'influence plus ou moins avancée de l'une ou, de manière simultanée, des deux sous-instances du « moi » dans le processus de conservation des Êtres humains. Et la civilisation est l'influence d'une culture sur une autre. Ces définitions sont plus explicites dans le Livre 7 (*La démocratie idéale*) de la collection *Psychanthropologie*.

A partir de ce bloc, trois alliances émergent et illustrent trois formes spécifiques de modernité.

Sous-section 1 : La modernité immatérialiste

La première se fonde sur l'alliance entre le « moi » et le « surmoi ». Cette alliance fait émerger des cultures fondées sur une valorisation très forte de la morale. Ce type de société accorde à la morale une autorité puissante et extrêmement contraignante. Généralement, c'est le socle de l'identité des sociétés religieuses[5]. Dans ce type de société, le niveau de stimulation du désir est très faible. Ceci se traduit par un très faible niveau d'exploitation du potentiel de « supermoi », instance du symbole du débridement du potentiel de l'intelligence humaine.

Cette première alliance est à la base de ce que nous pouvons appeler la modernité immatérialiste, à

---

[5] Nous étudierons le profil de la société religieuse dans la prochaine Application de cette collection.

cause de la très faible implication du « supermoi ».

Sous-section 2 : La modernité matérialiste

La seconde forme de modernité est celle fondée sur l'alliance entre le « moi » et le « supermoi ». Elle est à la base des cultures structurant les imaginaires individuels et collectifs à partir de la stimulation plus ou moins très avancée du désir. Il est dit supra et dans des Livres précédents que ce niveau de stimulation implique une exploitation proportionnelle du potentiel de l'intelligence humaine. C'est l'exploitation avancée de ce potentiel qui permet un niveau très élevé de production qualitative et quantitative des Biens & Services. Cependant, via une telle culture, les mécanismes visant à créer une harmonie et la pérennité dans/d'une société sont largement sous-optimaux. En effet, les mécanismes permettant l'ultra valorisation de cette alliance paralysent l'expression de l'amour, source de la compassion, de l'altruisme, etc. Ensuite, ce type de société fait face à un déficit cruel de morale. Car ses mécanismes fondateurs neutralisent structurellement, l'autorité de cette dernière. Et, dans une moindre mesure, ces mêmes mécanismes rendent inopérante l'autorité de la conscience, qualifiée par Kant[6] d'« *autonomie de la volonté* ».

---

[6] Emmanuel Kant, *Critique de la raison pratique*, 1788.

Cette alliance est le principal fer de lance des sociétés modernes matérialistes telles que, entre autres, la société économique. Nous allons l'analyser en détail dans la suite de cet ouvrage.

Sous-section 3 : La modernité encadrée

Une culture fondée sur l'exploitation plus ou moins avancée des deux alliances (« moi »/ « surmoi » et « moi »/« supermoi ») est celle qui illustre une modernité équilibrée et pérenne. C'est elle qui permet l'émergence d'une société prospère et harmonieuse. Car, les activités du « supermoi » sont balisées et contrôlées par un « surmoi » efficace. Pour dire les choses plus simplement ou de manière caricaturale, la « *raison pratique* »[7] est un moyen de contrôle indispensable à l'optimalité de la « *raison pure* »[8].

Section 3 : Le désir comme essence de la modernité matérialiste

Dans les Livres 2 & 3 de cette collection, nous arrivons à la déduction que le désir est en même temps la cause et la conséquence de la modernité. En effet, dans un premier temps, la stimulation du désir met à l'épreuve le potentiel de l'intelligence

7 Emmanuel Kant, op. cit.
8 Emmanuel Kant, *Critique de la raison pure*, 1781.

25

humaine. Cette mise à l'épreuve débouche sur diverses inventions qui s'agrègent et se coordonnent pour faire évoluer la société vers la modernité.

Dans un deuxième temps, la modernité est à la base de la stimulation du désir. Car, pour assurer sa pérennité, sa dynamique doit impérativement stimuler le désir sans discontinuer. On en déduit que c'est tacitement la politique de l'offre qui prévaut pour l'entretien et la croissance de/dans la modernité matérialiste. Nous allons continuer à l'étayer infra.

Section 4 : De la libération du potentiel du désir au consumérisme

Pour continuer à exister, voire pour toujours évoluer, la modernité matérialiste doit continuellement stimuler le désir. En d'autres termes, il faut créer en permanence des désirs en chacun des individus et y apporter des réponses. Poussée à l'extrême, la stimulation du désir crée une relation très étroite entre l'individu et les Biens & Services produits. En quelque sorte, par sarcasme, on peut dire que l'individu marche derrière l'offre des Biens et Services. Cette dernière agit telle une carotte. Par conséquent, en toile de fond, ceux qui organisent la production des Biens & Services ont, de par l'action de la dynamique de l'inconscient, intérêt à entretenir cet ordre. Ce sont eux qui décident[9]. Ils ont intérêt à maintenir cet effet carotte qui pousse les individus à consommer toujours plus. Comme c'est cette stimulation du désir qui entretient le fonctionnement de cette forme de modernité, cette relation devient structurelle sous l'impulsion de ces décideurs.

La modernité matérialiste étant tacitement indissociable de la stimulation du désir, il y a un impact structurel sur la configuration mentale des individus de ce type de société. Autrement dit, la pérennisation de cette forme de modernité dépend de la manière dont est structuré l'univers psychique de ces individus. Cette structuration doit lier leur existence individuelle et collective à la consommation des Biens & Services. C'est ce lien qui donne un sens à leur vie. En cela, modernité matérialiste se confond à la société de consommation. Dès lors, les individus de ce type de société s'inscrivent ou s'enferment tous dans une doctrine tacite : le consumérisme. Cette société évolue et change de statut. On parle désormais de société économique. Et les citoyens deviennent des homoeconomicus. Dans ce sillage, on définit le consumérisme comme étant une doctrine à partir de laquelle les homoeconomicus ne donnent un sens à leur vie qu'à travers la consommation des Biens & Services.

---

9 Plus d'explications sont proposées infra.

La liaison entre existence et consommation des Biens & Services n'est possible qu'à travers des dynamiques de conditionnement et d'endoctrinement. Ces dynamiques aboutissent à une addiction consumériste régie exclusivement par la dynamique de l'inconscient.

CHAPITRE 2

Ossature de la société économique

Il est possible de mettre en exergue l'axe central de la société économique. Les composantes de cet axe sont représentées par des éléments incontournables rendant possible son émergence et lui conférant une identité.

Section 1 : L'économie comme principal agrégat

L'économie, en toute évidence, est l'agrégat principal de la société économique. C'est par elle et autour d'elle que se bâtit le système de la société économique. En d'autres termes, elle est au cœur du système.

Section 2 : La frénésie du travail

Le travail est la principale activité de la société économique. C'est la seule activité qui permet de produire des Biens & Services. Il y a une autre façon d'interpréter l'apport du travail dans le contexte de ce type de société. Ce ne serait plus de dire seulement que, grâce au travail, les homoeconomicus peuvent produire des Biens & Services indispensables pour assurer leur conservation, mais ce serait aussi de dire que grâce à cette activité, ils peuvent réaliser le sens qu'ils donnent à leur vie à travers le consumérisme. Par conséquent, il y a une frénésie pour et autour du travail comme dans nul autre type spécifique de société[10]. Le travail est alors considéré comme un instrument. Avoir un travail est un moyen et la consommation des Biens & Services est une fin. Donc, en plus d'être un élément pouvant leur permettre de satisfaire à leurs manques basiques (besoins), le travail leur permet aussi de vivre selon un matérialisme contemporain. C'est-à-dire un matérialisme toujours renouvelé et mis régulièrement à jour. Car c'est à travers leur capacité à vivre selon ce matérialisme contemporain qu'ils « trouveraient un épanouissement »[11].

Par ailleurs, c'est aussi par le travail que l'on répond aux désirs exprimés et/ou créés à l'égard

---

[10] Dans la société religieuse, c'est à travers la prière que homoreligiosus donne un sens à sa vie. Le travail y est marginalisé.

[11] Dans le Livre 8 de la collection *Psychanthropologie* (*La formule littérale du bonheur*), des arguments démontrent que cette aspiration spécifique est vaine. Car les émotions de type e", produites par la satisfaction aux manques liés aux désirs, ne suffisent pas pour assurer un bonheur stable et complet.

des consommateurs. Donc cette activité s'impose autant aux offreurs de Biens & Services.

Section 3 : Le siège du désir

L'ensemble des manques du corps sont captés et régis par la dynamique de l'inconscient. Depuis le Livre 1 de cette collection (*L'intelligence de l'inconscient humain*), il est souligné que cette dynamique appartient à la partie basse de l'âme, le « ça ».

Section 4 : Le corps

Le corps, en tant qu'une des trois dimensions de tout Être humain, est le principal, voire l'unique, réceptacle des Biens & Services produits par l'activité économique. C'est d'ailleurs de lui que partent tous les manques humains à satisfaire, in fine, par ces Biens & Services.

Section 5 : L'économie dans un système plus vaste

Dans des analyses précédentes[12], nous montrons que l'axe de la société économique fait partie d'un système sociétal plus vaste. Ce système plus vaste intègre d'autres agrégats (Famille, Institution de

---

[12] Voir Livre 7 de la collection *Psychanthropologie* (*La démocratie idéale*).

piété et Ecole). Outre le travail, ce système intègre aussi diverses autres activités de base telles que l'action, la dévotion (ouvrant à la spiritualité) et l'œuvre.

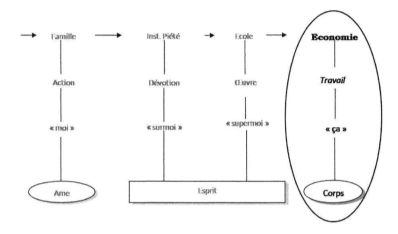

Figure n°2 : L'axe central de la société économique

Cette figure illustre les principales composantes produisant l'optimalité des choix et comportements dans l'espace et le temps chez l'Être humain. Elle est constituée de quatre blocs spécifiques pouvant, chacun, former l'ossature de base d'un système sociétal. A ce titre, le premier bloc est celui de la société familiale ou société sociale ; le second, celui de la société religieuse ; le troisième, celui de la société de la connaissance ; le quatrième, celui de la société économique. Bien que cohérents, ces systèmes sociétaux spécifiques sont tous sous-optimaux, car contre-productifs. Ils sont tous vecteurs structurels de la violence. Le bloc de la société économique, qui nous intéresse dans cet ouvrage, est encerclé dans cette figure.

A partir de l'axe central de la société économique, nous pouvons apporter des premières précisions concernant la nature de la société économique

Section 6 : La nature de la société économique

Fondée sur une modernité matérialiste, les composantes du système ne prennent en compte que des paramètres rationnels. Précisément, ce qui donne un sens à la vie des individus de ce type de société n'est basé que sur la dimension rationnelle. Ceci veut dire que, par exemple, contrairement à homoreligiosus, homoeconomicus ne croit pas en un Être irrationnel omniprésent et omnipotent. La structuration de son imaginaire ne se réduit qu'à la matérialité. Par extension, comme symbole, l'axe central de la société économique n'intègre que le corps. Or, le corps est, des trois dimensions de l'Homme, la dimension matérielle.

Le réductionnisme illustré par la liaison entre existence et consommation des Biens & Services représente un puissant vecteur de déstabilisation pour les Êtres humains le subissant.

CHAPITRE 3

LA SOCIÉTÉÉCONOMIQUE ET LA LIBERTÉ

Dans ce chapitre, nous allons aborder la question la plus sensible liée aux sociétés spécifiques telle que la société économique. C'est la notion de liberté. Elle est primordiale tant pour évaluer la qualité de ce type de société que pour déterminer ses caractéristiques.

Dans le Livre 4 de cette collection (*Les origines de la liberté*), nous avons traité assez précisément, du point de vue de la Psychanthropologie, ce qu'est la liberté. En l'occurrence, aucune liberté n'est possible sans émergence du libre arbitre. Nous rappelons que le libre arbitre représente l'espace du conscient à partir duquel l'individu pose des choix et prend des décisions sans aucune forme de déterminisme.

La doctrine tacite fondant la société économique, le consumérisme, permet-elle l'émergence du libre arbitre ?

Section 1 : Rappel du pouvoir de la dynamique de l'inconscient

Avant d'entrer dans le vif de l'analyse, rappelons certaines évidences fondées sur la Psychanthropologie.

Sous-section 1 : L'autorité de l'inconscient

Le principal facteur de servitude naturelle innée en tout Être vivant est la dynamique de l'inconscient. Cette dernière gère tout l'environnement endogène au corps. Entre autres, elle y capte tous les manques (besoins et désirs) du corps et les transmet à la dynamique consciente sous forme d'injonctions. La dynamique consciente a pour fonction principale de gérer tous les environnements externes au corps et d'y capter des ressources visant à satisfaire à ces injonctions. La transmission de ces injonctions se fait donc avec autorité. Dès lors, nous parlons d'autorité de l'inconscient. Cette dernière est dotée d'un potentiel phénoménal de pression sur la dynamique consciente. Le niveau de pression réel dépend d'au-moins trois facteurs.

- Le premier est l'espace de temps qui sépare l'expression d'un manque et la satisfaction à ce manque. Plus cet espace de temps est long, plus la pression augmente. Par exemple, la pression pour la réhydratation du corps exercée sur la dynamique consciente est très forte si vous passez deux jours sans boire, par rapport à deux heures.

- Le deuxième facteur est le conditionnement possible grâce à un ou plusieurs stimuli.

- L'accoutumance ou l'addiction se traduit par des automatismes, régis exclusivement par la dynamique de l'inconscient, à consommer un Bien ou un Service spécifique. Outre les addictions classiques, les sociétés modernes produisent de nombreuses autres formes d'addictions. Par exemple, à l'ère du numérique, de moins en moins de personnes peuvent se passer d'Internet ; de moins en moins peuvent se passer des réseaux sociaux ; etc.

L'autorité de l'inconscient est une des principales parties prenantes dans le processus d'émergence de la liberté humaine.

Sous-section 2 : L'impact des automatismes

Des actes ou des comportements répétés très souvent sont captés par la dynamique de l'inconscient et traduits progressivement en automatismes. Dès lors, dans des contextes adaptés, ces actes routiniers ne transitent plus par un arbitrage conscient. Plusieurs exemples peuvent être cités.

- L'exemple probablement le plus célèbre est celui illustré dans le film *Les temps modernes*[13] de Charlie Chaplin sur la chaîne de production et à la sortie d'usine.
- Programmer son réveil pour se faire réveiller tous les jours à 5 heures du matin. Après x temps, avec ou sans l'intervention du réveil, l'intelligence de l'inconscient active notre dynamique consciente en nous réveillant à 5 heures.
- Aussi, soulignons l'activité d'un pianiste. A force d'exercices et d'entraînement, l'association des sons aux touches du piano devient automatique. Dès lors, le pianiste pourrait être capable de jouer des notes même les yeux fermés.
- Aussi, chez un comptable, par exemple, l'encodage répétitif des chiffres apporte des automatismes pour cette activité.
- Etc.

D'innombrables autres exemples de ce type peuvent êtres cités. D'ailleurs, chacun d'entre nous, à

---

[13]   Charlie Chaplin, *Les temps modernes*, 1936.

travers son expérience personnelle, peut reconnaître un ou plusieurs cas d'actes routiniers traduits en automatismes autant dans l'univers professionnel que privé.

Section 2 : Rappel sur le processus de formation du libre arbitre

Afin d'éviter une rupture au cours de la lecture de cet ouvrage, nous allons brièvement rappeler comment émerge le libre arbitre, creuset de la liberté[14].

La liberté humaine est le fruit de plusieurs composantes antagonistes dont l'une est endogène au corps et d'autres, exogènes. La composante endogène est représentée par l'autorité de l'inconscient qui tend à imposer, par diverses injonctions, les doléances (manques = besoins et/ou désirs) du corps. Ces injonctions ne sont pas toujours socialement, humainement, culturellement, écologiquement acceptables. Dès lors, se dressent devant cette autorité endogène de multiples autres autorités généralement exogènes. Ce sont l'autorité de la morale, l'autorité des lois formelles, l'autorité parentale, l'autorité des us & coutumes, l'autorité de la nature, l'autorité de la

---

[14] Une démonstration exhaustive est réalisée dans le Livre 4 (*Les origines de la liberté*) de la collection *Psychanthropologie*.

conscience, l'autorité des expériences passées, l'autorité de la déontologie, etc. Ces diverses autorités antagonistes à l'autorité de l'inconscient posent des interdits et empêchent que les actes humains soient dictés par la dynamique de l'inconscient. C'est de cette confrontation qu'émerge le libre arbitre. Rappelons, une fois de plus, que le libre arbitre est l'espace du conscient à partir duquel l'Être humain pose des choix et prend des décisions sans aucune forme de déterminisme. A partir de ce libre arbitre, l'individu pose des choix en connaissance de cause. Il est libre. C'est pour cela que, du Livre 4 de cette collection, entre autres, nous avons déduit que la liberté est le fruit de l'interdit.

La figure illustrant l'espace du libre arbitre est la suivante :

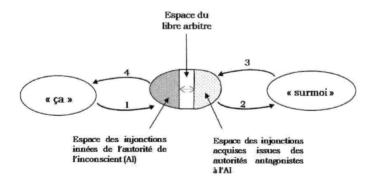

Figure n°3 : Création de l'espace du libre arbitre

C'est la dynamique de l'inconscient, symbolisée par l'instance du « ça », qui capte tous les besoins et désir du corps. Tous ces manques sont au préalable rangés dans une zone d'attente de la conscience en attendant un éventuel arbitrage. Cet arbitrage se réalise grâce aux diverses autorités antagonistes à l'autorité de l'inconscient intériorisées et rangées dans un autre espace du conscient. Cet espace spécifique est symbolisé par le « surmoi ». Sur cette figure, l'espace du libre arbitre est la zone immaculée au centre ne souffrant d'aucun parasitage. Tout parasitage serait signe de servitude pouvant provenir tant de l'autorité de l'inconscient que d'une quelconque autre autorité antagoniste exogène.

En considérant toutes ces données, comment se profile la liberté dans la société économique ?

Section 3 : Le libre arbitre émerge-t-il dans la société économique ?

Pour analyser méthodiquement la question de la liberté dans la société économique, il faut impérativement articuler la stimulation du désir avec l'activité de l'autorité de l'inconscient. Précisément, il faut garder en mémoire le fait que la stimulation du désir impacte le niveau de pression de l'autorité de l'inconscient. Avant d'aller plus loin, analysons les principales composantes susceptibles d'influencer l'émergence du libre arbitre chez homoeconomicus.

Sous-section 1 : De l'impact du désir au statut d'homoeconomicus

Comme il est souligné supra, le désir est l'essence de la modernité matérialiste. Sa stimulation sans discontinuer l'entretient et la fait évoluer. Il est à la base du consumérisme et, donc, pousse les individus de la société économique (homoeconomicus) à ne donner un sens à leur vie qu'à travers la consommation des Biens & Services. Les mécanismes permettant d'atteindre le statut d'homoeconomicus incluent tant le conditionnement que l'endoctrinement. Ils entraînent l'addiction.

- Le conditionnement

   Le désir étant l'essence de la société économique, l'organisation du système ouvre toutes les vannes susceptibles de le stimuler en profondeur. L'un des moyens incontournables de stimuli est la publicité. En principe, elle envahit le maximum d'espace possible. Elle est omniprésente dans toutes les formes de médias. Les appels à la consommation que lancent ces publicités touchent divers aspects de la vie quotidienne de manière à cerner chaque homoeconomicus.

A côté des stimuli publicitaires, chaque individu subit tacitement la pression sociale. En effet, vivre selon le consumérisme est le sens que homoeconomicus donne à sa vie. Mais, pour rester en phase avec la dynamique du système, il doit adapter sans cesse sa consommation à l'évolution de sa société. On dit alors qu'il vit selon un consumérisme contemporain. Dès lors, il cherche à s'inscrire dans le sillage des innovations ou des nouveautés. En d'autres termes, il consomme en fonction des innovations ou des nouveautés. Tout homoeconomicus qui, pour une raison ou l'autre, ne respecte pas ce principe de consumérisme contemporain, encourt un risque d'être marginalisé de part et d'autre au sein de son groupe. A ce titre, malheur à l'adolescent qui, dans la cour de son école, confond une tablette avec une petite table. Dans ce type de société, la pression sociale peut être un puissant facteur coercitif de consommation.

- L'endoctrinement

En l'occurrence, l'endoctrinement passe par le bourrage de la psyché des individus avec un message précis : rien d'autre n'est meilleur et acceptable que le consumérisme ; il n'y a pas d'alternative. Il impose une conviction sans arbitrage.

- L'addiction

Le conditionnement et l'endoctrinement concédés par l'individu passent à une étape supérieure. En effet, après un certain laps de temps, la fréquence de consommation des Biens & Services se traduit en automatismes. Dès lors, l'individu (son « moi ») perd totalement le contrôle de la situation et devient dépendant de la consommation. C'est d'ailleurs à partir de cette perte de contrôle que l'on peut acter le passage du statut de citoyen à celui d'homoeconomicus. Les automatismes inhérents à l'addiction sont exclusivement régis par la dynamique de l'inconscient. Perdre le contrôle par le « moi » signifie, dans la plupart des cas, qu'il n'y a aucune possibilité d'arbitrage psychique débouchant sur l'émergence du libre arbitre. Concrètement, l'addiction tend à asservir tout individu qui la subit. Car la pression exercée sur la dynamique consciente, univers du « moi », est phénoménale.

Ainsi, le conditionnement, l'endoctrinement et l'addiction sont de très puissants facteurs libérant une pression totale de l'autorité de l'inconscient. A côté de ces trois facteurs, l'accumulation illimitée des manques impacte aussi la pression de l'autorité de l'inconscient.

Sous-section 2 : L'impact du cumul des manques

La stimulation permanente du désir augmente mécaniquement, et de manière structurelle, les manques du corps. Dès lors, en plus des manques ordinaires fondamentaux, ceux des besoins, s'ajoutent continuellement d'autres manques liés aux désirs. Cette accumulation sans discontinuer de manques implique une augmentation systématique des fréquences d'injonctions de la dynamique de l'inconscient à l'égard de la dynamique consciente. Cette augmentation des fréquences impacte positivement le niveau de pression de l'autorité de l'inconscient sur l'individu. De prime abord, on peut considérer que la capacité à satisfaire à ces manques pléthoriques dépend du niveau de revenu de chacun. En tout état de cause, cette fréquence d'injonctions est une très mauvaise nouvelle pour toute personne dont les revenus sont limités. C'est d'ailleurs, le principal facteur d'instabilité potentielle de ce type de société. Il est à la base de l'augmentation du niveau du potentiel de propension à la violence. Nous y reviendrons infra.

Sous-section 3 : Le centre de décision psychique chez homoeconomicus

Sous l'impulsion soutenue tant du conditionnement que de l'endoctrinement menant à l'addiction, homoeconomicus (son « moi ») est en permanence sous la pression des injonctions consuméristes portées par la dynamique de l'inconscient. Cette pression tend à parasiter l'espace du libre arbitre et, donc, à neutraliser la liberté dans la société économique.

Ce parasitage est illustré par la figure suivante :

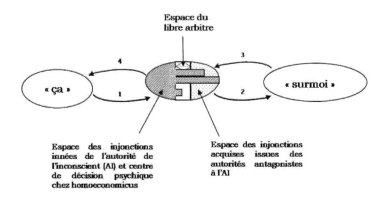

Figure n°4 : Parasitage de l'espace du libre arbitre par l'autorité de l'inconscient

Description et interprétation

Cette figure illustre les différents niveaux de parasitage de l'espace du libre arbitre par l'autorité de l'inconscient. Il y en a trois. Parmi ces trois, deux montrent l'existence et la légitimation de règles formelles ou informelles transgressées. Ce sont les première et troisième barres horizontales.

La deuxième barre horizontale illustre très précisément l'impact du consumérisme sur la liberté d'homoeconomicus. Elle pourfend totalement tant l'espace du libre arbitre que celui des autorités antagonistes à l'autorité de l'inconscient. Ce parasitage total s'explique par le fait logique de la non-interdiction de la consommation, voire du consumérisme. Dans la société économique, le comportement consumériste n'est pas un délit, bien au contraire. A priori, malgré les caractéristiques[15] tacitement valorisées et véhiculées par le système de la société économique, il est considéré et revendiqué le fait que consommer des Biens & Services (B&S), même au-delà d'un certain seuil, ne nuit pas aux intérêts de qui que ce soit. Ce sont l'immense pression de l'autorité de l'inconscient et l'absence de seuil[16] limite à la consommation de B&S qui expliquent cette incursion totale du consumérisme dans l'espace psychique des homoeconomicus. En d'autres termes, c'est cette configuration qui illustre la structure des imaginaires individuels et collectifs des homoeconomicus. C'est le consumérisme qui sédimente leurs imaginaires et régule en très grande partie leurs comportements. Par conséquent, cette configuration apporte un renseignement capital : homoeconomicus n'est pas libre. Ce qui donne un sens à sa vie est, pour lui, un puissant vecteur de servitude. La source de cette servitude totale est endogène, ancrée en lui. C'est la dynamique de l'inconscient. Par sarcasme, on dirait qu'homoeconomicus est prisonnier de lui-même, plus précisément d'une de ses propres dimensions.

---

[15] Voir infra.

[16] Au-delà de ce seuil, une autorité sanctionnerait toute consommation de B&S. Cette autorité serait alors antagoniste à celle de l'inconscient.

En bref, cette servitude résulte du fait que :

- La société économique pousse à l'extrême la libération du potentiel du désir.
- Pour assurer sa pérennité, les mécanismes du système de ce type de société imposent tacitement un conditionnement et une addiction à la consommation.
- Face à la pression consumériste, aucune autorité antagoniste à l'autorité de l'inconscient n'impose un niveau seuil à la consommation des B&S.

La servitude totale d'homoeconomicus par la dynamique de l'inconscient maintient son centre de choix et de décision dans la partie inconsciente du cerveau. Cette partie est symbolisée par la zone hachurée à gauche de cette figure. Précisément, le centre de décision d'homoeconomicus, en fonction de ce qui donne un sens à sa vie, se situe dans l'espace d'attente réservé aux injonctions innées de l'autorité de l'inconscient.

Si la liberté économique se réduit au productivisme et au consumérisme, alors cette liberté n'est rien d'autre que celle de la dynamique de l'inconscient. En d'autres termes, cette « liberté » n'est en réalité qu'une profonde servitude.

Enseignement : Il est impératif de réguler, certes jusqu'à un certain optimum. Car au-delà, on tombe dans une autre forme de servitude induite, non plus via le « ça », mais via le « surmoi »[17]. Dès lors, moins on régule, jusqu'à un certain seuil, plus on s'enferme dans la servitude. Autrement dit, plus on dérégule, jusqu'à un certain seuil, moins on est libre. La régulation, jusqu'à un certain seuil, induit la liberté. C'est ce qui ressort, entre autres, du Livre 4 de la collection Psychanthropologie (*Les origines de la liberté*).

Définition précise du consumérisme

Avec l'introduction de la notion de seuil, à travers son absence, on peut ajuster la définition du consumérisme. Dès lors, il représente une doctrine à partir de laquelle les homoeconomicus ne donnent un sens à leur vie qu'à travers la consommation frénétique des Biens & Services.

Comment interpréter, en articulation avec la société économique, le parasitage de l'espace du libre arbitre par ces trois barres horizontales? Par exemple, à partir de la deuxième barre horizontale, on peut dresser le profil précis d'homoeconomicus.

---

[17] Voir plus de détails et d'illustrations infra.

Section 4 : Les caractéristiques d'homoeconomicus

Les caractéristiques d'homoeconomicus, dont la vie ne prend un sens qu'à travers la consommation frénétique des Biens & Services, deviennent aisées à mettre en lumière avec le parasitage total de l'espace du libre arbitre par la dynamique de l'inconscient. En l'occurrence, comme le centre de décision d'homoeconomicus est maintenu dans l'inconscient, c'est la dynamique de l'inconscient qui, en très grande partie, influence les choix et les décisions d'homoeconomicus. Dès lors, sous l'emprise de la dynamique de son inconscient, les caractéristiques d'homoeconomicus seront exactement celles de la dynamique de l'inconscient. Dans les Livres 1 & 2 de cette collection, nous les avons explicitées et étayées de manière plus ou moins exhaustive. Ce sont : l'égoïsme, l'impatience, la convoitise, l'avidité, etc.

Ce sont d'ailleurs ces caractéristiques qui, suite à l'immense pression de l'autorité de l'inconscient, drainent un niveau de potentiel très élevé de propension à réaliser le potentiel de violence de l'Être humain.

CHAPITRE 4

LA SOCIÉTÉ ÉCONOMIQUE, LA COMPÉTITION ET LA VIOLENCE

Qui ne regarde que son nombril ne voit pas l'abîme vers lequel il avance.

La violation totale de l'espace du libre arbitre par l'autorité de l'inconscient, source des caractéristiques d'homoeconomicus, définit structurellement la nature des interactions entre ce dernier et le reste des Êtres vivants.

Section 1 : De l'individualisme à la compétition

Chacune des caractéristiques des homoeconomicus déterminées supra leur impose un comportement spécifique. Précisément, toutes ces caractéristiques peuvent se résumer en une seule : l'individualisme. Chaque homoeconomicus ne vit que pour lui et ne recherche donc exclusivement que ses intérêts.

Ainsi, la société économique ne se réduit qu'à une somme d'individualismes.

Par conséquent, il est évident de déduire que si, de manière structurelle, chacun ne cherche exclusivement que ses intérêts dans une société, alors les interactions entre les membres de cette société et au-delà ne seront fondées que sur des rapports de force et, donc, la compétition. Dès lors, le potentiel de propension à la violence est nettement plus élevé.

Section 2 : Le consumérisme comme vecteur de violence

Le consumérisme, résultat du conditionnement, de l'endoctrinement et de l'addiction à la consommation frénétique des Biens & Services est un puissant vecteur de violence.

Sous-section 1 : La violence pure, sans état d'âme

Dans le Livre 2 de la collection *Psychanthropologie* (*Les origines de la violence*), nous parvenons à démontrer que les caractéristiques de la dynamique de l'inconscient sont de puissants vecteurs de violence. A fortiori, il y est démontré que, par exemple, tout Être vivant aura un niveau potentiel d'égoïsme et de convoitise élevé s'il doit fournir plus d'efforts que d'autres pour assurer sa conservation (survie et bien-être). Dans le cadre de la société économique, les efforts supplémentaires sont liés à la multiplicité des désirs stimulés en chacun des homoeconomicus. Et, finalement, comme ces efforts sont intenses et permanents, alors il est doté d'un niveau supérieur de potentiel de violence par rapport à n'importe quel autre type d'individus (homoreligiosus, homofamilus, homopoliticus, etc.). En effet, l'analyse de chacune de ces caractéristiques, lorsqu'il est question des interactions entre Êtres vivants, montre qu'elles débouchent toutes sur la violence.

- L'égoïsme

Dans un groupe, si chacun ne cherche que ses intérêts, alors il trouve en l'autre un adversaire. L'égoïsme est à la base de la logique de la *"loi de la jungle"*, la loi du chacun pour soi. En tant qu'adversaire, chaque individu est prêt à tout pour évincer l'autre pour assurer sa propre conservation (survie et bien-être). L'explication originelle[18] de cette caractéristique est liée, d'abord, au rapport de la dynamique de l'inconscient avec le corps. Ce rapport est celui de sa mission : assurer les homéostasies biologique et émotionnelle du corps. A ce titre, à travers

---

[18] Voir Livre 1 de cette collection : *L'intelligence de l'inconscient humain.*

l'intelligence de l'inconscient, en toute circonstance, elle ne cherche exclusivement que les intérêts du corps auquel elle est attachée. Ensuite, il faut souligner son champ de compétence et, donc, ses limites. En effet, la dynamique de l'inconscient n'a pas vocation à gérer les environnements externes au corps auquel elle est liée. Cette gestion est l'apanage de la dynamique consciente. Dès lors, comme elle n'est pas dotée de raison, elle n'est pas conçue pour comprendre les intérêts des autres corps appartenant à ces environnements externes. Sous son influence, l'individu ne peut pas se mettre à la place des autres. Au mieux, même avec l'intervention de l'amour exclusif qu'elle véhicule[19], elle ne cherche avant tout que les intérêts du corps auquel elle est liée.

- La convoitise

La convoitise est la deuxième caractéristique la plus saillante de la dynamique de l'inconscient de tout Être vivant. Consécutivement à la libération très avancée du potentiel du désir, à cause de l'immense pression exercée par l'autorité de l'inconscient sur la dynamique consciente,

---

[19] Voir Livre 5 de cette collection : *Anthologie de l'amour.*

homoeconomicus est caractérisé par un niveau de convoitise supérieur. Parce que la raison est largement balayée par cette immense pression[20], il n'hésitera pas à convoiter et à s'accaparer les intérêts d'autrui.

- L'impatience

La troisième caractéristique principale de la dynamique de l'inconscient est l'impatience. Pour les mêmes raisons développées ci-dessus, homoeconomicus montrera un niveau d'impatience très largement supérieur et permanent par rapport à tout autre type d'individu (homoreligiosus, homofamilus, homopoliticus, etc.). L'impatience s'explique et s'illustre originellement par l'intransigeance de la dynamique de l'inconscient dans le processus de maintien ou de rétablissement des équilibres des homéostasies biologique et émotionnelle. Cette intransigeance se justifie par l'urgence de la sauvegarde de l'essentiel : la conservation du corps, qui est la mission principale de l'intelligence de l'inconscient. Un besoin ou un désir exprimé par le corps doit être résolu au plus vite, peu importe les

---

[20] Voir explication infra.

moyens utilisés. L'illustration la plus évidente est l'arc réflexe. L'observation du comportement des nourrissons instruit sur d'autres illustrations de l'intransigeance et de l'impatience. Par exemple, lorsqu'ils ont faim, ils le manifestent à travers des pleurs. A partir de ce moment, en situation ordinaire, les pleurs ne cesseront que lorsqu'ils auront été nourris. Ils ne peuvent pas comprendre la nécessité de patienter. Car la patience est une caractéristique valorisée principalement par la raison, élément développé dans la dynamique consciente. A ce moment de l'existence, c'est exclusivement la dynamique inconsciente qui régit leurs actions : il n'y a pas d'arbitrage[21].

Lorsque la satisfaction à un besoin ou à un désir passe par la dynamique consciente, par exemple, si le taux de pression d'une injonction spécifique (dans l'hypothalamus) de l'autorité de l'inconscient sur ce dernier est faible, ce sont les valeurs et les normes intériorisées via le « surmoi » qui postposeront cette satisfaction. Mais plus le taux de cette pression s'élèvera, plus les valeurs et les normes sociales s'écarteront pour laisser s'exprimer l'intransigeance, et donc l'impatience, de la dynamique de

---

[21] Voir Livre 4 (*Les origines de la liberté*) de cette collection.

l'inconscient.

- L'avidité

- Etc.

L'exacerbation de ces caractéristiques dans la société économique entraine donc, de manière proportionnelle, un niveau élevé du potentiel de propension à la violence. A fortiori, le fait que l'autorité de l'inconscient parasite totalement tant l'espace du libre arbitre que le « surmoi » montre qu'homoeconomicus est capable d'exercer, sans état d'âme, toutes les formes de violence, même la violence dite « gratuite ». Cette violence gratuite s'explique par la neutralisation de l'autorité de la conscience qui appartient à l'instance du « surmoi ». Cette neutralisation empêche l'émergence du remords. C'est la grande particularité de la violence exercée par homoeconomicus.

Pour mieux illustrer l'explosion de la violence inhérente aux mécanismes de la société économique, il faut se tourner vers les sociétés matériellement pauvres susceptibles d'adopter bon gré, mal gré, les principes de ce type de société.

Sous-section 2 : Consumérisme et explosion de la violence dans les pays pauvres

Nous reviendrons dans un futur ouvrage sur le rapport du consumérisme à l'instabilité et à la dégénérescence des pays pauvres. En attendant, mettons en lumière la causalité entre adoption tacite ou explicite de cette doctrine et l'explosion de la violence dans ces pays.

Dans le Livre 4 (*Les origines de l'intelligence*) de cette collection, nous démontrons que ce qui explique, en grande partie et de manière structurelle et dynamique, la pauvreté matérielle de beaucoup de nations est l'insuffisance d'accumulation d'automatismes d'aisance à exploiter le potentiel de l'intelligence humaine. Lorsqu'il est question de déficits d'automatismes généraux, ce sont généralement les nations appartenant aux zones tropicales et équatoriales qui en souffrent le plus. En amont, en autarcie[22], les populations de ces nations n'ont vécu quasiment que sous l'impulsion des besoins pendant des centaines de milliers d'années. Les conditions climatiques favorables ne leur ont pas permis de débrider, avec une accumulation d'automatismes d'aisance à le faire, le potentiel de leur intelligence. En d'autres termes, la faible

---

[22] Absence totale de contact avec la culture des zones tempérées.

stimulation du désir n'a pas permis de libérer progressivement le potentiel de l'intelligence au cours des milliers d'années.

Que se passe-t-il lorsque la culture de la zone tempérée rencontre celle de la zone tropicale ?

Cette rencontre aboutit à des échanges culturels, voire à une domination civilisationnelle des zones tempérées sur des zones tropicales. En guise de rappel, nous définissons la civilisation comme étant l'influence d'une culture sur une autre. Parmi les facteurs influençant les cultures des peuples issus des zones tropicales, on cite, entre autres, la stimulation du désir. Car beaucoup de Biens & Services proposés par les nations issues des zones tempérées sont créés suite à la stimulation, parfois très avancée, des manques superflus du corps. Or, il y a une inadéquation entre l'expression de ces manques superflus et les possibilités structurelles d'y répondre de manière endogène en zone tropicale. Car les populations de ces zones sont dépourvues tant de l'accumulation, par voie culturelle, des connaissances permettant de produire ces Biens que de l'accumulation, par voie génétique, d'automatismes d'aisance à exploiter le potentiel de l'intelligence (au départ, bridé indifféremment chez tous les groupes d'Êtres humains). Pendant un laps de temps très long, les nations appartenant à ces zones tropicales doivent importer tous les Biens devant satisfaire à ces manques superflus. Or, étant pauvres, il leur est impossible d'importer effectivement en quantité suffisante[23] ces Biens qui sont généralement dotés d'une forte valeur ajoutée.

Ainsi, on observe un décalage entre stimulation plus ou moins avancée du potentiel du désir et capacité à satisfaire à cette stimulation. Dès lors, à travers l'immense pression structurelle exercée par l'autorité de l'inconscient née de cette stimulation, il y a systématiquement libération du potentiel de violence dans ces pays pauvres. En d'autres termes, la violence, sous toutes ses formes, et la corruption explosent avec la libération du potentiel du désir. Cette corrélation est très bien illustrée par Cathy Scott-Clark et Adrian Levy[24]. *« En 1998, le roi du Bhoutan a déclaré que l'objectif du pays serait d'atteindre le plus haut niveau de bonheur national brut. Mais en 1999, il a commis une « erreur fatale » : il a levé l'interdit de posséder une télévision. Rupert Murdoch a aussitôt fourni quarante-six chaînes, à travers son réseau Star TV. Et ainsi les habitants du royaume ont vu le lot habituel de sexe, violence, publicité, romances que les habitants des pays riches regardent aussi. Le résultat ne se fit pas*

---

[23] Concrètement, on pourrait se rendre compte que ces importations sont très marginales.

[24] Cathy Scott-Clark & Adrian Levy, *Fast Forward into Trouble*, The Guardian, 14 juin 2003.

attendre. Les divorces, la criminalité, la consommation de drogue ont immédiatement augmenté »[25].

Cette analyse portant sur la stimulation du désir dans les pays pauvres permet de dégager un enseignement général.

Enseignement

D'une manière générale, peu importe l'espace où cela s'applique, la propension potentielle à la violence explose avec la libération du potentiel du désir.

Section 3 : La société économique et le bonheur

En considérant le sens que les homoeconomicus donnent à leur vie et le caractère « insatiable » du désir, on assiste à une sorte de course à l'échalote dans la société économique. Les homoeconomicus courent derrière une carotte (le bonheur) qu'ils ne peuvent saisir. A fortiori, cette course est parasitée par la causalité entre désir et violence. Le bonheur n'est que très faiblement compatible avec le système de la société économique à cause de « l'insatiabilité » du désir.

D'une manière générale, les sociétés qui ne croient

---

[25] Daniel Cohen, *Homoeconomicus : Prophète (égaré) des temps nouveaux*, p.19, Albin Michel, 2012.

obtenir le bonheur qu'à travers les émotions de type *e''*, celles produites par l'aspect matériel de la vie, iront toujours de désillusion en désillusion. Les émotions de type *e''* ne sont qu'une composante, parmi tant d'autres, du bonheur. Nous traitons, de manière exhaustive, la question du bonheur dans le Livre 8 de cette collection (*La formule littérale du bonheur*).

Section 4 : La société économique frappée par la myopie

Le consumérisme, doctrine individualiste, repose essentiellement sur les caractéristiques explicitées supra. Toutes convergent vers la production de la violence (sous-optimale et hors contrôle) et, donc, de la destruction. Etant la doctrine principale sédimentant les imaginaires individuels et collectifs des homoeconomicus, il n'y a pas de compensation structurelle à la violence. Au contraire, la violence gagne en ampleur avec la stimulation perpétuelle du désir. Au cours de cette course effrénée, la destruction (des vies) s'accélérerait avec une possible extension de cette doctrine dans l'espace.

A tort, le système de la société économique considère que le comportement consumériste ne nuit pas aux intérêts de l'ensemble. Ceci est une vision essentiellement court-termiste tirant ses sources des caractéristiques de ce type de société. Précisément, l'impatience qui régit homoeconomicus l'empêche d'avoir une vue d'ensemble, une vue à long terme. Régit par la dynamique de l'inconscient, son comportement automatique l'empêche d'intérioriser des limites au consumérisme. Il ne vit que pour l'instant présent en regardant principalement son nombril. Or, s'il ne regarde que son nombril, alors il ne voit pas l'abîme vers lequel il avance.

Dès lors, nous pouvons en déduire que la doctrine consumériste ou, plus globalement, la société économique est frappée d'une myopie. Elle ne considère que l'instant présent. Cette vision réduite est incompatible avec l'écologie.

Par ailleurs, c'est l'exacerbation des caractéristiques de la dynamique de l'inconscient, fondant l'accroissement du potentiel de propension à la violence, qui, plus que dans n'importe quel autre type de société, impose l'adoption d'une pléthore de lois dans la société économique.

CHAPITRE 5

LA SOCIÉTÉ ÉCONOMIQUE ET LA BOULIMIE DES LOIS

L'immense pression de l'autorité de l'inconscient exercée sur la dynamique consciente impose au système de la société économique d'entretenir une relation particulière avec les lois.

Section 1 : Les composantes de la liberté dans la société économique

Dans cette section, nous analyserons le niveau de pertinence, la compatibilité et les possibilités d'implémentation des autorités antagonistes à l'autorité de l'inconscient. Ceci est important pour évaluer tant le niveau de stabilité de la société économique que les principaux éléments sur lesquels repose cette stabilité.

Dans le livre 4 (*Les origines de la liberté*) de cette collection nous dressons et analysons une liste des principales autorités antagonistes à l'autorité de l'inconscient. Elles sont à peu près au nombre de neuf : l'autorité de la morale, l'autorité des lois formelles, l'autorité parentale, l'autorité de la nature, l'autorité de la conscience, l'autorité des us & coutumes, l'autorité des expériences passées, l'autorité de la déontologie, etc. Quel est le niveau de compatibilité et de pertinence de chacune de ces autorités antagonistes à l'autorité de l'inconscient dans la société économique ? Comment s'articulent-elles avec le système de cette dernière ?

Sous-section 1 : L'autorité de la morale

Elle est incompatible avec la société économique. Car la nature de ce type de société est exclusivement matérialiste et, donc, rationnelle. Contrairement à homoreligiosus, homoeconomicus ne croit pas en un Être omnipotent et omniprésent. Il ne croit qu'en lui-même. Homoreligiosus postpose son paradis pour une vie après la mort, tandis qu'homoeconomicus tend à construire et à vivre son paradis pendant sa vie rationnelle sur Terre. Chacun des deux se comporte suivant ces perspectives respectives. Dès lors, homoeconomicus souhaite « maximiser » son bien-être pendant son bref passage sur Terre. Pour ce faire, il diversifie autant que possible ses sources d'émotions : stimulation accrue du désir. Ainsi, l'autorité de la morale, pourtant la plus efficace pour la stabilité et l'harmonie des sociétés (voir Livre 4 de la collection *Psychanthropologie*), est neutralisée par les fondements et les mécanismes de la société économique. C'est donc l'amoralité qui régit la société économique.

Sous-section 2 : L'autorité de la conscience

Dans les Livres 1 & 4 de la collection *Psychanthropologie*, nous démontrons que la dynamique consciente est subordonnée à celle de l'inconscient dans le processus de conservation de l'Être humain. L'autorité qu'elle a sur celle de la dynamique de l'inconscient est potentiellement très faible. En l'occurrence, en considérant l'immense pression exercée par l'autorité de l'inconscient sur la dynamique consciente, le pouvoir de l'autorité de la conscience est nul. En d'autres termes, le principe de « *l'autonomie de la volonté* » de Kant n'a aucun pouvoir de résistance face au conditionnement et à l'addiction consuméristes. Par conséquent, cette autorité est très facilement neutralisée.

Dans la société économique, la seule autorité susceptible de faire contrepoids, autant que faire se peut, à celle de la dynamique de l'inconscient est l'autorité des lois formelles élaborées par des pouvoirs ou institutions étatiques.

Section 2 : L'omniprésence et la multiplicité des lois formelles

En considérant l'immense pression de l'autorité de l'inconscient chez les homoeconomicus, il faut un pouvoir fort ou des institutions crédibles susceptibles de sanctionner efficacement tout acte malveillant. A cause de cette immense pression, les homoeconomicus chercheront en permanence des failles pour satisfaire indûment aux multiples désirs qui s'imposent en eux. Dès lors, pour assurer la pérennité et la stabilité du système de la société économique, les institutions multiplient des lois afin de se prémunir de ces velléités malveillantes. Ainsi, du global au moindre petit détail, ces institutions tendront à légiférer sur tous les aspects de la vie quotidienne des homoeconomicus. Pour les raisons évoquées supra, rien ne sera laissé à l'appréciation de la conscience ni au bon sens éthique des homoeconomicus. En d'autres termes, cette pléthore de lois montre qu'homoeconomicus n'est absolument pas digne de confiance. Divers mécanismes, outils (caméras) et institutions de surveillance particulièrement efficaces pourraient être mis en place pour scruter ses moindres faits et gestes dans la lumière comme dans l'ombre (espace privé, lieux publics sans témoins ou sans présence concrète de l'autorité des lois formelles, etc.).

C'est tant cette multiplicité des lois que la crédibilité des sanctions accompagnant ces lois qui permettent l'émergence partielle de certains espaces du libre arbitre chez homoeconomicus. Ces espaces, sur la figure n°4 supra, sont ceux qui ne sont pas parasités par l'autorité de l'inconscient. Il n'est pas vain de préciser que ce libre arbitre ne concerne que tout ce qui est interdit : l'acte malveillant. Il ne concerne pas le consumérisme, essentiel pour la société économique.

Face à la fréquence et à l'amplitude très élevée des injonctions de l'autorité de l'inconscient, avec l'adoption d'une quantité pléthorique et proportionnelle des lois, un autre levier est indispensable pour empêcher l'écroulement du système de la société économique. C'est la disponibilité, voire l'accessibilité, des ressources devant satisfaire à la multiplicité des désirs exprimés en permanence.

Section 3 : La disponibilité des ressources

Le levier basique et évident permettant d'empêcher l'exercice du potentiel de violence, via la convoitise, l'avidité, l'impatience ou l'égoïsme, est la disponibilité des ressources. Cette disponibilité permet de satisfaire, de manière potentielle, à tous les manques exprimés par le corps de chacun des homoeconomicus. En effet, si, dans le temps, chacun a de quoi satisfaire à l'ensemble de ses besoins et désirs, le potentiel de violence est globalement maîtrisé et, donc, la paix sociale acquise. La disponibilité des Biens et Services permet de répondre au niveau élevé de la pression de l'autorité de l'inconscient.

Mais, comme l'univers de la société économique se fonde sur la compétition à travers la loi du *chacun pour soi*, la disponibilité des ressources ne suffit absolument pas. Car il se pose le problème de l'accessibilité à ces ressources par tous.

- Celui qui, pour une raison ou l'autre, n'a pas les moyens de satisfaire à ces manques sera poussé (par l'autorité de l'inconscient) à piétiner, si possible, les intérêts des autres membres de la société : vol, divers trafics, etc. Mais ces actes malveillants sont contrés par une autorité des lois puissante et crédible. Grâce à cette opposition, l'espace du libre arbitre est maintenu intact. Cependant, il pourrait arriver que les homoeconomicus les plus démunis ou les classes populaires exploitent des possibles failles pour transgresser la loi.
- Ceux appartenant à une éventuelle classe moyenne[26] auront aussi tendance à piétiner

---

[26] La bande représentant la classe moyenne dans la société économique est très mince.

les intérêts des autres membres de la société. Car, dans ce type de société, à cause de l'avidité renforcée par le conditionnement et l'addiction, le désir sera toujours supérieur aux revenus[27]. En toute circonstance, tout revenu court derrière le désir. Car ce dernier est insatiable.

- Paradoxalement, les riches et les plus riches, ceux qui, a priori, ont les moyens financiers d'accéder aux ressources, piétineront aussi les intérêts des autres. Ceci s'explique aussi par la supériorité, en toute circonstance, du désir sur les revenus. Le niveau de qualité d'exigence du désir est supérieur (faire du tourisme dans l'espace, changer de yacht tous les deux ans, etc.). Tous courent aussi derrière le désir. Mais, nous apporterons plus de précisions dans la deuxième partie de cet ouvrage, les plus riches font généralement partie du cercle des élites. Suivant les analyses menées dans le Livre 7 (*La démocratie idéale*) de cette collection, on devrait s'attendre à ce que ces élites sacralisent ce cercle afin de s'affranchir de l'autorité des lois. A titre de précision, si l'on considère la définition de la notion du « sacré » proposée par Émile Durkheim, « *les*

---

[27] Pour plus d'explications, se référer au Livre 3 de cette collection : *Les origines de l'intelligence.*

choses sacrées sont les choses séparées, marquées par une frontière qui délimite deux ensembles hétérogènes. Frontière entre l'espace enclos dans le temple et l'espace qui s'étend autour de lui, entre les jours ouvrables et les jours fériés, entre les activités ouvertes à tous et celles réservées aux initiés, etc. »[28]. Cette idée laisse sous-entendre que tous les homoeconomicus ne sont pas égaux devant la loi. Certains, ceux qui les conçoivent, s'en mettent à l'abri. Ce contexte est illustré par la première barre horizontale en partant du haut dans la figure n°4 supra. Cette barre montre que l'autorité des lois n'est pas suffisante pour contrer l'immense pression de l'autorité de l'inconscient chez les élites homoeconomicus.

Dans les classes sociales défavorisées et dans beaucoup de nations pauvres, c'est le désir qui est la principale porte de prison.

Enseignement

Fondamentalement la liberté économique, fondée sur le consumérisme, et donc sur le productivisme, n'existe pas. Ce diptyque étant les doctrines

---

[28] Camille Tarot, « *Le symbolique et le sacré* », préface, p.17, La Découverte/M.A.U.S.S., 2008.

71

motrices de la société économique, les homoeconomicus ne sont pas libres.

A travers les fondements de la société économique, comment s'organise-t-elle ?

PARTIE 2

LA DYNAMIQUE DE LA SOCIÉTÉ ÉCONOMIQUE

Dans la partie précédente, nous avons montré que les homoeconomicus subissent un envahissement complet de l'espace du libre arbitre lié aux injonctions donnant un sens à leur vie. Cette servitude endogène permet, a priori, de remettre en cause structurellement la compatibilité de la société économique avec la démocratie. Dans la seconde partie, nous allons continuer à passer au scanner ce type de société afin de mettre en lumière son profil.

CHAPITRE 1

LES COMPOSANTES DU SYSTÈME
DE LA SOCIÉTÉ ÉCONOMIQUE

Le système de la société économique s'organise nécessairement, de manière cohérente, autour de son axe central exposé dans la première partie. Cet axe est le fil rouge, la référence, qui protège son identité et valorise les paradigmes susceptibles de l'induire[29]. Dans ce système, l'économie n'est pas prise comme simple agrégat producteur de valeurs matérielles, mais comme élément central permettant à des individus de donner un sens à leur vie. Suivant cette logique, l'Économie a, en plus d'une capacité de production qualitative et quantitative des Biens & Services exponentiellement plus élevée, une valeur symbolique. C'est ce qui marque une des grandes différences entre la société économique et les autres types de sociétés modernes.

---

[29]Par exemple, il y a une proximité très étroite que l'on peut établir entre le paradigme néolibéral et l'émergence de la société économique.

Cet agrégat est donc le point de départ. C'est autour de lui que sont greffées d'autres structures cohérentes apportant viabilité et performance au système. Rappelons, à titre de précision, que « *tout système social est un ensemble de structures socio-économiques, socio-politiques, techno-économiques, ... On y distingue des normes et règles, des organisations, modèles culturels. [...] Au cœur de tout système socio-économique se trouve une constellation d'éléments structurels fortement reliés les uns aux autres, qui favorisent l'émergence, le développement d'éléments compatibles et rend non-opérationnels ceux qui ne le sont pas.* »[30].

Ainsi, pour que le système de la société économique soit viable et performante, il faut que s'agrègent, en tout ou en partie, d'autres agrégats autour de son axe principal. Ces autres agrégats doivent tous concourir à la réalisation du sens qu'homoeconomicus donne à sa vie. En d'autres termes, ils doivent être cohérents avec le consumérisme. Ils sont déjà analysés en profondeur dans le Livre 7 de la collection *Psychanthropologie* (*La démocratie idéale*). Ils sont au nombre de deux. Ce sont : la Famille et l'École. A côté de ces principaux agrégats, il en existe d'autres qui sont accessoires.

---

[30] Jean-Pierre Gern, *La problématique de la transition*, in Économie *en transition*, pp. 20-21, Maison-Neuve & Larose, 1995.

Section 1 : L'Économie

De toute évidence, la société économique ne peut pas exister sans l'agrégat de l'Économie (en tant qu'institution). C'est le support de la société économique. Cet agrégat est au cœur du système.

Section 2 : La Famille et l'émergence des classes sociales

Comme pour tout type de société, la Famille est indissociable de la société économique.

Sous-section 1 : La Famille comme source procréatrice des homoeconomicus

La Famille est la base de toute société. C'est d'elle que proviennent l'ensemble des individus. Pour la société économique, ces individus représentent la main-d'œuvre, les consommateurs, les producteurs, les élites, etc. La société économique ne peut donc se passer de la Famille. Pour que la société économique se construise sans la famille, il faudrait qu'elle lui trouve des alternatives en tant que structures de procréation d'individus indispensables pour la performance de son système. Par exemple, une idée qui pourrait sembler farfelue serait la production industrielle, à la chaine, des Êtres humains grâce à des manipulations ou techniques scientifiques. C'est-à-dire des individus produits hors cadre familial. En attendant, la famille reste encore la principale structure qui fournit à la société économique des homoeconomicus.

Sous-section 2 : La Famille au-delà du sens classique

Dans le Livre 7 (*La démocratie idéale*) de la collection *Psychanthropologie,* nous élargissons la notion Famille en lui donnant un sens couvrant toute la société. En effet, Jean-Jacques Rousseau[31] présente l'individu comme étant la base de la famille. Et la famille est la base de la société. En d'autres termes, la constitution de toute société humaine commence par l'individu. Comme il vient au monde d'une mère et d'un père, c'est naturellement la famille qui représente la première société humaine. C'est l'agrégation des individus et des familles, au sens classique, qui fondent les sociétés humaines classiques. Dès lors, la société est une grande famille.

Sous-section 3 : Émergence naturelle des classes sociales

D'une part, comme il est démontré supra, en considérant la logique du chacun pour soi qui

---

[31] Jean-Jacques Rousseau, *Du Contrat Social*, 1762.

prévaut dans la société économique, ce sont des rapports de force qui y régissent les interactions individuelles. Précisons que, par défaut, les rapports de force s'observent naturellement et systématiquement entre Êtres vivants.

Cependant, d'abord, la propension à exercer ces rapports de force est beaucoup plus élevée chez l'Être humain à cause de l'extrême précarité de sa condition de Base[32]. Ensuite, ils sont encore plus exacerbés dans la société économique à cause de la très forte pression de l'autorité de l'inconscient décrite dans la première partie. En d'autres termes, la propension aux rapports de force est, de très loin, la plus élevée chez homoeconomicus que chez n'importe quel autre Être vivant (Êtres humains non-homoeconomicus, Animaux, Plantes).

D'autre part, chez les Animaux comme chez les Être humains, l'issue des rapports de force établit toujours une hiérarchie entre les vainqueurs et les vaincus. Dès lors, le sort de ces derniers dépend toujours des premiers. Chez les Animaux, les perdants sont soit mis à mort, soit bannis du groupe. Chez les Êtres humains, en plus d'être mis à mort ou d'être bannis, ils peuvent être utilisés comme esclaves (être soumis). L'esclavage est la tendance présentant une continuité de gains, en plus de celui du rapport de force : c'est une main

---

[32]Démonstration exhaustive dans le Livre 2 (*Les origines de la violence*) de la collection *Psychanthropologie*.

d'œuvre gratuite ou à très faible coût. Peu importe les paradigmes admis ou les systèmes établis par les Être humains, sans acquisition de l'amour agape[33], c'est cette logique, liée à l'instinct primaire, qui a toujours prévalu[34], parfois en toile de fond ou alors explicitement. Elle fait partie d'un des déterminismes imposés par la dynamique de l'inconscient.

Dans le Livre 7 (*La démocratie idéale*) de la collection *Psychanthropologie*, en rapport avec les sociétés modernes, il est mis en lumière trois statuts spécifiques issus des rapports de force :

- Les élites

   Les élites sont les principaux vainqueurs des rapports de force. Elles sont représentées par le symbole SE-D, avec S pour Survie, E pour Émotions et D pour Domination. Précisément, à travers les moyens qu'elles disposent, d'abord, les élites assurent facilement leur survie. Ensuite, elles peuvent aisément satisfaire aux diverses émotions

---

[33]Voir Livre 5 (*Anthologie de l'amour*) de la collection *Psychanthropologie*.

[34]Notons que lorsque cette logique n'est pas ostentatoire ou flagrante au sein de certains types de sociétés modernes entre individus, elle peut être observable entre nations. C'est la pratique d'une autre logique : égoïsme collectif (versus égoïsme individuel).

interchangeables de type e" produites grâce à la stimulation du désir[35]. Enfin, ce sont elles qui, d'une manière directe ou indirecte, explicite ou implicite, organisent la société et lui donnent un cap. Dans le cas précis de la société économique, c'est la dynamique consumériste qui entretient l'âme de ce type de société. Dès lors, comme ce sont les institutions économiques et les élites économiques qui rendent possible le consumérisme, elles influencent significativement la destinée de ce type de société. Autour de leur cercle, s'arriment les principaux pouvoirs influençant tant l'organisation de la société que les opinions publiques. En d'autres termes, il y a fatalement une collusion entre le monde économique, le monde politique, des médias, etc. Or, les élites homoeconomicus, mues par les caractéristiques spécifiques d'égoïsme, de convoitise, d'impatience et d'avidité n'influencent les décisions politiques et les opinions que pour servir leurs intérêts particuliers et consolider leur position dominante. A cause de « l'insatiabilité » du désir, l'accumulation des gains ne connaît

---

[35] Plus de détails concernant les différentes natures d'émotions dans les Livres 7 & 8 de la collection *Psychanthropologie*.

pas de limite.

- La classe moyenne

Elle est représentée par le symbole SE (S pour survie et E pour émotions). Suivant la logique régissant la société économique et le statut de dominés, les homoeconomicus de la classe moyenne subissent, d'une façon ou d'une autre, les décisions produites par les élites (SE-D). Nous avons démontré dans le Livre 7 que les individus situés en SE perdent leurs privilèges de bêtes politiques et d'architectes de leur univers.

- La classe des démunis

Elle est représentée par le symbole S (Survie). Les homoeconomicus les plus démunis, contrairement à ceux situés en SE, ne vivent pas mais survivent en permanence. Ils sont très loin de réaliser le sens que tout homoeconomicus donne à sa vie. En d'autres termes, ils n'ont que très peu l'occasion de satisfaire à la multiplicité des désirs créés par les mécanismes du système. Dès lors, ils ne vivent que très peu les émotions interchangeables e" produites grâce à la satisfaction des désirs. Ils connaissent donc un niveau de frustration extrêmement élevé. En proportion, la densité de la pauvreté devrait être quantitativement et qualitativement plus élevée dans ce type de société que dans la plupart des autres types de sociétés modernes.

- o Quantitativement
  La pauvreté matérielle s'explique par la logique du chacun pour soi. Il n'y a pas de sécurité sociale permettant de la juguler.

- o Qualitativement
  La pauvreté intellectuelle est la conséquence, avant d'être la cause, de la pauvreté matérielle. L'absence de sécurité sociale impose tacitement un accès sélectif à l'enseignement. A fortiori, le coût de l'enseignement supérieur leur est hors d'atteinte.

Ces pauvretés quantitative et qualitative figent les positions des classes sociales. Sous l'impulsion de la dynamique de l'inconscient des élites, on devrait s'attendre à ce que les plus démunis, comme les homoeconomicus situé en SE, subissent un des sorts réservés aux perdants : la mise à mort, le bannissement ou l'esclavage (ou la soumission subtile dans certains contextes). La tendance la plus avantageuse pour les vainqueurs est logiquement l'esclavage, les deux autres devraient s'exercer de manière très marginale. Ces vaincus représenteraient la main d'œuvre exploitée du système.

Ainsi, les plus démunis font donc face à une équation très difficile, voire impossible, à résoudre pour sortir de la spirale négative dans laquelle le système les enlise. Cette frustration est un puissant faisceau d'exercice de l'immense potentiel de propension à la violence propre à la société économique. Mais, comme il est mis en lumière dans la partie précédente, la boulimie des lois dans ce type de société vise à contrer cet exercice de violence. Conscients de ce qu'ils risquent et mis sous une forte pression permanente de l'autorité de l'inconscient suite à l'addiction consumériste, les plus démunis exploiteront autant que possible les moindres failles du système pour tenter de satisfaire aux désirs s'imposant à eux (à leur « moi »). Ces tentatives ne seront pas toujours fructueuses. Dès lors, ce type de société devrait être celle qui compte le plus grand nombre d'incarcérations. En d'autres termes, il compterait le plus grand nombre de prisons et de prisonniers. Par sarcasme, on peut en déduire que le désir représente la plus grande porte d'entrée de prison.

La Famille, dans le système de la société économique, n'est exploitée que comme productrice d'homoeconomicus. Pourtant, elle possède d'autres vertus qui, sous d'autres contextes, apportent cohésion et harmonie dans un groupe. Cette vertu est basée sur la production de l'ocytocine encore appelée « hormone de l'amour ». Les interactions, fondées sur autre chose que la compétition impulsée par l'addiction consumériste, créent mécaniquement des affinités consolidées proportionnellement par cette hormone. De manière formelle, les effets de cette hormone (générosité, altruisme, compassion, patience, etc.) sont à l'opposé des caractéristiques d'homoeconomicus (égoïsme, convoitise, impatience, avidité, etc.).

Quelle place occupe l'École dans la société économique ?

Section 3 : L'École, de la spécialisation à la paupérisation

L'École est certainement, dans la perspective de performance de la société économique, l'un des agrégats les plus importants. C'est grâce à cet agrégat que les individus de la société économique peuvent espérer atteindre le sens qu'ils donnent à leur vie. En effet, l'École, comme institution, permet l'apprentissage et libère le potentiel créatif des individus. En d'autres termes, l'École permet à chacun d'exploiter le potentiel de son intelligence[36]. Grâce à cette exploitation, les Êtres humains améliorent de manière qualitative et quantitative la production des Biens & Services. Ceci est en complète adéquation avec la doctrine productiviste et, donc, consumériste, lorsqu'il est question de la société économique. Sous l'impulsion de cette doctrine, les individus pourront vivre en permanence selon un matérialisme contemporain que nous avons défini ci-dessus. Autrement dit, les individus de la société économique pourraient avoir largement de quoi donner un sens à leur vie.

Cependant, comme la société économique est une société spécifique, on assistera à une spécialisation (implicite et explicite) des programmes scolaires et académiques. Cette spécialisation s'observera en intra-discipline. Par exemple, la formation en sciences économiques tendra à promouvoir les doctrines productiviste et consumériste. Les autres doctrines économiques à contre-courant du

---

[36] Plus précisément, il est question ici de l'intelligence psychique, celle de la dynamique consciente. Cette dénomination est faite pour la différencier de celle de l'intelligence de l'inconscient.

système de la société économique seront marginalisées.

De même, seront aussi marginalisées et implicitement évincées les disciplines ne concourant que très faiblement, voire pas du tout, à la stabilité et à la performance de la société économique. Dans ce sillage, les débouchés liés à ces disciplines seront très faibles. Dès lors, leurs cotes de popularité seront aussi très faibles, voire nulles. Par exemple, on cite principalement la philosophie. Cette spécialisation est synonyme de paupérisation des programmes scolaires et académiques. Sur cette problématique de paupérisation, nous apporterons plus de précisions infra

Donc, de manière tacite, l'agrégat École ne sera que partiellement intégré dans le système qui régit la société économique.

Section 4 : Les agrégats accessoires

En plus des principaux agrégats de base, il existe divers autres agrégats accessoires. Ces divers autres agrégats sont plus ou moins indispensables. Ceux-ci peuvent être intégrés dans le système régissant la société économique et contribuer à sa performance. On cite, entre autres, la force militaire (agrégat Défense), la Diplomatie, le Sport, etc.

Par ailleurs, d'autres agrégats ne contribueraient pas à la performance et seraient même en contradiction avec le système de la société économique. Ces derniers ne seraient pas intégrés dans ce système.

Section 5 : Organisation structurelle de la société économique

A ce stade, voici les places respectives des principales composantes de la société économique dans le système.

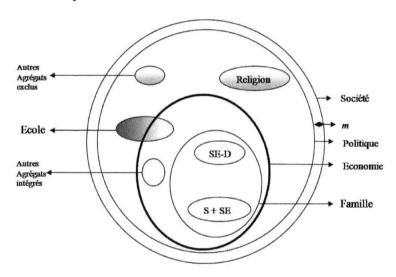

Figure n° 5 : Composantes du système de la société économique

Description et interprétation

Cette figure montre les différentes composantes de la société économique. Elle indique la centralité de l'Économie dans le système[37]. Car c'est autour de l'Économie, en tant qu'institution, que se définissent la place et le rôle de tous les autres agrégats. C'est à partir de l'Économie que se donne le tempo de la société. On peut constater que :

- Certaines composantes sont complètement immergées dans l'Économie. C'est le cas de la famille, au sens large (ensemble des individus homoeconomicus intégrés dans le système), et de certains autres agrégats contribuant à la viabilité et à la performance de la société économique.

- Nous pouvons observer que l'École est partiellement intégrée dans la structure du système régissant la société économique. Cette intégration partielle, tacite ou explicite, permet de renforcer, de consolider et d'améliorer la performance de l'Économie et, donc, de la production des Biens & Services. Rappelons que c'est ce niveau de production

---

[37] Cette centralité sera beaucoup plus explicite dans l'analyse de la dynamique du système réalisée dans le chapitre 2 infra.

qui rend possible le consumérisme.

- Par contre, certains autres agrégats sont complètement éjectés du système, car incompatibles avec la nature (rationalité) et/ou les fondements et objectifs (consumérisme) de la société économique. C'est le cas de la religion fondée sur des perspectives irrationnelles. En effet, le sens qu'homoreligiosus donne à sa vie se fonde sur une espérance de vie meilleure après la mort, tandis qu'homoeconomicus souhaite avoir une meilleure vie pendant son court passage sur Terre. De même, les exhortations religieuses[38] (solidarité, altruisme, compassion, etc.) sont contradictoires avec la logique structurelle à la base des fondements de la société économique (égoïsme, convoitise, impatience, avidité, etc.). Avec la religion, divers autres agrégats accessoires font aussi l'objet d'une éviction. A noter cependant que ces autres agrégats éjectés du système, mais pouvant évoluer en marge, peuvent influencer de manière informelle le comportement d'une certaine quantité d'individus dans la société.

Notons aussi que, radicalement, toute société économique absolue ne tolère pas, même en marge du système, des

---

[38] En ce qui concerne, par exemple, le christianisme.

agrégats contradictoires à la logique du système.

- Notons l'existence et la position de (*m*). Ce symbole représente l'espace et les individus qui, pour une raison ou l'autre, ne sont pas intégrés dans le système de la société économique. Ils évoluent en marge (*m*) du système et ne l'impactent que marginalement.

- Dans ce dispositif, la politique joue un rôle de coordination entre les divers agrégats et acteurs du système. De même, elle protège sa logique et procède à ses ajustements.

Cette configuration présente les composantes et leurs positions respectives dans le système. Sur base des analyses menées jusque-là, on peut établir minutieusement le déploiement de ce système et les interactions entre toutes les composantes concernées.

CHAPITRE 2

La dynamique de la société économique

Dans le chapitre précédent, nous avons posé toutes les bases permettant de mettre en lumière le déploiement (dynamique) du système de la société économique.

Section 1 : Les articulations de la structure du système

Dans le chapitre précédent, nous avons précisé que ce sont les élites, les homoeconomicus positionnés en SE-D, qui prennent en main la destinée de la société économique. A titre de comparaison, nous verrons dans une autre Application de la collection *Psychanthropologie* que ce sont les élites religieuses qui mènent la danse dans les sociétés religieuses. Nous avons montré supra que ce sont ces homoeconomicus situés en SE-D qui donnent le cap à la société. Ce sont leurs choix qui s'appliquent en ce qui concerne les grandes lignes de la destinée de la société. Par conséquent, régis par les caractéristiques propres aux homoeconomicus (égoïsme, convoitise, impatience, avidité, etc.), ces élites s'accaparent tous les privilèges et privent, par ce fait, les plus faibles de leur statut d'acteurs ou de bêtes politiques[39]. Dans le Livre 7 de cette collection, nous avons aussi montré que les bénéfices des politiques initiées par les élites se répartissent suivant le principe de l'investissement altruiste décroissant. Elles sont les premières bénéficiaires de leurs politiques. Ceux situés en S, les plus grands perdants des rapports de force, et ceux situés en SE, les autres perdants, ne bénéficient que de ce que décident les élites à travers le système : à peine de quoi survivre pour la grande majorité ! Cette répartition, profondément inégalitaire, des richesses et des privilèges est aussi un déterminisme déductible à travers les connaissances portant sur la dynamique de l'inconscient humain.

Afin de mettre en lumière la dynamique du système de la société économique, faisons usage de la figure n°5 ci-dessus.

---

[39]Une acception détaillée et cohérente est déjà realisee dans le Livre 7 (*La démocratie idéale*) de la collection *Psychanthropologie*.

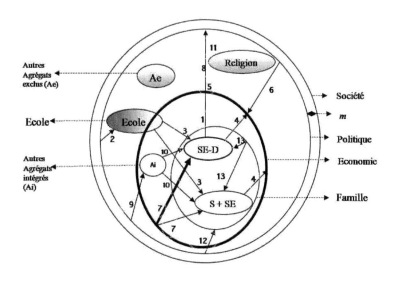

Figure n°6 : Dynamique de la société économique

Cette figure n°6 représente la dynamique du système de la société économique. Elle illustre les interactions qui se font entre les individus et les agrégats. La cohérence de ces interactions (Int) tire sa source des différentes logiques développées supra.

Section 2 : Des interactions avec les agrégats intégrés en tout ou en partie

La dynamique de la figure n°6 détermine les articulations qui existent entre les acteurs et les divers agrégats du système.

Sous-section 1 : La loi du plus fort (Int n°1)

Nous avons démontré que, dans la société économique, c'est la loi du plus fort qui prévaut. Cette logique est très fortement accentuée par la pression incommensurable exercée par l'autorité de l'inconscient due au conditionnement et, au final, à l'addiction consumériste. Cette addiction neutralise l'autorité de la conscience (équivalent au principe de « *l'autonomie de la volonté* » de Kant[40]). Dès lors, ce sont les vainqueurs des principaux rapports de force, ceux appartenant à la classe sociale SE-D (les élites), qui décident de la destinée de la société. En d'autres termes, ce sont ces élites qui, en réalité, font de la politique. Elles ne décident qu'en veillant toujours à la sauvegarde de leur position sociale et à la fructification de leurs intérêts. A ce titre, dans un tel système légitimant l'individualisme, on peut logiquement s'attendre à ce que les défenseurs de l'intérêt général, élu(e)s, gouvernant(e)s, etc., fassent passer avant tout, voire exclusivement, leurs intérêts particuliers. Car c'est la logique de base du système structurant ou colonisant la psyché de tous les homoeconomicus : chacun cherche avant tout et principalement ses intérêts. Tous les homoeconomicus appartenant aux classes sociales SE et S, classes des vaincus, subissent les choix et les décisions politiques de ces élites. A

---

[40] Emmanuel Kant, *Critique de la raison pratique*, 1788.

noter que, même en cas de suffrage universel, les individus de la masse ne voteraient que pour des programmes proposés par les élites. A très peu de choses près, ces programmes respectent toujours la nature et les fondements de la société économique. En effet, dans une société économique, il y a des lignes standards sur lesquelles s'agrègent ou s'arriment tous les programmes. Par exemple, un programme intégrant des propositions antagonistes aux principes du consumérisme n'a aucune chance d'être avalisé et légitimé. Autrement dit, il y a comme une forme implicite de similitude, de consensus et d'unanimité sur les questions qui touchent les fondements de la société économique.

Bref, en ce qui concerne les grandes questions, les individus de la masse, les perdants des principaux rapports de force, perdent leurs privilèges d'acteurs et de bêtes politiques.

Sous-section 2 : L'exploitation avancée du potentiel de l'intelligence (Int n°2, n°3 et n°4)

La nature et la finalité de la société économique passent par l'exploitation permanente du potentiel de l'intelligence psychique. Cette exploitation est à la base des innovations et de la maîtrise des connaissances existantes. Elle permet de produire en quantité et en qualité des Biens & Services garantissant le consumérisme. Par contre, comme nous l'avons énoncé supra, l'École est amputée en partie. En effet, plusieurs disciplines sont mises à l'écart. Ce sont des disciplines qui ne contribuent pas à la performance de l'Économie. A contrario, ce sont principalement les disciplines, directement ou indirectement, dites productives qui sont valorisées dans ce système. A l'évidence, à travers la tendance à la spécialisation des programmes académiques, les caractéristiques d'impatience et la pression exercée par l'autorité de l'inconscient, la société économique éteint tacitement l'esprit critique des homoeconomicus. En d'autres termes, il n'y a pas, chez ces derniers, beaucoup de possibilités d'avoir de la hauteur ou de prendre de la distance par rapport à la logique du système.

Donc, vu le degré d'importance de l'École et son caractère décisif, la formation de ce qui est couramment appelé « capital humain » est la première priorité des élites de la société économique. Grâce à cette logique, nous pouvons affirmer que le capital humain impacte en premier lieu l'Économie.

Bref, l'École permet l'accès à des connaissances favorables à l'essor du système qui régit la société économique. Elle enseigne (Int n°3), selon la doctrine choisie par les élites (Int n°2), les techniques et les connaissances permettant un meilleur essor du productivisme (Int n°4) et, donc, du consumérisme.

Sous-section 3 : Inégale redistribution des richesses (Int n°5, n°6 et n°7)

Grâce à l'exploitation du potentiel de l'intelligence organisée via l'École, les homoeconomicus se mettent au service de la consolidation, voire de l'expansion, de la société économique. Ceci aboutit à une création faramineuse de richesses.

La façon dont ils doivent se mettre au service de l'expansion de la société économique dépend, une fois de plus, des choix et des décisions des élites (Int n°5). En effet, ce sont ces choix et décisions des élites qui définissent l'organisation et les stratégies des institutions économiques (Int n°6). Globalement, se mettre au service de l'expansion de la société économique est une activité rémunératrice. L'ensemble des richesses produites dans le système sont réparties entre tous les membres de la société économique (Int n°7).

Cependant, suivant la logique régissant la société économique, comme d'ailleurs toutes les sociétés de domination[41], les vainqueurs de rapports de force, les élites, sont ceux qui se taillent la « part du lion ». Autrement dit, l'orientation fonctionnelle du système fait en sorte que ce soit les élites qui tirent sur toutes les ficelles. A ce titre, Il existe des

---

[41] Société structurée par et autour des rapports de force.

techniques ou des mécanismes légaux, voire illégaux mais tolérés par tous[42], qui permettent cette répartition inégalitaire des richesses. On peut citer, entre autres, les privatisations des Entreprises publiques, la protection (via des bases militaires) des intérêts des Entreprises privées (ou capitalismes privés) financée par les perdants (les contribuables), une fiscalité avantageuse pour le capital par rapport au travail, l'optimisation fiscale, l'évasion fiscale, etc. Il existe aussi des avantages nés de la sacralisation (selon l'acception de Durkheim) des pratiques liées à diverses déloyautés faites par les élites. Etc.

Afin de symboliser cette répartition inégale des richesses, nous avons marqué d'un trait épais le revenu des élites sur la figure.

Sous-section 4 : Consolidation du système (Int n°8, n°9 et n°10)

Si certains agrégats sont fondamentaux dans la construction du système de la société économique, d'autres y participent de manière plus ou moins indispensable. Nous avons cité plusieurs exemples.

---

[42] C'est parfois lié aux difficultés structurelles de s'y opposer et d'avoir gain de cause, pour autant que l'on puisse être capable de prendre de la distance avec le système. Dans chaque classe, dont celle des élites, on devrait se serrer les coudes.

Ce sont des institutions de Santé, de Défense, de Sport, de Diplomatie, etc. Chacun de ces agrégats accessoires contribue, à sa manière, à la performance de la société économique. Par exemple, plusieurs travaux montrent le lien évident entre la performance économique et la politique de santé. A ce titre, Amartya Sen affirme que « *santé et développement* [économique] *sont indissociables* »[43]. De même, dans un monde qui se bâtit exclusivement à travers des rapports de force, une politique de Défense efficace est indispensable pour la société économique, autant qu'une stratégie politique (officielle et/ou officieuse) impériale. Donc, la force militaire contribue aussi à la stabilité, voire à l'expansion, de la doctrine de la société économique.

Sous-section 5 : Déshumanisation (Int n°11, n°12 et n°13)

A la suite des analyses menées dans le Livre 5 (*Anthologie de l'amour*) et l'Application 1 (*Phénoménologie du racisme*) de la collection *Psychanthropologie*, sur une certaine série de critères (individu, famille, tribu, région, nation, race, humanité) de préférence des individus, l'humanité n'arrive qu'en dernier lieu. A ce titre,

---

[43] Sen Amartya, *Santé et développement*, allocution prononcée à la 52e Assemblée mondiale de la santé à Genève, 1999.

par défaut, on aime plus son enfant que celui du voisin de la même tribu ; [...] ; etc. A fortiori, les mécanismes accentuant l'individualisme ne permettent pas aux homoeconomicus de créer des contacts indispensables pour la production de l'ocytocine, encore appelée « hormone de l'amour ». De même, subissant une pression phénoménale de l'autorité de l'inconscient, comme c'est la dynamique de l'inconscient qui le guide, homoeconomicus évolue à « l'aveugle ». Il est totalement incapable de se mettre à la place de l'autre. Dès lors, l'humanité n'est absolument pas la préoccupation de tous les homoeconomicus (élites et individus de la masse). Ils ne connaissent ni compassion, ni empathie. Ce qui compte principalement c'est leur stricte personne.

De même, en rappelant que c'est la compétition qui détermine les positions de chacun dans une classe sociale spécifique, il n'est pas dans l'intérêt des élites de rendre la vie facile aux homoeconomicus situés en SE et en S. Tous restent des adversaires réels dans le système. Bref, leur sort individuel, en tant qu'Êtres humains, n'est pas une priorité pour les élites. Ce « triste » sort n'impacterait pourtant pas la performance de la société économique. Car le système réussit quand même à assurer et à promouvoir le consumérisme. Les questions « morales » sont très facilement balayées par la logique et les mécanismes fondant le système.

Avec la routine, la productivité n'est plus fonction du bien-être dans la société économique. Des réalités de forcing imposent cette dissociation et son intériorisation jusqu'à la dynamique de l'inconscient. Le principal mobile de cette dissociation est l'interchangeabilité des travailleurs homoeconomicus. D'abord, en effet, ces travailleurs intériorisent le fait qu'ils sont tous interchangeables. Celui qui flanche est aussitôt remplacé. Comme il n'y a pas de sécurité sociale, associer la productivité au bien-être est un luxe. On pourrait les faire travailler debout toute la journée en leur imposant, si besoin, de faire pipi sur eux dans des langes qu'ils portent au préalable avant de commencer le travail, qu'ils ne broncheraient pas. Ils peuvent travailler à temps plein toute l'année et passer leur vie dans leur voiture qu'ils ne broncheraient pas. Etc. Dans la société économique, ces situations honteuses par ailleurs n'émeuvent presque personne. C'est la logique impitoyable du chacun pour soi.

Ce rapport au travail propre à la société économique instaure ce que l'on pourrait appeler aliénation par le travail. L'Être humain, précisément l'homoeconomicus perdant du principal rapport de force, n'est réduit qu'à un facteur de production du système : il est déshumanisé.

Par métaphore, voire par sarcasme, on peut oser

dire, avec logique à l'appui, que les homoeconomicus situés en S et SE perdent leur statut de bêtes politiques : ce sont les élites qui régissent la société. Ce statut se décline en celui de bêtes de somme. De même, toujours avec métaphore et de manière sarcastique, ils ne travaillent plus pour un salaire, mais pour une pitance. Bref, il ne travaille pas pour eux, c'est-à-dire pour leur propre épanouissement et suivant leurs propres choix, mais pour un système qui profite essentiellement aux vainqueurs des rapports de force situés en SE-D, les élites.

Par ailleurs, en dépit des politiques implicitement ou explicitement défavorables à l'épanouissement de l'individu à travers la Famille[44] ; en dépit du fait que ces politiques soient éventuellement tentées de convertir implicitement l'Être humain en automate[45], il y a une réalité immuable complètement indépendante de tout système sociétal. C'est le caractère inné des sentiments, principalement l'amour exclusif ou amour philéo. Partout où il y aura des contacts sans motifs de compétition entre les individus, entre les individus et d'autres Êtres vivants ou même des choses, en

---

[44] Les émotions positives produites par les sentiments ne sont pas valorisées.

[45] Cette transition est fortement plausible à cause de l'immense impact de la dynamique de l'inconscient sur le comportement des homoeconomicus. Or, cette dynamique est le siège des automatismes des Êtres vivants.

l'absence de griefs, il y aura automatiquement production d'ocytocine. Mais, d'une part cette production est largement insuffisante pour compenser le vaste champ d'expression des caractéristiques de la dynamique de l'inconscient, celles d'homoeconomicus. D'autre part, c'est le maximum qu'homoeconomicus puisse connaître. Car, d'abord, les mécanismes du système tendent à marginaliser les contacts pacifiques (caractérisés par l'absence de compétition) ; ensuite, pour des raisons que nous avons soulignées supra et dans les Livres 4 & 5 de cette collection, les mécanismes de la société économique neutralisent l'autorité de la morale et celle de la conscience. Ils empêchent homoeconomicus de vivre selon les principes de l'amour inclusif ou amour inconditionnel.

Note : Contrairement à certains types de sociétés spécifiques, les interactions concernant la Famille n'arrivent qu'en dernier ressort dans le système de la société économique. Ceci indique ou confirme le fait que les émotions de type e', celles issues des sentiments d'ordre affectifs, sont ultra marginalisées dans ce système. En d'autres termes, les homoeconomicus ne manifestent que très faiblement de l'empathie, de la compassion, etc.

Un des éléments principaux à retenir est la place de choix accordée aux élites par le système de la société économique. Elles seules décident de la destinée de la société. Ceci est illustré par les interactions n°1, 5, 8 et 11. Ce sont elles qui font la politique. Les individus de la masse, ceux qui sont situés S et en SE, sont des suiveurs. Ces derniers ont perdu leur privilège d'acteurs et architectes de leur société.

Section 3 : Les agrégats complètement évincés du système

Dans la société économique, peuvent exister des agrégats qui évoluent complètement en marge du système. Nous ne nous attarderons pas sur les raisons qui fondent l'existence de ces autres agrégats. Mais, a priori, toutes les sociétés humaines ont un héritage historique. Et cet héritage historique peut tapisser encore leur univers sans plus objectivement impacter la destinée ou bien le futur de ces sociétés. Ces agrégats restent en marge parce qu'ils ne contribuent pas explicitement à la performance du système qui régit la société économique. Au mieux, ils sont tolérés. Mais dans certains cas, leurs préceptes peuvent même subir un discrédit parce qu'incompatibles avec le système de la société économique.

A ce titre, dans la société économique, nous avons souligné la contradiction qui existe entre le système de ce type de société et la religion. Cependant, cette marginalisation ne signifie pas l'absence d'interactions. Par exemple, tout en restant dans le système, certains individus peuvent adopter et vivre selon des préceptes religieux malgré la contradiction entre ceux-ci et les principes de la société économique. Par conséquent, ils sont en permanence tiraillés entre des doctrines diamétralement opposées. Ils sont obligés, dans ce cas, de faire des compromis ou bien d'être en permanente contradiction dans leurs choix individuels.

Par ailleurs, on peut aussi citer d'autres agrégats pouvant demeurer dans la périphérie du système sans concrètement influencer le cours du destin de la société. En tout état de cause, du moment que les préceptes de ces agrégats ne représentent pas une réelle menace pour le système qui régit la société économique, ils restent tolérés.

Toutes ces démonstrations nous permettent de proposer une <u>définition complète</u> de la société économique. C'est une société de domination dont le système est exclusivement conçu et régi par les dominants (les élites) pour accroître la performance de la production des Biens & Services à partir desquels les homoeconomicus donnent un sens à leur vie.

Section 4 : Les Marginaux

Parmi les individus de la société économiques, certains peuvent choisir de vivre en marge du consumérisme. Ceci peut être la conséquence, entre autres, de la prise de conscience des mécanismes aliénants du système. Sur cette figure, ils sont représentés par le symbole (*m*).

Ces deux derniers chapitres ne permettent pas encore de déterminer toutes les caractéristiques de la société économique. Une analyse des effets de la hiérarchisation sociale dans la société économique est nécessaire.

CHAPITRE 3

SOCIÉTÉ ÉCONOMIQUE
ET TOTALITARISME

Le totalitarisme induit par un système n'intervient que lorsque ce système neutralise les possibilités permettant aux individus de penser par eux-mêmes afin de poser des choix, voire de prendre des décisions en toute liberté. Les élites prennent des décisions à leur place. Quels arguments liés au système de la société peuvent permettre d'imputer à la société économique l'étiquette du totalitarisme ?

Section 1 : La servitude exogène

Dans les chapitres précédents, nous avons mis en lumière une hiérarchie de classes induite tacitement et entretenue par le système de la société économique. Ce système donne beaucoup de privilèges aux élites, une toute petite minorité, dont celui de décider des grandes orientations de la société. Cette exclusivité est synonyme de servitude subie par les homoeconomicus situés en S et en SE, car privés de l'essentiel de leur liberté politique. Concrètement donc, une servitude naît avec cette configuration.

Nous pouvons illustrer cette servitude structurelle, de champ exogène, dans la figure suivante.

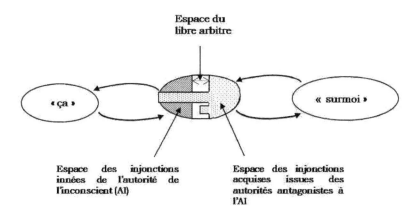

Figuren°7 : Servitude exogène chez homoeconomicus

Description et interprétation

Cette figure illustre le parasitage de l'espace du libre arbitre des homoeconomicus, situés en S et SE, par le fait du système de la société économique. Le contexte réel où les élites imposent leurs choix et décisions en ce qui concerne les grandes orientations de la société témoigne, en l'espèce, d'une absence de liberté politique chez ces homoeconomicus. Deux niveaux de parasitage, ayant des impacts différents, peuvent être observés. Il faut déterminer lequel est le plus adapté à la société économique.

Sous-section 1 : Parasitage partiel

Le parasitage partiel de l'espace du libre arbitre est symbolisé par la seconde barre horizontale, celle du bas, sur la figure n°7 ci-dessus. Ce parasitage partiel indique que les homoeconomicus de S et SE feraient valoir leur désir de liberté ou instinct de liberté via la dynamique de l'inconscient, mais cet instinct est piétiné par une autorité exogène puissante. En d'autres termes, ces homoeconomicus seraient conscients de l'entrave à leur liberté et pourraient l'exprimer d'une manière ou d'une autre. A ce stade, nous n'avons pas encore d'arguments cohérents pour dire si c'est simplement ce parasitage partiel qui s'opère dans ce type de société. Si tel était le cas, on ne parlerait pas de totalitarisme. Mais, pour se mettre sur une piste, on peut analyser cette problématique sous un autre angle en se posant d'abord des questions simples. Homoeconomicus est-il conscient qu'il a perdu l'essentiel de sa liberté politique ? Si oui, pourquoi s'en accommoderait-t-il ?

Sous-section 2 : Parasitage total

Sur cette figure, on observe que la première barre horizontale, celle du haut, parasite totalement l'espace du libre arbitre et celui de l'espace réservé aux arguments de la dynamique de l'inconscient. Ceci signifie que l'autorité antagoniste à celle de l'inconscient est tellement puissante que, en plus de neutraliser le libre arbitre, elle annihile l'instinct de liberté chez les homoeconomicus des classes S et SE. Annihiler cet instinct, c'est neutraliser toute possibilité de laisser entrer cette valeur dans la conscience et d'éventuellement la revendiquer. Dès lors, ils sont structurellement et fatalement incapables de prendre de la distance par rapport au système qui les asservit et de revendiquer un autre sort. En d'autres termes, ils sont asservis sans en être conscients. Si tel était le cas chez ces homoeconomicus, on parlerait alors de totalitarisme. Mais il reste à déterminer par quels mécanismes s'opère cette neutralisation. Pour ce faire, il faut prendre en compte l'impact de la servitude endogène.

Pour déterminer lequel de ces deux niveaux de parasitage est conforme à la société économique, il faut considérer le phénomène de double servitude chez homoeconomicus

Section 2 : Le phénomène de double servitude chez homoeconomicus

La première partie de cet ouvrage met en lumière une servitude structurelle dont les mécanismes sont endogènes à homoeconomicus. La dynamique de l'inconscient, à travers son autorité, est le moteur de cette forme de servitude. Quant à la servitude exogène, elle se met en place sous l'action d'autorités situées dans des champs externes au corps. L'exercice du pouvoir de ces autorités se décline en autoritarisme pouvant aboutir au totalitarisme. En l'occurrence, les injonctions qu'elles émettent parasitent l'espace du libre arbitre des homoeconomicus de la masse.

Ce phénomène de double servitude est illustré par la figure ci-dessous.

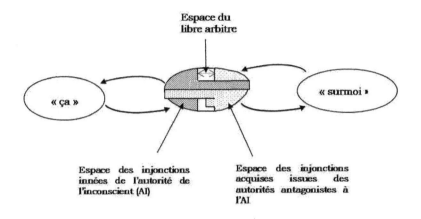

Figure n°8 : Double servitude chez homoeconomicus

Description et interprétation

C'est une certitude : homoeconomicus est otage de deux autorités antagonistes extrêmement puissantes. Cependant, même si les mécanismes psychanthropologiques sont différents, cette double prise d'otage n'est pas une spécificité d'homoeconomicus. On peut aussi l'observer, à une faible ampleur, chez homoreligiosus qui est pris en otage tant par ce qui donne un sens à sa vie que par les autorités religieuses. C'est de faible ampleur parce que, par voie endogène, le parasitage de l'espace du libre arbitre n'est pas impulsé par la dynamique de l'inconscient, mais par une conviction. Or, le siège des mécanismes d'émergence de la conviction se situe dans la

113

dynamique consciente. Ce raisonnement est le même en ce qui concerne homopoliticus.

Cette figure illustre les deux formes possibles de totalitarisme. La première, c'est déjà acté, est endogène. Elle est représentée par la traversée totale des espaces tant de l'espace du libre arbitre que celui des autorités antagonistes à l'autorité de l'inconscient. La seconde est exogène. Mais ceci demande à être confirmé.

Nous devons maintenant préciser si l'incursion de l'autorité du système dans l'espace du libre arbitre est partielle ou totale.

Section 3 : Totalitarisme exogène ?

Homoeconomicus subit-il un totalitarisme exogène ? Deux hypothèses peuvent permettre de trancher sur cette question.

Sous-section 1 : La liberté politique semble accessoire

Pour ce faire, rappelons-nous que c'est le conditionnement, l'endoctrinement et l'addiction qui entraînent le totalitarisme endogène. La force de ce triptyque, débouchant sur le consumérisme, permet à la dynamique de l'inconscient chez homoeconomicus d'accomplir dans le temps sa mission de base, assurer les homéostasies biologique et émotionnelle[46]. Dès lors, toutes autres doléances telles que, entre autres, la liberté politique, deviennent accessoires. Par conséquent, ce besoin de liberté n'est plus une doléance ou une injonction présentée par cette dynamique. Dans ce cas, les homoeconomicus ne sont absolument pas conscients de leur servitude. Car le besoin de liberté politique est une doléance instinctive qui n'entre pas dans leur conscience.

Sous-section 2 : Homoeconomicus se veut-il être cohérent ?

Homoeconomicus ne veut pas combattre le système qui donne un sens à sa vie. Cette idée suppose l'incursion partielle (troisième barre horizontale, celle du bas, sur la figure n°8 ci-dessus). Il serait donc conscient de cette servitude mais préférerait un statut quo. Il serait ainsi une victime consentante. Cette hypothèse nous semble invraisemblable. Car elle ne peut pas résister dans le temps : elle n'est pas structurelle.

Ainsi, c'est la première hypothèse que nous retenons. Donc les homoeconomicus des classes S et SE subissent un totalitarisme structurel de

---

[46] Voir Livre 1 (*L'intelligence de l'inconscient humain*) de la collection *Psychanthropologie*.

sources exogènes.

Au final, voici la principale configuration psychique et psychanthropologique de la très large majorité des homoeconomicus, en lien avec le système.

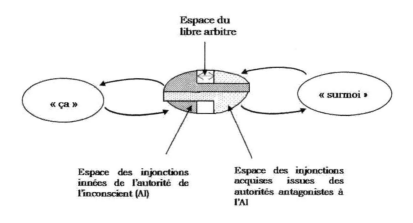

Figure n°9 : Principale configuration psychique d'homoeconomicus

Cette figure illustre parfaitement le phénomène de double servitude que subissent les homoeconomicus dans leur très grande majorité.

En parlant de totalitarisme, d'aucuns pourraient brandir, sur base de faits concrets, la compatibilité entre société économique et démocratie. En effet, certaines sociétés actuelles, proches de la société économique, ont des institutions qui valorisent et défendent, par exemple, la liberté d'expression et des élections.

Qu'en est-il exactement ?

Section 4 : Une instrumentalisation de la démocratie

L'émergence de la société économique n'est pas spontanée (naturelle). C'est une construction a posteriori. Son système doit donc s'accommoder de diverses valeurs antérieures. Mais, il est dit supra que ces valeurs doivent être compatibles avec le système pour assurer sa pérennité, voire sa performance. Sinon elles sont combattues et éjectées de ce système. Parmi ces valeurs, nous pouvons citer la liberté d'expression, les élections, etc. Comment expliquer le paradoxe d'une cohabitation entre totalitarisme, liberté d'expression et élections dans la société économique ?

En tant que système totalitaire, la bonne question à se poser est celle de savoir si le système de la société économique redoute la liberté d'expression et les élections.

Quid de la liberté d'expression ?

Les institutions de la société économique ont-elle

quelque chose à craindre de la liberté d'expression ?
La réponse sans détour est : NON !

Les principaux arguments étayant la faible influence de la liberté d'expression sur le totalitarisme du système de la société économique sont les suivants :

- La neutralisation de la critique à l'égard du consumérisme

  Le parasitage total des espaces du libre arbitre et des autorités antagonistes à celle de l'inconscient neutralise totalement l'émergence de la critique du consumérisme. C'est ce parasitage qui illustre le sens que les homoeconomicus donnent à leur vie. Dès lors, il ne leur viendrait pas spontanément à l'idée de remettre en cause ce sur quoi ils fondent leur raison d'être. Ils (leur « moi ») sont pris dans un piège qui les dépasse. Ce qui donne un sens à leur vie ferme toutes les voies d'occurrence de la critique. Dès lors, les champs de la liberté d'expression ne concerneront jamais la remise en cause de la nature et du fonctionnement du système.
  La raison, instance de la critique, est littéralement balayée par la bande parasitant

les espaces tant du libre arbitre que des autorités antagonistes à celle de l'inconscient. Dans le chef des homoeconomicus, il y a comme une sorte de lobotomie qui s'opère avec ce parasitage.

A fortiori, ils baignent dans une propagande permanente (consumériste et pro-système) qui les endoctrine et rend ainsi étroite leur capacité à prendre du recul.

- Les laissés-pour-compte du système

Les laissés-pour-compte, les homoeconomicus les plus pauvres, sont très nombreux. Leur niveau de pauvreté est tel qu'il ne sera même plus question de consumérisme, mais de survie. Mais, le conditionnement, l'endoctrinement et le principe de la carotte entretiendront la doctrine consumériste dans leurs imaginaires individuel et collectif. Donc la critique porterait sur autre chose que sur la nature et les fondements du système. Principalement, cette critique serait fondée sur la frustration liée au très faible niveau de consommation. En d'autres termes, elle porterait plus sur les inégalités ou sur les obstacles à l'accès aux ressources disponibles que sur la remise en cause du système.

Ainsi, la liberté d'expression n'est absolument pas une menace pour le système de la société économique. Bien au contraire, c'est un puissant allié instrumentalisé pour légitimer abusivement ce système.

Quid des élections ?

Nous avons déjà évoqué le sillage uniforme dans lequel s'inscrivent les électeurs homoeconomicus. Les programmes qui leur sont proposés ne trahiront jamais les principes du système. Ce dernier tend structurellement une carotte qui ne sera jamais attrapée par la très grande majorité. En d'autres termes, à cause du conditionnement, de l'endoctrinement et, in fine, de l'addiction au consumérisme, même s'ils sont conscients des réalités qu'ils subissent[47], les homoeconomicus ne voteront que pour des programmes entretenant le sens qu'ils donnent à leur vie.

A fortiori, en cas de totalitarisme, la critique n'entre jamais dans leur conscience. Dès lors, la nature des institutions de la société économique ne sera jamais menacée par les élections. En d'autres termes, suivant cette configuration, les élections ne font peser aucun risque sur le système totalitaire. On en déduit que les homoeconomicus de la masse

---

[47] Hypothèse non-retenue supra.

sont des victimes ignorantes de leur servitude.

Notons que ce contexte pourrait prendre une autre tournure si, pour une raison ou l'autre, la critique consumériste entre dans la conscience des individus. Dans ce cas, l'autoritarisme du système ne se cacherait plus derrière les élections et la liberté d'expression. Il montrerait son vrai visage en sortant des bois.

C'est tacitement cynique de la part des institutions de la société économique de revendiquer la démocratie. Tant que les individus de la société économique ne briseront pas leur statut d'homoeconomicus, ils continueront toujours à légitimer un système qui entretient leur servitude.

Tout système tend à intégrer les principes et mécanismes susceptibles de renforcer sa stabilité, sa pérennité et sa performance. C'est le cas des principes appartenant à la démocratie. Ils ne sont qu'instrumentalisés pour la forme afin de pacifier et de pérenniser un système, au fond, totalitaire.

CHAPITRE 4

LES SIGNES D'UNE TRANSITION VERS LA SOCIÉTÉÉCONOMIQUE

La société économique n'est pas spontanée. Une allusion en est faite supra. Ses mécanismes, très élaborés, s'installent ou s'imposent progressivement dans les paysages sociopolitique et socioéconomique. Ces mécanismes tendent, d'une part, à neutraliser, voire à évincer, des structures, des principes et certains éléments incompatibles avec son système ; et, d'autre part, à renforcer, voire à spécialiser d'autres éléments apportant stabilité et performance. A l'échelle de la planète, les sociétés étant de natures disparates, divers signaux indiquent, à géométrie variable, une migration structurelle de ces sociétés vers la société économique.

Pour faire plus simple, considérons une société historiquement dite démocratique avec une protection sociale. Sans être exhaustif, en considérant les analyses menées jusque-là, on peut expliciter les principaux signaux structurels montrant une transformation de cette société en une société économique.

Section 1 : L'éviction de l'économie du giron politique

Cette éviction se traduit par le désengagement de l'État par rapport à la pratique d'activités économiques. Il y a autonomisation des institutions économiques par rapport à la sphère politique. En d'autres termes, le Politique perd le contrôle sur l'Économie. Certes il y a des intersections, mais ces deux mondes évoluent en parallèle : l'un, démocratique et l'autre, technocratique. Les signaux indiquant cette éviction sont nombreux. Entre autres, on peut citer les cas où :

- L'État entame des politiques massives de privatisation des Entreprises publiques.
- Il abandonne sa souveraineté monétaire à une technocratie généralement supranationale, garante du consumérisme.
- Il réduit les pouvoirs de sa banque nationale. Désormais, il emprunte aux banques privées.
- Etc.

Dès lors, L'État perd de précieux leviers de financement de ses politiques publiques. Il doit s'endetter davantage pour financer l'ensemble de ses dépenses.

Pourtant, il est démontré dans le Livre 7 (*La*

démocratie idéale) de la collection *Psychanthropologie* que l'Économie est une des composantes essentielles de la politique permettant de rendre possible la démocratie. Par conséquent, cette éviction, purement idéologique et opportuniste, est antidémocratique. A fortiori, il est démontré supra qu'il ne faut absolument pas compter sur le sens de la raison ou de la bonne conscience des homoeconomicus. Car la raison est littéralement balayée par le parasitage de leur espace psychique par la dynamique de l'inconscient. Donc, il ne faut absolument pas leur faire confiance. Leur confier votre bourse ou vos actifs, sans garanties contraignantes, est une perte certaine. Sauf s'ils tirent un intérêt supérieur à vous les remettre. Par exemple, si pour une raison quelconque, vous leur confiez 400 € sans garanties contraignantes, ils ne vous les rendront que s'ils en tirent un bénéfice (estimé ou réel) supérieur à 100 %, c'est-à-dire au moins 401€.

Section 2 : L'influence grandissante des institutions économiques sur les décisions politiques

L'éviction de l'économie du giron politique a des conséquences automatiques. Fatalement, elle conforte l'État dans une trappe d'endettement. Cette spirale négative d'endettement engendre une dépendance vis-à-vis de ses créanciers privés. Ce sont généralement des institutions économiques qui, à un certain stade, pourraient s'octroyer le droit de « s'imposer », et donc de s'ingérer, dans la gestion des politiques internes des nations concernées. Être débiteur subordonne de fait l'État à ses créanciers. A ce titre, ce lien de subordination est corroboré par un adage populaire selon lequel « *la main qui donne est la main qui dirige* ».

Section 3 : Prééminence de la politique de l'offre

La politique de la demande est moins dynamique et, donc, moins consumériste que celle de l'offre. Comme cela s'explique-t-il ?

L'explication est assez simple si l'on considère toutes les analyses réalisées depuis le début de cet ouvrage. En fait, c'est la stimulation du désir qui entretient et pérennise le consumérisme. En d'autres termes, sans cette stimulation, la production de Biens & Services stagne. Or, dans la perspective de gains, la dynamique de stimulation est logiquement plus élevée de la part des offreurs des Biens & Services. Plus ceux-ci stimulent, plus on consomme. Et plus on consomme, plus ils augmentent leurs gains. Il est donc de l'intérêt des offreurs de stimuler le désir. La perspective de gains est une source substantielle de motivation. Pour ce faire, ils font usage de leur créativité pour créer la demande.

Du côté de la politique de la demande, dans le Livre 3 (*Les origines de l'intelligence*) de cette collection (*Psychanthropologie*), il est démontré que l'auto-stimulation est tacite. Elle s'inscrit essentiellement dans le sillage de la satisfaction aux besoins. Or, les sociétés modernes ne vivent plus suivant la motivation par le besoin. Cette désuétude tend à neutraliser l'auto-stimulation du désir.

Donc, dans un système consumériste, l'offre précède nécessairement la demande.

Section 4 : De l'égoïsme collectif à l'égoïsme individuel

La migration vers la société économique passe par l'éclatement ou la minimalisation de la sécurité sociale. La sécurité sociale n'est pas une logique compatible avec les fondements individualistes de la société économique. Précisément, elle n'est pas compatible avec le principe du « chacun pour soi ». Cet éclatement passe par l'affaiblissement (discrédit, marginalisation, dénigrement, dévoiement/fayotage, etc.) des syndicats. Progressivement, suite à l'immense pression exercée par les protagonistes et les institutions œuvrant pour la migration vers la société économique, certains de ces syndicats offriront des ponts d'or pour cet éclatement, légitimant ainsi implicitement la transition. Leur fayotage à l'égard des politiques de ces institutions trahira leur subordination progressive.

Section 5 : Paupérisation des programmes académiques

Nous avons expliqué supra que les programmes académiques doivent concourir à la stabilité et à la performance du système de la société économique. Donc, en cas de transition, avec la pression négative exercée sur la sécurité sociale, les lendemains deviennent de plus en plus incertains en ce qui concerne la survie. Dès lors, en matière d'études, les choix deviennent pratiques, voire pragmatiques : on choisit les filières offrant des débouchés certains. Ces filières sont en phase avec la stabilité et la performance du système de la société économique. En d'autres termes, très peu d'étudiants prendraient le risque de choisir des filières n'offrant que très peu de débouchés. Ainsi, pourraient progressivement être marginalisées certaines filières « n'apportant rien de concret » au système de la société économique. On pourrait citer la Philosophie, l'Histoire, etc. A fortiori, la privatisation possible des universités rendrait non rentable l'enseignement de ces filières. On parlerait alors de paupérisation de l'enseignement. Il faut converger, à travers une structuration spécifique des imaginaires individuels et collectifs, vers la pensée unique. Précisément, par exemple, loin de former des intellectuels, la société économique ne forme que des spécialistes et techniciens servant une cause d'ordre matérialiste. En effet, d'après la Psychanthropologie, l'intellectuel est celui qui est capable d'exploiter, de manière avancée, la « *raison pure* » encadrée par la « *raison pratique* ». En d'autres termes, cela concerne tant l'approfondissement des connaissances que, en prenant du recul, la qualité des analyses et d'interprétations de ces connaissances. Cette qualité d'analyse et d'interprétations tend toujours à la contribution de l'amélioration des conditions de vie de tous les Êtres vivants[48]. Or, homoeconomicus ne sait pas prendre du recul à cause de l'immense pression exercée par l'autorité de l'inconscient sur la dynamique consciente. De même, l'ensemble de ses caractéristiques ne militent pas pour l'altruisme. Dès lors, en matière d'approfondissement des connaissances, il file tout droit, il va droit au but, notamment sous la forte influence de la caractéristique de l'impatience.

Par ailleurs, on constaterait aussi une spécialisation intra-disciplinaire concernant les disciplines phares (pour le système de la société économique). Cette spécialisation concernerait, principalement, les programmes des sciences

---

[48] A cause du potentiel de la raison de l'Être humain qui instaure tacitement une aspiration d'harmonie et stabilité dans l'espace et le temps.

économiques. Ces programmes tendraient à promouvoir les doctrines productiviste et consumériste au détriment des doctrines économiques à contrecourant du système.

Section 6 : Croissance continue des inégalités économiques

De l'analyse de l'ensemble de ses principaux agrégats et de son système, il ressort que la société économique est profondément et structurellement inégalitaire. A fortiori, elle crée autant de richesse que de pauvreté. Les inégalités structurelles et profondes sont indissociables de ce type de société. Donc l'observation progressive d'inégalités structurelles, illustrées par la formation nette des classes sociales, est aussi l'un des principaux signes de la transition d'une société démocratique vers la société économique.

Section 7 : Le travail comme principale activité

Hannah Arendt, dans son œuvre *la condition de l'homme moderne*[49], décrit trois principales activités de l'homme. Elle cite *le travail, l'action et l'œuvre*. A ces trois activités, on peut ajouter une quatrième

---

[49] Hannah Arendt, *"La condition de l'homme moderne"*, p. 37, Ed. Pocket, 1994.

activité : la spiritualité verticale[50].

Dans la société économique, le travail est la principale activité. D'ailleurs, pour des raisons évoquées et développées supra, le statut de citoyen est réduit à celui de travailleur. C'est l'activité qui fait vivre le système. Plus que dans n'importe quel autre type de société, elle est au cœur des programmes, des controverses et des polémiques. Dès lors, sont progressivement marginalisées les autres activités principales (l'œuvre, l'action et la spiritualité). Le travail prend de plus en plus de place tout le long de la vie des individus des classes populaires et moyennes (futurs homoeconomicus de S & SE). Le temps de travail s'allonge ; la retraite est repoussée dans les lisières de l'énergie active, à la frontière avec l'impotence. Ces individus, futurs homoeconomicus, tendront à servir le système jusqu'à leurs dernières forces. Avec la pression négative exercée sur la sécurité sociale, ils y sont contraints. Au cours de cette transition, voire après, il ne fait pas bon d'être chômeur. Le chômage est un calvaire et tend à devenir une calamité. Le chômage est une honte.

Section 8 : Perte de cohésion sociale et violence

Des analyses menées plus haut, il ressort que le

---

[50] Voir Livre 6 (*Anthologie de l'esprit*) de collection *Psychanthropologie*.

système de la société économique est fondé sur l'individualisme. Ce système augmente, plus que dans n'importe quel autre type de société, le potentiel de propension à exercer la violence. Ceci est dû, d'une part, à la stimulation toujours plus avancée du désir et, d'autre part, tant à l'infériorité systématique des revenus par rapport aux désirs stimulés en permanence qu'à la pression négative exercée sur la sécurité. Il sera donc possible d'observer, au cours du processus de migration vers la société économique, plus de violence, moins d'empathie, moins de compassion, moins de cohésion et un phénomène de repli progressif sur soi, etc.

Section 9 : Uniformisation de l'offre politique

A priori, l'offre politique tend à s'uniformiser. Progressivement, à très peu de choses près, ces programmes respectent la nature et les fondements de la société économique. La diversité de cette offre tendra à se réduire comme une peau de chagrin. Les programmes à contrecourant de la société économique seront marginalisés, discrédités et dénigrés.

A posteriori, peu importe qui arrive au pouvoir, il fera face à une évidence : les principaux leviers, notamment économiques, monétaires et financiers, susceptibles de rendre possible n'importe quel programme sont aliénés à des institutions parallèles technocratiques supranationales « garantes » de la transition. Ce sont elles qui, en principe, imposent les grandes lignes politiques. Les possibilités d'appliquer des programmes allant à contrecourant sont de plus en plus faibles pour devenir nulles plus tard. En d'autres termes, l'alternance démocratique ne change en rien la nature des grandes orientations politiques : il faut converger vers la société économique. Dès lors, les programmes, éventuellement à contrecourant des fondements de la société économique, sont explicitement ou insidieusement dévoyés dans la pratique au cours de l'exercice du pouvoir.

Cette configuration est synonyme d'affaiblissement des États concernés.

Section 10 : Affaiblissement de l'État

L'ensemble des 9 sections précédentes amènent à déduire que la migration de toute société vers la société économique entraîne automatiquement l'affaiblissement de l'État. D'après la Psychanthropologie, un État faible est celui-là qui limite structurellement les possibilités d'épanouissement de l'ensemble de ses citoyens, qui ne promeut pas les valeurs d'humanisme et de cohésion. C'est un État qui adopte des doctrines oppressant son propre peuple et, plus loin, l'humanité, abandonnant ainsi certains (la grande majorité en l'occurrence) à leur triste sort. A ce titre, la société économique débouche sur un statut d'État puissamment faible. Dès lors, c'est un État archaïque.

Section 11 : Société économique et archaïsme

Le système de la société économique subordonne, voire neutralise, toutes les structures permettant de contenir la très grande influence de la dynamique de l'inconscient sur le comportement des individus. En d'autres termes, ce système libère fortement le potentiel de cette dynamique. Or, cette libération est fortement antagoniste à toute initiative ou comportement humaniste. C'est un retour aux comportements archaïques et originels des premières sociétés humaines. Cette forme de société fait émerger un niveau très élevé de potentiel de propension à exercer le potentiel originel de violence inné en chaque Être humain[51]. Ceci veut dire que le statut d'homoeconomicus est potentiellement plus violent que n'importe quel autre statut (homoreligiosus, homopoliticus, etc.). L'exercice de ce potentiel est principalement contenu ou freiné par la grande disponibilité des

---

[51]   Voir Livre 2 (*Les origines de la violence*) de la collection *Psychanthropologie*.

ressources, produites par le système, susceptibles de satisfaire aux injonctions liées au désir. Sans cette disponibilité des ressources, il y aurait explosion de la violence.

Donc la marche vers la société économique ne tend que vers une modernité ambiguë. Car, d'une part, elle promeut une production de Biens & Services permettant de sortir de l'archaïsme matériel et, d'autre part, elle détruit tous les gains liés aux progrès humains en imposant une logique structurelle d'autodestruction (destruction de toute forme de vie). Humainement, la marche vers la société économique renvoie à un profond archaïsme. Dès lors, en considérant cette ambiguïté, la société économique n'est qu'une forme de modernité ne marchand que sur une seule jambe.

CONCLUSION

La société économique est une forme typique de société. Son système s'organise nécessairement, de manière cohérente, autour d'un axe central spécifique. Cet axe est le fil rouge, la référence, qui protège son identité. Dans ce système, l'Économie n'est pas prise comme simple agrégat producteur de valeurs, mais comme élément permettant à des individus de donner un sens à leur vie. Suivant cette logique, économie a, en plus d'une productivité qualitative et quantitative des Biens & Services très élevée, une valeur symbolique[52] forte. C'est ce qui marque la grande différence entre la société économique et les autres types de sociétés. L'existence, la stabilité et la croissance de la société

---

[52] Représentation renvoyant a une dynamique cohérente plus vaste.

économique reposent sur deux doctrines interdépendantes : le productivisme et le consumérisme, la seconde étant le contrepoids de la première. A partir de cette double doctrine, les individus de la société économique, les homoeconomicus, donnent un sens à leur vie à partir de la consommation des Biens & Services. A ce titre, la société économique se confond à une société de consommation. La concrétisation de ces doctrines est l'objectif de tout paradigme tendant à faire émerger ce type de société.

Dans cet ouvrage, nous avons analysé méthodiquement tout le processus induisant le consumérisme. Dans les faits, fondamentalement, cette doctrine naît de la stimulation avancée et permanente des désirs humains. Or, les désirs, tout comme les besoins, sont des manques du corps captés par la dynamique de l'inconscient et transmis à la dynamique consciente. A force de conditionnement, d'endoctrinement et d'émotions positives diversifiées qu'ils procurent, par des mécanismes spécifiques, ces désirs se transforment en addiction à la consommation des Biens & Services.

Techniquement, au cours du processus menant au statut d'homoeconomicus, une phase essentielle permet de comprendre les caractéristiques tant d'homoeconomicus que de la société économique.

Cette phase spécifique est celle du moment de contact entre la dynamique de l'inconscient, à travers l'autorité de l'inconscient, et celle du conscient. L'addiction produite suite à la stimulation avancée et permanente du désir décuple la pression exercée par l'autorité de l'inconscient sur la dynamique consciente. Cette immense pression est exercée pour faire satisfaire à toutes les injonctions liées aux désirs. Comme, au contraire d'être interdit, le consumérisme est encouragé, cette immense pression parasite les espaces tant du libre arbitre que des autorités antagonistes à l'autorité de l'inconscient. Ce parasitage total de la psyché d'homoeconomicus par la dynamique de l'inconscient est décisif pour cerner tous les contours ainsi que le profil d'homoeconomicus et de la société économique. A priori, il colonise et structure les imaginaires individuel et collectif des homoeconomicus.

La colonisation totale de la psyché des homoeconomicus par les injonctions de la dynamique de l'inconscient entraîne avec elle la transposition systématique des caractéristiques de cette dynamique sur les comportements de l'individu-victime. Précisément, toutes ces caractéristiques sont exactement celles d'homoeconomicus. Les principales sont : l'égoïsme, la convoitise, l'impatience, l'avidité. Dès lors, la société économique est profondément et structurellement individualiste. Car, à travers ces caractéristiques, l'individu ne peut pas comprendre la nécessité de l'altruisme ou de la compassion. Il ne vit exclusivement que pour lui-même : seuls ses intérêts comptent.

Toutes ces caractéristiques sont à la base de la violence. Car elles poussent chacun à ne chercher que ses intérêts. En effet, qui ne cherche que ses intérêts trouve tacitement en son congénère un adversaire. Comme ces caractéristiques sont structurelles, le potentiel induit de propension à exercer la violence le sera aussi. Ainsi, le système de la société économique porte en lui de la violence. Il instaure un climat permanent d'interactions conflictuelles entre les individus. En d'autres termes, ce sont des rapports de force qui structurent la société économique. Or, l'issue de tout rapport de force détermine toujours un vainqueur et un vaincu. Et, dans l'espace et le temps, chez les Animaux comme chez les Êtres humains, le sort des vaincus dépend toujours du vainqueur. Soit il est mis à mort ; soit il est banni ; soit il est réduit en esclave ; soit il doit payer « un droit de vie » (taxes ou rentes « indues » versées aux vainqueurs). En l'occurrence, ce contexte aboutit systématiquement à l'émergence marquée des classes sociales dans la société économique. Les plus forts, les vainqueurs, ont intérêt à se coaliser pour rendre robuste leur position. Ils forment le cercle des élites. Les vaincus, d'une façon ou d'une autre, se mettent au service des élites. Ils forment la grande masse. Dès lors, et c'est inéluctable, le système de la société économique est un puissant vecteur de production d'inégalités structurelles.

De par ses fondements, la société économique crée autant de richesses que de pauvreté. Ceci est la conséquence d'abord de l'association entre stimulation avancée des désirs et, de manière proportionnelle, l'exploitation du potentiel de l'intelligence. Cette association permet une création exponentielle des richesses (Biens et Services). Ensuite, sa structuration par les rapports de force impose naturellement une répartition inégale des richesses créées.

Les analyses menées dans cet ouvrage montrent aussi que le système de la société économique est profondément et structurellement liberticide. A fortiori, il est totalitaire. Ce totalitarisme tire ses sources du phénomène de double servitude que subissent les homoeconomicus de la masse. La première est endogène. Elle est liée au parasitage total des espaces tant du libre arbitre que des autorités antagonistes à celle de l'inconscient. La seconde, beaucoup plus subtile, est exogène. Elle est liée à l'accaparement exclusif de la gestion de la destinée de la société économique par les élites. Dès lors, la société économique est profondément incompatible avec la démocratie.

De même, les analyses menées dans cet ouvrage nous amène à conclure que la société économique n'est pas structurellement compatible avec l'Ecologie. Car les ressorts de son système imposent une pression phénoménale et abusive sur les ressources naturelles.

D'une manière générale, la marche vers la société économique ne tend que vers une modernité ambiguë. Car, d'une part, elle promeut une production de Biens & Services permettant de sortir de l'archaïsme matériel. D'autre part, elle inhibe la conscience et, dès lors, détruit tous les gains liés aux progrès humanistes en imposant une logique structurelle d'autodestruction (destruction de toute forme de vie). Humainement, la marche vers la société économique renvoie à un profond archaïsme. Dès lors, en considérant cette ambiguïté, la société économique n'est qu'une forme de modernité ne marchant que sur une seule jambe.

BIBLIOGRAPHIE

- ARENDT Hannah, *"La condition de l'homme moderne"*, Ed. Pocket, 1994.
- CHAPLIN Charlie, *Les temps modernes*, 1936.
- COHEN Daniel, *Homoeconomicus : Prophète (égaré) des temps nouveaux*, Albin Michel, 2012.
- GERN Jean-Pierre, *La problématique de la transition*, in *Economie en transition*, Maison-Neuve & Larose, 1995.
- KANT Emmanuel, *Critique de la raison pure*, 1781.
- KANT Emmanuel, *Critique de la raison pratique*, 1788.
- PLATON, *La République*, Les Belles Lettres, 2002.
- ROUSSEAU Jean-Jacques, *Du Contrat Social*, 1762.
- SEN Amartya, *Santé et développement*, allocution prononcée à la 52ᵉ Assemblée mondiale de la santé à Genève, 1999.
- TAROT Camille, « *Le symbolique et le sacré* », préface, La Découverte/M.A.U.S.S., 2008.
- SCOTT-CLARK Cathy & LEVY Adrian, *Fast Forward into Trouble*, The Guardian, 14 juin 2003.

TABLE DES MATIÈRES